FIGHT LIKE A GIRL

THE TRUTH BEHIND HOW FEMALE MARINES ARE TRAINED

KATE GERMANO
WITH KELLY KENNEDY

 Prometheus Books

59 John Glenn Drive
Amherst, New York 14228

Published 2018 by Prometheus Books

Cover image © PJF Military Collection / Alamy Stock Photo
Cover design by Jacqueline Nasso Cooke
Cover design © Prometheus Books

Inquiries should be addressed to
Prometheus Books
59 John Glenn Drive
Amherst, New York 14228
VOICE: 716–691–0133 • FAX: 716–691–0137
WWW.PROMETHEUSBOOKS.COM

22 21 20 19 18   5 4 3 2 1

Library of Congress Cataloging-in-Publication Data

Names: Germano, Kate, 1973- author. | Kennedy, Kelly, 1970- author.
Title: Fight like a girl : the truth behind how female Marines are trained / by Kate Germano;
    with Kelly Kennedy.
Other titles: Truth behind how female Marines are trained
Description: Amherst, New York: Prometheus Books, [2018] | Includes index.
Identifiers: LCCN 2017049748 (print) | LCCN 2017050749 (ebook) |
    ISBN 9781633884144 (ebook) | ISBN 9781633884137 (pbk.)
Subjects: LCSH: Germano, Kate, 1973- | United States. Marine Corps—Women—Training
    of. | United States. Marine Corps. Marine Regiment, 11th. Battalion, 4th—Biography.
    | United States. Marine Corps—Women—Social conditions. | United States. Marine
    Corps—Officers—Biography. | Women marines—United States—Training of. | Women
    and the military—United States. | Sexism—United States.
Classification: LCC VE23 (ebook) | LCC VE23 .G47 2018 (print) |
    DDC 359.9/6092 [B] —dc23
LC record available at https://lccn.loc.gov/2017049748

Printed in the United States of America

To Joe, without whom neither I, nor this book, would be here. RR forever.
And to all those who fight every day to eliminate obstacles for
women in the military and beyond, I salute you.
#MeToo.

CONTENTS

ACKNOWLEDGMENTS

When you experience a terrible event in life, you must make a conscious daily decision to be grateful or face drowning in a shame and self-doubt. You can choose to be bitter, or relearn how to be happy and self-assured by taking stock in the people to whom you are most indebted. I would be remiss if I did not publicly thank those people who held my hand and walked with me during my darkest days, including Joe, Popster, Kathy, and the rest of our family, and our dearest friends Chris Lorence, Brian Emerson, and Lynn Lowder. I would also like to sincerely thank Kelly Kennedy, who served as my confidant, counselor, cheerleader, and coach throughout this process—I am indebted to her for her belief in me as a good human being and Marine.

Much gratitude goes out to all of the service men and women, veterans, colleagues, friends, and strangers who offered their support every step of the way. I'd also like to thank John Silbersack, of the Trident Media Group, for believing in me, and the many great folks at Prometheus Books, including Jade Zora Scibilia, for their hard work and impeccable judgment in fine-tuning my story.

Finally, many thanks to the members of the media who dug into the story of my relief to provide a more balanced view of who I am and what I was trying to achieve for the Marine Corps. Your work was invaluable in shedding much-needed light on the challenges faced by women in segregated boot camp and the significant work that remains to be done to end gender bias and truly level the playing field for Marine women.

Continue to shine a light.

CHAPTER 1

TEARS AND CUPCAKES

Good Morning Ma'am,

    I just had to email you and let you know that it still shocks me to hear/read that you are no longer at Parris Island. I may not know the details of the situation and I've only read what *Marine Corps Times* has posted. When you stepped on deck at Parris Island, you hit the ground running with high expectations, and, with a lot of hard work, the results started to show. I'm at a loss for words, having worked for you. It pushed me to develop my Marines and my recruits beyond their limits—to understand that the bare minimum is not acceptable. In my opinion, the battalion was finally headed the right way, and with you being gone, I'm afraid that it will go back to the way it was when I first got there: complete chaos. Regardless, Ma'am, I will always remember what you've taught me: "C.A.P" (Confidence, Accountability, Pride). I will continue to lead Marines and set the example, the way you did for all of us.

    R/

    SSgt Cristal [former Fourth Battalion drill instructor]

As I prepared to take command of Fourth Battalion, the boot camp for brand-new female recruits, I told myself I would have to stop cussing so damned much.

I would have to reconstruct my "resting bitch face" into a countenance brimming with sunshine and light.

I would work to encourage a culture of compassionate listening, and I would try not to yell.

It was, after all, the Marine Corps.

I was excited to take over—proud that I had been hand-selected, and eager for a new challenge. In every position I had ever held, I did my best to leave it a better place. I aimed for efficiency and to improve the Marine Corps overall, but I also worked hard to improve the quality of life for Marines under my watch.

After years of deployments, the last thing I wanted was a Marine feeling stressed out over recruiting duty or a drill-instructor tour.

This job—commanding officer of Fourth Recruit Training Battalion— seemed perfect for me. I hoped to take the lessons I had learned as a Marine— but also as a *female* Marine—and build up a group of women who understood just how capable they were. I wanted to prepare them to succeed in a Marine Corps that might not always be supportive or understanding of their goals; and I wanted them to come out with a strong vision of themselves and their abilities. I wanted it for my drill instructors. I wanted it for my officers. And I wanted it for my recruits. The Marine Corps had treated me well, and I knew that strong, capable women could only help the service.

I found the Marine Corps accidentally after a Navy recruiter rejected me for my math SAT scores, but I was attracted to the Corps from the beginning because I felt that it was a place for me to make my mark. From the start, I knew the Marine Corps was the smallest, most elite branch of the military, with the fewest women and the highest standards. I had always had high expectations for myself, so this resonated with me in a way no other profession or organization had. Plus, without the Marine Corps, I would never have met my husband, Joe. He has saved my life on more than one occasion, including on Parris Island. Over the years, my feelings of affection and loyalty to the Corps increased because it was the one place where I felt I could make a difference.

It was where I wanted to believe I belonged.

Ultimately, I loved how much I learned with every new mission, and I expected to learn just as much on this tour of duty. I had already established some goals for myself, and some of them were direct results of being a woman. Although some of my challenges may have been enhanced by my wholehearted Marine-ness, I don't think they are far off from what women who haven't served in the military also face. (Before any non-military readers get too far, I suggest you take a look at "Marine-Speak 101," at the back of the book, for an understanding of how Parris Island is structured, and a basic primer on "Marine-Speak.")

In my previous command, I had pushed to make good changes for Marines— to make sure they had more time off and less stressful jobs. I wanted to see fewer divorces, fewer drunk-driving cases, and fewer suicide attempts. But to do that, I shoved my curvier peg into the Marines' extraordinarily square hole. I cursed. I yelled. I was extremely strict. Even though we were able to reach our goals and life got better, a lot of the Marines didn't like me much. I constantly fought not to be "other," by acting the way the male Marines acted; but because I was the only female commanding officer, I was never part of the group. And the things I did to fit in? The yelling and cursing? They only made me stick out worse. Even in the Marine Corps, those are not the traits expected of a woman—unless that woman is "mean" or "a bitch." Worse, none of those attributes matched my personal leadership style.

So, as I took charge of women's boot camp for the Marine Corps, overseeing some of the world's fiercest drill instructors, I decided to be true to myself.

I thought, "How awesome would it be to leave a command at the end of my tour as commanding officer and not have any regrets like, 'Maybe I shouldn't have said this?' or 'Maybe I shouldn't have yelled about that?'"

I had served eighteen years in the military, including stints at Marine Corps Air Ground Combat Center on Twentynine Palms in California and a tour in Iraq, but I had never planned to stay in more than twenty years. My husband, Joe, and I had an agreement that we would launch second careers, and that agreement had allowed me to push hard to Marine Corps standards without worrying about the politics that career service members play to so they can make rank. But even with the yelling, I had always received excellent reviews. I was seen as a straight-shooting go-getter who could get things done.

I went to Parris Island thinking, "This is my redemption tour. I'm going to retire after twenty years in the Marine Corps, and this tour is going to allow me to feel good about leaving the service."

We all see how that worked out.

To say it was a tumultuous year would be like calling the *Titanic* disaster a "bad day at sea." But despite the significant obstacles I faced, I never lost sight of the feelings of absolute pride I felt in my Marines at Fourth Battalion as they proved women recruits could, in fact and obviously, perform better if they were simply expected to shoot well and run faster. But no matter how we worked to overcome decades of apathy and low standards for performance within my battalion, there were men at the highest levels of command on the recruit depot who expected—even wanted—the women to fail because they didn't want to see women fully integrated into the Corps. And there were women who fell so fully in line with the status quo that it never occurred to them to see what the female recruits could achieve.

My job was to oversee a battalion of fourteen officers, one hundred drill instructors, and 3,200 recruits. Parris Island is the only place in the Marine Corps where female Marines are made, and I wanted to ensure that every day of their thirteen weeks of training counted, so they could graduate faster, smarter, tougher, and better shots. But on Parris Island, the women trained separately from the men—which is different from the other services, where men and women train alongside each other. The women at Parris Island train separately simply because of an outdated study suggesting they would perform better that way. That proved to be incorrect in so many ways, but it also proved to be my downfall, along with a history of neglect, no support from my local leadership, and Pentagon-level bosses who saw better statistics as a step closer toward women joining infantry units. They wanted women to serve only in support roles.

Going in, I knew that working only with women would be a challenge. Before I arrived at Parris Island, my predecessor warned me, "They're either baking you cupcakes or on your couch in tears."

In hindsight, I see that her comment summed it up perfectly and encapsulated the perception of the battalion throughout the depot and the Marine Corps. Everyone had the expectation that Fourth Battalion, my battalion, was incapable. It could achieve enough to get by, but there was not an established tradition of excellence—a stated need to be better and best. Because it was an all-female unit, even the regimental sergeant major called Fourth Battalion the "Fourth Dimension." In other words, it operated in a different world with different expectations from the male recruit battalions. There was always an undercurrent of women being too emotional and cruel—to each other and to the recruits—and, because the expectation existed, that's how some of the women behaved.

They shouldn't have. They were strong and capable.

I started doing turnover with my predecessor in February 2014 by phone and email, and then I went to visit the battalion in April, before starting in June. During turnover, you learn the ropes of the new position and gain some of the cultural background of a new place. My predecessor could tell me where there might be problems, as well as point out on whom I could rely. That's when she told me the duty was either tears or cupcakes.

The problems went deeper than that. Female drill instructors were sleeping with female recruits, and with each other. Drill instructors abused the recruits. Drill instructors abused other drill instructors.

In my battalion, I would have to work through inappropriate sexual relationships, screaming as an accepted form of communication, and even fistfights. There were hazing investigations going on in April and a court-martial case later that month. A court-martial is when a military court is called upon to enforce military law. The issues with drill instructors sleeping with recruits were being brushed under the rug. A lot of the issues with recruits being abused? Those were being brushed under the rug, too.

It was a big rug.

I had to get everyone focused on good order and discipline, and then deal with the gender-related issues. It turned out the two areas of focus were intimately connected.

When I finally arrived to take over command at Parris Island in June 2014, I thought, as I always do, "How am I going to make it better?" But as I dug into performance statistics to see how to do that, even obvious improvements met with sometimes violent resistance. We found that women hadn't performed better than men in essentially any category since the records had been kept. That included weapons qualification rates, academic performance, injury rates, and even how well women marched. Gender differences shouldn't have played into academics or marching, so I struggled, at first, to understand why the women would perform worse in those areas. But I also figured that if we could boost up all the numbers, we'd be making the Marine Corps look better, and everybody would be happy. I was naive.

The abusive drill instructors didn't want to change, because they felt that new recruits—and new drill instructors—should have to pay their dues, just as they had. They also did not want to be held accountable for bad behavior.

The enlisted Marines—the drill instructors—had run the show for so many years that officers—the Marines in charge of the drill instructors—essentially had nothing to do. This was bad for two reasons: They had no control. And they rebelled hard when forced to take control, because it meant more work.

My boss didn't want change, because he didn't want to rock the boat.

On top of all of that, the culture within Fourth Battalion was often petty and mean, riddled with rumors and false claims. This was reinforced by leadership that encouraged gossip and arbitrarily enforced Marine Corps standards. This led to a miserable climate within the battalion, but it also reinforced the idea within the male battalions that women could not operate without "drama."

I was walking into a minefield, but because I had never encountered anything like it, I went in blind. I needed to hold my officers and drill instructors accountable; I needed to reorganize my staff to reward excellence and remove abuse; and I needed to help my Marines and their recruits understand that they were capable of meeting much higher standards. But without senior leadership that supported those changes, the task would impossible.

During my first month in South Carolina, my boss invited me to talk about my goals, as well as to give me a rundown of his command philosophy. The colonel didn't seem too interested in what I had to say, but I wrote down the words he emphasized: "I prize harmony among my staff members above all else."

In other words, he didn't want to deal with any turbulence. He just wanted everyone to get along.

That stuck with me.

The same month, I had my first conversation with Brigadier General Loretta Reynolds, who was, at the time, the commanding general of the depot. She was the first woman to fill that position.

I wrote down what she said, too: "Go with your gut, and never back down if you think something is right."

They gave me two perspectives completely at odds regarding how I should go into this command tour. If I had chosen the first, there would be no story to tell.

That first month, I chose to take Reynolds's advice and go with my gut.

There would be no mercy at Fourth Battalion.

And that applied first and foremost to the cockroaches—they were everywhere. I would grind the filthy, no-good cockroaches into the ground! When the recruits marched along the catwalks, you could hear the cockroaches crunch under their feet. Ugh. And they flew! The barracks were clean, but headquarters was a mess, including my office. I even found cockroaches under that damned rug.

As we sent the cockroaches scurrying back to their hovels, I started working with my Marines on what else needed to be fixed. Everything was subpar for the women. Everything. Their living quarters. Their standards. Their training. And it led to lower scores for female recruits across the board: academics, physical fitness, shooting, drill—everything. They didn't have room to train; because of the physical setup of Fourth Battalion within the regiment, female Marines received less fitness training; maintenance was last on the priority list for our living quarters; and because the women were set apart from the men, they seemed to be forgotten.

It felt intentional.

Many of the female recruits were not able to or were barely able to meet the standard on basic Marine skills. They fell out of hikes and runs. They shot marksman—the lowest passing qualification—at the range. They injured themselves because they hadn't been properly trained to prevent such injuries. How much respect could female Marines possibly earn from male Marines if we female drill instructors and staff had such low expectations of ourselves? After their separate boot camps, the men and women would train together at Marine Combat Training school, where they would hike and go through obstacle courses and learn how to respond to attacks. The men would see that the majority of the women could not meet the required standards, let alone keep up. (That's different from the other service branches. In the Army, Air Force, and Navy, men and women train together at all stages of their military careers, and they go straight from basic training or boot camp to their job-training schools—to learn to be cooks, clerks, cops, or infantrymen.)

To me, it was crucial to improve the female Marines' skills, knowledge, and leadership. It wasn't only a matter of competing with the men or proving women's abilities. It was a moral imperative.

I remember calling Joe one night and saying, "We're sending women to combat. We've been doing this for fifteen years, and for fifteen years, we've been sending women who can't shoot as well as they should."

These women serve as military police officers out on patrol. They serve as truck drivers on roads that have faced constant attack. They serve as convoy leaders, as members of small teams that go out into communities to provide services, as translators, and as medics.

Many of them aren't even comfortable pulling their weapon apart to clean it—because they don't know how to put it back together.

Let me fall back and say that there have been many female Marines who are and have been capable of all of those skills, and more.

All female Marines should be.

This was something I had to work on myself—as I'll talk about later—but as an officer, I did not go through boot camp at Fourth Battalion. Male and female officers do, in fact, train together, and I fired expert during my initial training.

But, at Fourth Battalion, the foundational level of training, the female recruits were expected to fail. The slowest member of the platoons set the running pace for everybody else during physical training. Trainers told them that their arms were too short to fire weapons properly and that girls couldn't shoot. They didn't even hike the same distance for the Crucible—the proud culmination of a recruit's training—as did the men, because the drill instructors hadn't measured the course properly. From the moment I arrived, it was obvious that the Marine Corps was locked in an era of tight girdles and smelling salts.

I'm not exaggerating. By graduation, female Marines had been performing push-ups, running for miles, hiking with packs, shooting rifles, and generally sweating their asses off for thirteen weeks. Often, the recruits were covered in mud, mosquito bites, and sunburn. But at the Marine emblem ceremony following the Crucible hike, a row of chairs provided a safety net behind the newly minted female Marines. Why? In case any of them felt faint.

The men did not get chairs.

I changed that immediately.

No, the men did not get chairs.

It sounds ridiculous, and it is. Nobody wants lowered standards for their Marines, but, paradoxically, that's exactly what we have. The paradigm requires someone at the policy level and at the implementation level to say, to acknowledge, "Why, yes, we have been holding women to lower standards, but now we're going to change that." I think that's important.

As we worked to improve rifle scores, reduce injuries, and build strength, we encountered similarly dated ideas. While men were allowed to eat what they liked, women were not allowed to have sweets. They were told that if they used stretch bands and foam rollers after exercise, they were "weak." And they were told they were a "distraction" on road marches when we finally managed to integrate our hikes.

My team and I realized we had to change the mind-set of the recruits and my staff. Every new recruit, as well as the officers and drill instructors who made up my staff, learned that she was capable in every way—from running to leadership to shooting—and that we expected her to excel. As we trained differently, we saw improvement in all of those areas.

But we also needed to make life better for my drill instructors and company-grade officers. We did not have enough women—a product of senior leadership stealing women away to act as typists, even if they didn't have that skill set, as well as of drill instructors getting pregnant to get out of a stressful duty. That meant longer hours for the women, more 24-hour shifts for the women, and more stress for the women.

That stress, mixed in with an isolated culture, led to bad behavior, including scaring recruits until they peed their pants, or not allowing new drill instructors to drink water in August in South Carolina. We addressed the bad behavior, of course, but we also combated the stress with everything from reorganized duty schedules to yoga classes within the battalion.

I felt like things were going well. I had great interactions with my Marines. Culture within the battalion improved. Abuse decreased. The recruits? They didn't know any better—each fresh group knew only the new training and new attitude, so we could make change quickly.

However, change is hard—even good change. Books have been written about it, because it's hard. You can't expect big changes to happen in an organization and for everyone to be happy. Sometimes it's hard to recognize that the change is good; sometimes people simply become set in their ways; and, sometimes, people believe everybody should be subjected to the same kind of nonsense they dealt with as a young person. You see that in fraternities that embrace hazing as a rite of passage, in military units that believe it's the only way to prove strength, and in career women who believe everyone should have it as hard as they did.

That's a fallacy. The goal, as a society, is evolution. As we work to improve teamwork and respect and integrity, we have to ensure that our Marines (and co-workers and service members and kids) trust each other. There's no trust in abuse.

Not all of my Marines wanted change—particularly in two companies with a history of abuse. In those companies, the training results across the board were lower in every category than the other company's results.

Still, many of my Marines worked hard, and our numbers improved—especially on the rifle range. Some officers took charge of their drill instructors, and we saw magical things happen in their companies: Culture improved; mentoring increased; training became fun.

But.

I clashed with my boss. We clashed over emails; we clashed in person; and we clashed when my officers claimed I was being too hard on them when I demanded that we make things better for their drill instructors and their recruits. Officers were in charge of enlisted Marines; drill instructors are enlisted Marines; drill instructors were in charge of recruits. All of them reported to me, and I, as a lieutenant colonel, reported to a colonel who was responsible for my battalion, as well as three other battalions.

All of this resistance is to be expected in any unit, and, I suspect, any business that is going through a sea change. If your leadership supports you, you can work through the bumps. If they don't—if there's a need to maintain the status quo from the top—then you're staring failure straight in the face from the beginning and may not even know it.

Throughout my whole year-long tour, I felt as if my boss were harboring a grudge. He never said anything directly, and it was impossible for me to figure out what, in his eyes, I was doing wrong. Improving physical-fitness scores? Training harder on the rifle range? Expecting my Marines to be ethical? If he believed I was being too tough on them or that I was overstepping boundaries, he never said so. Everything felt passive-aggressive. He would purse his lips hard, and his face would go totally scarlet—he fumed like a whistling teakettle. But he never said, "This is why I'm angry." He certainly never counseled me or wrote anything down.

The best that I could figure was that he didn't want the women to do better. He didn't want the friction that comes with forcing change.

I thought making the female Marines stronger would make the Corps stronger, and I assumed that I would have support up and down and sideways through the chain of command.

I was wrong.

In my case, the need to maintain the status quo came from much higher up than my boss. That said, I believe our relationship was simply a personality clash that, timing-wise, worked out in his favor. In fact, throughout my tour, the higher-ups at the recruit depot told me to keep doing what I was doing and to just wait him out. His tour was to end one year after I arrived at Parris Island.

But there were problems that had to be addressed immediately, that couldn't wait months until my boss left town. I had a company commander who regularly cried in front of her Marines. She came into my office twice, in tears, to quit, because she didn't get along with her first sergeant. The first sergeant also tried to quit—because she didn't get along with her company commander. These were grown women. A drill instructor was admitted as an in-patient for alcohol abuse caused by the pressure of bad leadership. Another drill instructor punched someone who outranked her, in front of new recruits. And my executive officer—my second-in-command—responded to a negative job review by encouraging gossip about me within the battalion.

Again, that's typically just stuff people deal with, especially if they're making change to try to address exactly that kind of behavior. And, typically, a functional command both allows the leadership to hold accountable the 10 percent who are causing problems and reinforces that accountability. A dysfunctional command allows the 10 percent to control the 90 percent.

I did not have command support.

Instead, when the 10 percent complained that I was mean or that I rolled my eyes, my boss decided to fire me.

At no point did he offer any mentoring, counseling, or even spoken delivery of what he expected or of what I had done wrong. How on Earth could rolling my eyes be more egregious than the recruit abuse that had gone unchecked prior to my tenure? How could it be more egregious for me to lay out a commander for not training her Marines than for me to enable drill instructors who couldn't perform their jobs? Under my leadership, morale was up, disciplinary issues were down, and recruits were treated better. But my boss told me that I was too aggressive, that I was too blunt, that I didn't listen, that I went over his head, and that I disobeyed his orders.

I didn't understand. He had never talked to me about any of those issues. I had gotten his permission to carry out the very orders he said I didn't follow. It made no sense. Being a commanding officer and not knowing where you stand with your boss is the worst possible place to be, because you never know what his expectations are.

I had thought, going in, "I'm going to be happy all of the time. I'm going to smile all of the time. I'm never going to call people in and yell at them. I'm never going to use foul language"—which, by the way, isn't the easiest thing for a Marine to do. But, I figured, "You know what? If the drill instructors aren't allowed to use foul language with the recruits, then I'm not going to use foul language with the drill instructors or my company staff. I don't want them to think it's okay for me to do it but not for them to do it."

So, even though I had never thought of myself as abrasive, I was still working to change other people's perceptions of me for the better. I feel like I was successful; but I hated it! I didn't feel like I was mean to begin with. I didn't feel like I should smile unless I was happy. I mean, I'm fine with toning down my language and not yelling, but even that wasn't enough. I had to contort my countenance to combat "resting bitch face." I feel like I'm a pretty happy person. I love to joke. I love to have a good time. But I had people—men—at Parris Island tell me, "You should smile more. You should be nicer." (You have probably experienced this, too, if you're a woman.) I was like, "Are you effin' kidding me? I'm here doing my job. We're seeing results, but you're telling me I need to be nicer?"

When was the last time you heard someone tell a male Marine he needed to smile more? Or a man, period?

As things got worse after several months at Fourth Battalion, I sent an email to the sergeant major of the depot—a woman. I said, "Hey, look. I need your help. I need to know what you see. Am I doing something wrong?" And she wrote back: "Don't worry. We see it, too." This is what I had heard from the commanding general, too: "We know what's happening. Keep doing what you're doing." I started thinking, "I just need to get through this."

Those days—those months and months of days—were like a bad dream. I'd wake up in the morning and think, "Wait. The system's going to work."

Instead, it got so bad that I asked that a mediator be present every time I had to work with my boss. But nothing happened. Instead of looking into my concerns, my senior leadership appointed an investigating officer to look into me as a leader.

After I had asked that a mediator be present, my boss gave me my annual job review. In the Marine Corps, we call that a "fitness report."

My boss began my fitness-report counseling with: "I've been giving you enough rope to hang yourself."

While I had been working to mentor my Marines and improve my recruits, my boss had been giving me enough rope to hang myself.

Isn't that uplifting?

He had never talked to me about how to improve or what I had done wrong. He didn't offer suggestions. He didn't once come to visit my battalion and sit in on a training session. Instead, when he realized I wasn't going to hang myself with his rope, he pulled out the chair from beneath my feet.

In this meeting, he told me he had ranked me last, not only of all the battalion commanders at the recruit depot, but of all lieutenant colonels with whom he had ever worked.

Ranked me last.

None of our achievements mattered, even though they were historic for the Marine Corps.

Nothing mattered.

After that meeting, everything felt gray. I drove home from Parris Island to my bottom-floor apartment in a crazy, pink historic home. After all of our hard work and success—which was achieved despite resistance, criticism, and undermining—I was hit with the worst possible ranking.

I just wanted to be done.

I was thinking really dark thoughts.

I could end it.

Here's the thing: I'm a Marine, through and through. That's my identity. I'm so proud of the people with whom I work. My pals are Marines. There's some bad-assery that comes with being a Marine, especially with being a female Marine, and I had enjoyed that cachet for almost twenty years. I loved my Corps.

Ranked me last.

My career was in a shambles.

That meant my self—my core identity—had been decimated.

But as I pulled into my driveway, Mr. Fitzwizzle popped up and leaned on the windowsill. He looked at me, and he meowed.

"Oooh," I thought. "Someone has to feed the cat."

He's a great cat.

Not to put him second, but Joe also gave me reasons to stay the course and see it through. He called constantly to cheer me up or to help me work through how to deal with all of this. I had met Joe when we were both young lieutenants at Twentynine Palms. He had grown up in Ohio, but, by the time he got to college, he was obsessed with climbing. And he climbed with women—learned from them, admired them, understood that some were better climbers, and respected that. Actually, he didn't just respect that women were sometimes better climbers; he enjoyed their strengths and didn't think about gender. By the time he met me, he already knew he wanted a partner in the truest sense of the word. We went on one date, and, man, we were together from then on. He makes me laugh like no one else can—tears-running-down-my-face laugh. We've always supported each other, as well as called each other on our crap. He's my best friend, and he's gotten me through a lot. Everything. He's kept me alive.

That night, we talked about an escape plan. Our conversations were no longer about how to work with a difficult boss; they were about how to leave Parris Island with my career, my reputation, and my sanity intact.

Somehow, I still had hope that someone higher up the chain of command would both recognize what was happening, and acknowledge the progress the Marines and the recruits were making.

In the meantime, Joe was working his contacts at the Pentagon, and he started hearing some of the background noise on my situation. Joe had just retired from the Marine Corps and was friendly with a number of senior folks on the commandant's staff. As I was dealing with what felt like local issues with my boss, they were telling Joe about all the meetings and briefings about my situation that were taking place all the way up to the commandant level. He was told that people were even asking about my medical status in these meetings because they were looking for ways to get rid of me if they couldn't relieve me for misconduct. From what he learned, it was clear that they were playing out all of these options.

I thought, "What the hell? They're already talking about how they can get rid of me, and they haven't even investigated whether I've done anything wrong?"

Here I was, thinking I was just a battalion commander fighting with her boss down in South Carolina. Why on Earth would the bigwigs at the Pentagon care? I mean, I can't even get a replacement drill instructor, but a pissing match over whether I roll my eyes too much is now a matter of national security? It didn't make sense.

Until it did.

When I took command of Fourth Battalion, the Marine Corps began its gender-integration study. While they were working to show that women are incapable of working with men in combat situations because they don't have the strength or skills, I was showing that we could improve women's strength and skills simply by having higher expectations for them.

For political reasons that had nothing to do with my performance—at least, not for my "bad" performance—they were going to sacrifice me.

It started to sink in that I was going to be relieved, and that all of the work we had done would be swept under that giant rug—the good with the bad. On the third of June, a year after I had arrived at Parris Island, I drafted a letter to my Marines telling them how sorry I was to go, and that I was responsible for everything that had happened in the battalion, including the things that had gone wrong. I told them how proud I was of what they had accomplished. I told them, "Demand your seat at the table, because no one is ever going to give it to you, and you've done more than anyone ever thought you could—certainly more than headquarters Marine Corps thought you could." I begged my sergeant major to get it to my Marines if I were relieved.

As I prepared for what I knew was coming, I agonized about the end of my career. I am so proud to be a Marine, and I love the institution. I love the people I served with. I love what I learned about myself. I loved the challenges I faced and accomplished. And I hated that I was doing my best—and succeeding—but was being treated as a failure. Even as I understood and hated the bureaucracy and the opposition to change, I still bought into the motto *Semper Fidelis*. Always faithful.

On June 29, 2015, I got a call from my boss, telling me I needed to be at the commanding general's office at 7:30 the next morning. At that point, I knew they were going to fire me. The commanding general would not have had my colonel call me if he was going to hold the colonel accountable. I tried not to hear the glee in his voice.

Still, I felt prepared. That night, I copied all of my files from my desktop. I packed up my office.

This was two weeks before my boss was scheduled to change command of the regiment and leave for his next duty station. I hadn't been able to "wait him out."

When I walked into the commanding general's office, my boss was there, and the inspector general who had investigated me was there. Both the commanding general and the inspector general had told me to keep doing what I was doing—that I was doing good work. Now they were both there to lead me to the hangman's tower.

And I had removed the fainting chairs.

The general asked me to sit down. My boss was behind me, so I couldn't see him. The general started reading to me from a script. I thought that was cowardly. *Please just tell it to me straight while you look me in the eye.*

Five minutes into the script, he stopped. He said, "I hate to do this. I'm a big fan." And then he went back to the script.

"I'm relieving you for lack of trust and confidence."

I hate to do this.

I'm a big fan.

As I sat there, it didn't make any sense. It didn't jive with any of the meetings I'd had with him before that. This was the guy who came to see me on four separate occasions between January and May to tell me to keep doing what I was doing. "I know you're having problems with your boss," he told me. "It's my job to fix colonels. Keep doing what you're doing."

I think he expected me to fall apart when he relieved me of my duty.

I didn't. I'd had months to prepare. I wasn't going to give them the satisfaction of crying in front of them.

I know I'm not perfect. There were times when I did, in fact, roll my eyes when I got frustrated with some of the Marines. There were times when I interrupted people when they were giving me excuses. But none of that is a sign of a bad commander who doesn't care about her Marines. I knew they weren't firing me for my performance, for "lack of trust and confidence."

He asked if I had any questions.

I demanded an immediate transfer to Washington, DC. I'll never forget the shocked expression on the general's face.

I wanted to be with Joe. I wanted to be home. I wanted copies of the investigations. And I wanted all of that immediately. I asked for approval to go on leave. I wanted to drive far away from Parris Island. When I had said my piece, I stood abruptly. I had no need for their words. As I turned my back on them and left the room, they had none.

At the crazy, pink house, I packed what I needed and began the drive home. It was only then that I fell apart, distraught. Once again, even with Mr. Fitzwizzle demanding attention while curled up in my lap, my thoughts grew dark.

I thought again of killing myself.

Looking back on it, I feel like a coward for feeling that way; but, even now, it's hard for me to imagine anything worse than what I had gone through.

I can't express to you how horrible I felt. My whole identity was tied up in the Marine Corps, and the Corps said I was an abusive failure. I cared about nothing more than promoting my Marines, and about making sure they were safe and supported—from recruit command to Fourth Battalion. Everything I had been working toward for the past twenty years had been for the Corps, and all of a sudden, they told me I was the worst leader on the planet, and they said it in a very public way.

Normally, the Marine Corps sends out some vague announcement about it being a "lack of trust and confidence." But before I received copies of the investigations, the Corps had not only sent out a detailed statement regarding my relief but also had released the investigations to the media. That's highly unusual. Even the media were shocked. The brass worked hard to publicly make me look like a tyrant.

Any time you get relieved of your command, it's horrible. But if you're a commander, and you're relieved for abusive behavior? The only thing that could be worse is to be fired for dereliction of duty after causing Marines to be killed.

I had rolled my eyes.

They thought I wasn't going to fight back.

They thought I would abandon the progress we had made, and that I would desert the female Marines just as the opportunity arose to show how much they could achieve. I think the leadership at the Pentagon believed that, after I saw my tattered reputation in the morning newspapers, I would crawl in a hole and die.

They should have known better.

I'm a Marine.

CHAPTER 2

THE FIRING SQUAD

Kate,

This is your old EWS facad [faculty advisor], Sumo. I have just read about what happened to you. Let me know if I can help. I don't know the whole story and really only see the tip of the iceberg, but I believe if you were a male there would be no issues with anything you did or didn't do.

By the way, I don't jump to the aid of all my old Marines just because I hear about them in the paper. You are the first.

Hang in there and stay true to yourself.

Respectfully,

Sumo

Colonel Thomas K. Hobbs, USMC

Marine Attache, DAO Tokyo

As I worked to show that female recruits held to higher standards succeeded at higher rates, the Marine Corps worked to show the Pentagon that female Marines only held back the men.

Why?

The Marine Corps leadership did not want women in the infantry.

According to Marine Corps leadership, women in what I would argue is the Defense Department's most elite branch could not be trained to meet high standards in marksmanship, physical fitness, and leadership. As I was showing that they could, the Marine Corps put together a study to show that they could not.

This is why I was fired.

Just as I took over Fourth Battalion, the Marine Corps began its gender-integration study. Women would participate in teams with men to perform combat skills. The integrated teams would compete against all-male teams. The catch? The women had been trained in Fourth Battalion—before I got there and before anyone expected them to succeed. They started at a disadvantage.

Still, I had hoped to participate in the study, and I remember being surprised, at the time, that nobody reached out to me. I was, after all, conducting the Marine Corps' initial training for female recruits. If you want female Marines to succeed at higher levels of training, it seems as if you would want them to come out of boot camp strong.

Oh. Right.

I made my first mistake at Fourth Battalion by coming at the role from a position of logic. I thought about success from a traditional standpoint: "Making better Marines = Success!"

I should have been thinking about it from a position of politics.

I, and my team, had a lot of work to do at Fourth Battalion to make things better, and there were a few people who did not like those changes. But I had the support of my top leadership at Parris Island . . . until I made one key mistake. I wrote a paper for the *Marine Corps Gazette*, documenting our success. It was accepted for publication in March, to be published in the September 2015 issue. I provided a copy to the Parris Island depot sergeant major so that she could brief the depot general. I didn't want to go around him, and I knew that he supported what we were doing. (After all, he had told me to stay the course and keep doing what I was doing.) I just wanted to make him aware of the forthcoming publication of my article.

But before the paper was published, it was briefed to the generals at the Pentagon. Somehow, a paper written by a lieutenant colonel in charge of a battalion of women had made the rounds in the highest ranks. *Sweet! They'll see what we're doing and see that it's good, and we'll be supported in it!* You would think the statistics would be cause for celebration, right? Spoiler alert: They were not.

Immediately, the talk turned to, "How do we get Germano out of there?"

This is what they heard during the briefing, based on what I wrote in that article and on what Joe's friends and coworkers who attended the briefing say they heard: Women at Parris Island for decades had qualified at rates between 67 percent and 78 percent during their initial qualification test on the rifle range, while men qualified at between 85 percent and 93 percent. In Fiscal Year 2015, we raised the women's qualification rate to 92 percent.

The generals learned that our injury rate for women went down to a rate comparable to the men's when we instituted better strength training, such as hiking, rather than taking a bus, to classes and other training, while carrying rucksacks and weapons. We also taught the women how to stretch properly before and after physical training.

The generals learned that women ran faster when we place them in groups based on ability, rather than expecting all of the women to run together based on the slowest member of the group.

These achievements, compared to Marine Corps lore, seemed almost miraculous; yet no one seemed at all interested in how we did it, according to Joe's sources. The generals heard the statistics, and that was enough to determine that they should push my firing, for "abrasive" behavior and being too hard on my Marines and recruits.

I'm fairly certain lollipops and gold stars—rather than an expectation that women can shoot well and will be thrilled with an expert marksmanship badge as a reward—would not have improved the female recruits' scores. But I'm also fairly certain that the "how" of it wasn't important to the Marine Corps generals. Why?

When the generals conducted their gender-integration study, the outcomes were much different from the outcomes at Fourth Battalion.

The Marine Corps began working on its Marine Corps Force Integration Plan in January 2013, when the secretary of defense rescinded the Direct Ground Combat Definition and Assignment Rule, which prohibited women from being assigned to ground-combat units and jobs like the infantry. Women could work in support roles, such as supply or clerical jobs, but they could not have jobs that might involve combat, such as infantry or artillery, and they could not be assigned in support roles to those units. In February 2012, the Defense Department decided women could be on the ground with combat units that were likely to engage in direct combat. They were already filling 315 of 337 available job specialties. They were obviously serving in combat in Iraq and Afghanistan, and they had done so years before, during Desert Storm in 1991. But the Defense Department had not looked specifically at women in combat since 1992, during the Presidential Commission on the Assignment of Women in the Armed Forces.

When the Marine Corps finished the gender-integration study, they cited the twenty-five-year-old findings of the 1992 Presidential Commission—apparently deciding the best way through a tough decision is backward. "Risking the lives of a military unit in combat to provide career opportunities or accommodate the personal desires or interests of any individual, or group of individuals, is more than bad military judgment," the Corps quoted the old report, "It is morally wrong."[1]

Marine Corps leaders have made that argument before—the "social experiment" argument. You may have heard it:

Gen. Clifton D. Cates, the Commandant of the Marine Corps, wrote in 1949 that the military could not "be an agency for experimentation in civil liberty without detriment to its ability to maintain the efficiency and high state of readiness so essential to national defense," according to Morris J. MacGregor's book, *Integration of the Armed Forces, 1940–1965.*[2]

Cates was referring to African American service members.

To make its case against women, the Marine Corps placed one hundred female volunteers in a battalion with three hundred male volunteers, and they found that the all-male squads performed better than the squads composed of both men and women.

Why?

The men shot better, climbed over obstacles faster, and had fewer injuries.

When I read it, the study makes me so angry, I feel like my head is going to spin in a complete circle like Linda Blair in *The Exorcist*—with no injuries, of course, because I've had plenty of training in head-spinning anger over the past year. I've learned how to stretch properly.

The US Army, Air Force, and Navy have all recommended that women be allowed to serve in ground-combat jobs. In those branches, the men and women train together from the beginning of their time in service. Just before the Marine Corps' gender-integration study came out, two women graduated from the Army's Ranger School. This is amazing—not so much because women are capable, but because they were allowed to try. They made it because the training they had received to that point properly prepared them for it.

The Marine Corps women had not been properly trained for the gender-integration study. They had gone through Fourth Battalion before the standards were raised there. I have no doubt that women who have gone through boot camp with high expectations from their leadership can perform well in gender-integrated units. We showed in just one year of changes at Fourth Battalion that women can do exactly the things that the Marine Corps used their study to prove women cannot do.

I'm not the only one who believes the gender-integration study was meant to fail. Navy Secretary Ray Mabus—the civilian in charge of both the Navy and the Marine Corps—told NPR's *Morning Edition* that because male Marines are biased against female Marines, the outcome of the study was "almost presupposed."[3]

In other words, if you have low expectations, you'll meet them.

CHAPTER 3

NOT SMART ENOUGH
TO BE A SAILOR

Dear Lieutenant Colonel Germano,

Ma'am, your courage is an inspiration to me. My career is nearing its end, but I am proud to have spent the last two decades of my life in an organization populated by people like you. My Aunt Roslyn is the CEO of the Dallas Women's Foundation and one of the great true feminists of her generation. I share articles I see about you with her every chance I get.

Best of luck, Ma'am. Our Corps needs more like you!

Sincerely and Respectfully,

GySgt Colin D. Davis

Communications Maintenance Chief

GCSS Using Unit Account Manager

5th ANGLICO

When I was a kid, it never occurred to me that, because I was a girl, people expected less of me.

I never understood boundaries. As a toddler, I'd wobble my way out of the house, through the yard, down the sidewalk, and to the neighbor's mailbox, where I would promptly commence ripping letters to shreds. Too many times, my mortified mother suffered through another apology at the Garrisons' house for my destructive interest in their correspondence. Fortunately, they never pressed charges.

As I grew older, I continued to simultaneously amuse and frustrate my mom and dad by getting up before they did, jumping onto my bike, and playing in the woods all day. As dusk settled and the streetlights came on in the neighborhood, their calls for me to come home echoed from so far away. My imagination had taken me back centuries to build forts with my friends in the woods.

Being a girl never limited me, and I never shied away from a good challenge. It's like the time I wrestled an alligator named Mona.

Stick with me here.

About a year after my mom died, Joe and I took my dad to Disneyworld. Joe and I were close to my parents, and my mom's sudden death from a second round of breast cancer devastated us all. When the dreaded holidays rolled around, we didn't want to spend Christmas at home without my mom. Momma Bear, my affectionate name for her, had always held the family—and all of the holidays, schedules, and households—together. My parents had been married for thirty years when she died. We all worried that, without her, we wouldn't know how to function as a family. Since my dad had always wanted to go to Disneyworld, we figured it would be a good way to spend time together away from home and the many memories of my mom's illness and death.

By the last day in Florida, the thought of another amusement park ride or Disney tune left us feeling as if the world were perhaps too small, after all. As a joke, I suggested that we go to Gator World or Gator Land or Gator Planet or something.

"This is it," I said. "I'm going to wrestle me an alligator."

Unfortunately, I said it out loud. I was kidding, but we got there, and—of course!—you could buy tickets to wrestle an alligator. Then it became a thing—a dare, almost. "Kate's going to wrestle an alligator," all 5'4" and 115 pounds of me. And, of course, because I said it, I had to do it.

So we bought a ticket. My dad and Joe and I were up in the stands at Gator Galaxy when they announced that anyone with a ticket to wrestle an alligator should come down into the arena. I acted totally excited—clapping my hands and bouncing in my seat—but in my head, I thought, "Once again, Germano, you have gone and gotten yourself into something just to prove a point." As I ran down the bleachers—still excited!—I dreaded seeing the beast. I thought back to that National Geographic special in which I learned that alligators can travel up to fifty miles per hour in a sprint, and, in the water, they use their tails to jump up five to six feet in the air. But, as with most challenges, I figured I would look that gator straight in the eye and give him a what for. "And for what?" I asked myself as I slowed down a bit near the bottom of the bleachers. No boundaries. Man or woman, wrestling reptiles isn't the best of plans. I could picture the headline, "Maryland Woman . . ." As I jumped off the bleachers and headed out into the arena, I smiled and laughed at my guys, my ticket all sweaty in my palm like I was five years old again.

And then I looked around. There was nothing but six- and seven-year-old kids in line with me.

Am I the only adult who is going to wrestle an alligator?

But I couldn't back out, because I had my ticket, and I felt somehow obligated to my dad and Joe—even if in the back of my mind I'm wondering if they didn't know that I was going to end up in an alligator pit with children.

Now, to a first-grader, Mona was a giant. Huge and scary.

To me, she looked like something out of a glass menagerie. Small and frail. She measured probably six feet from tip to tail.

If I had known in advance, I would never have done it. I pride myself on giving money to the American Society for the Prevention of Cruelty to Animals (ASPCA), and I treat my chickens like children. (The chickens would not approve of Mona.) I cry every time one of those Sarah McLachlan commercials about saving the animals comes on TV, for Pete's sake. But it was the point. I had committed myself to wrestling an alligator, and I couldn't back down.

Unbeknownst to the people in the stands, the keeper had bound Mona's mouth shut with electrical tape. And unbeknownst to me, you didn't really wrestle Mona so much as just sort of sit on her shoulders—one leg on each side of her head—for pictures. So I walked up to Mona, and then I sat on Mona, trying to be as gentle as possible.

Oomph.

I heard her say it: "Oomph."

The whole thing was just sad, and, again, I wish I had known going in that the activity should be limited to kids who weigh fifty pounds or less—or, more likely, not allowed at all.

But I had different expectations when the idea to conquer one of the world's fiercest predators struck me. I was going to wrestle me an alligator and prove that I was a big-and-strong Marine. It would be a contest of will and wile, and I would risk life and limb.

And then it turned out that a six-year-old could handle Mona just as easily as I could, and that suddenly diminished my achievement.

I'm teasing a bit, of course, but this is how many Marines—or many men—see women. If I'm a big, strong dude, and I can wrestle an alligator, or, you know, make it through the Infantry Officer's Course, but then a woman comes along and does it, then somehow that makes me less of a real dude. If a woman can do it, then it's probably not as manly a thing to do as I thought. So maybe I'll come up with reasons for why she was able to make it: They taped its jaws shut, or they gave her a head start. We heard many men say this about the first two women who graduated from the Army's Ranger School.

In fact, it wasn't until after I joined the Marine Corps that I realized that lowered expectations for women in the military was even a thing. It hit me hard and quickly. As confident as I had been as a kid, after I joined the service, I too fell prey to the belief that women aren't as good at certain things as men are.

Shortly after I earned my commission, or my military appointment as an officer, I questioned whether I was good enough to be a Marine. It started when I got to the Basic School (or TBS), the six-month-long course of instruction all commissioned officers in the Marine Corps must successfully complete before being assigned their military occupational specialties—jobs—and moving on to their first duty stations. It turned out to be way different from Officer Candidates School, which I loved. Officer Candidates School was fun and funny, and we did ridiculous things like running with telephone poles or wading through a god-awful, stinky creek called "the Quigley" with our weapons and all of our gear. (OCS is what officers do instead of boot camp.)

But soon after I got to TBS, I realized that in everything from physical fitness to land navigation, people believed female lieutenants lacked the strength and capabilities of the male lieutenants. I started to believe it, too. It's all about stereotypes, as well as the expectations those stereotypes breed—just like when we tell schoolgirls that boys are better in math and science, and then, suddenly, the girls don't perform as well as the boys.

In the Marine Corps, the perception that women can't do some things as well as men quickly becomes reality, because of how we conduct entry-level training. For officers, it starts with little comments here and there at TBS: "Stay with your teams—make sure the 'females' make it over the walls in the obstacle course." "We're running fast this morning, so the women will be falling out." "Listen, I don't care if you ace this land-nav course—women never do; I just need you to *pass* the damned thing."

Land navigation, land nav, is basically the ability to look at a map, figure out coordinates for longitude and latitude, and use a compass to find a path to a location plotted on the map. It is an incredibly important skill to have when your unit drops you off in the middle of nowhere in combat and you have to lead your Marines to an objective. Since we won't always be able to rely on satellite navigation, all of the services still teach map reading and navigation using a compass.

I will never forget my first trip out to the woods with my map and compass.

Oh man—I was lost! I couldn't have found the nearest stream if I fell out of a boat. Big ol' BOLO. At the time, it didn't occur to me that perhaps I wasn't as capable as my male peers because most of them had grown up navigating with maps. Little boys do that in Boy Scouts, along with learning how to tie knots and run through obstacle courses. Little girls tend to earn sewing and baking badges, which reinforces the idea that one sex is better at certain skills than the other. Land nav was the first time I had ever failed at anything, and it blew my confidence. It didn't help that I was issued a faulty compass, which I realized later. Unfortunately, even though he saw me struggling and doubting myself, my captain never sat me down and said, "Germano, get your head out of your ass. You can do this, and I will show you how."

He simply assumed I failed because I'm a woman.

After I failed land navigation, I had to spend every Saturday in the woods doing remedial training while my peers were on liberty—Marine talk for off duty. Talk about demoralizing. Every Saturday session of being lost in the woods reinforced that maybe I wasn't meant to be a Marine officer.

Compounding my feelings of inadequacy, I also struggled with writing patrol orders, like a lot of other women. I couldn't write a simple sentence with a subject, a verb, and an object—the declarative style that made it easier for a Marine to follow an order. Instead, my sentences tended toward literary.

I had excelled in my writing efforts in college, but there, my professors wanted prose. I could do prose. Oddly, the Marine Corps didn't seem to like flowery sentences. Looking back, it seems a simple thing for a leader or mentor to say, "Hey. If you can write complex sentences, you can write simple sentences. Here's how to do it, but let's also talk about *why* you need to do it." But there was, of course, a less simple explanation: I had grown up couching my demands in pleasing-sounding, kowtowing language to avoid sounding like a bitch. Giving orders is not polite. Young girls are trained to be polite and unassuming—there's no Boy Scout badge for that.

So, my leaders took one of my best skills and turned it into a failure. It set me on a downward spiral that reduced my confidence in my ability to do anything other than an easy job as a lieutenant. My parents did not raise me this way.

I grew up in Aberdeen, Maryland, surrounded by the military. I came from a family with a proud military history. My dad's father had been in the Army—a career soldier. He enlisted and served in World War II and the Korean War, and then he became a warrant officer. He retired while he and my grandmother were stationed at Fort Bliss in El Paso, Texas. My mom's dad was also in the Army.

After completing his tour, he became a civil servant and continued to work with the Army at El Paso, developing missiles.

My mom was raised in Texas, but her mother was British, so when she was a kid they spent a lot of time going back and forth from the States to England. That's probably part of the reason why mom was so independent: it took a lot of confidence to be the odd kid out. She and my dad met when she was a single parent in El Paso, working at the Taco Box. My dad was in the Reserve Officer Training Corps while at college, and, after he earned his commission, my parents got married. After he completed his tour in Texas, they moved to Maryland when my sister and I were little. But then he was assigned to Germany for a three-year tour. Mom packed up the rest of the family after he had been there for a year, and we all moved to Germany. Before we left, she had to give up her job as the manager of a retail store to go be with my dad. She was miserable in Germany. It was difficult for military spouses to get employment overseas. Only so many wives can work at the commissary or the post exchange, and that didn't suit her interests, anyway. She became a secretary, but she hated sitting behind a desk all day. After a while, she didn't know who she was anymore.

So, my mom put her foot down. We moved back to Maryland, and my mom said, "I'm not moving around again." Mom went back to work and quickly moved up through the retail-clothing ranks. She worked as the manager at the Limited, which, during the 1980s, was a big deal. It was one of the cool mall stores—like the Gap—back when teenagers were mall rats, and Valley Girls inspired the nation's style. Mom eventually became the manager at Macy's, which also used to be a big deal. Dad went to grad school in Virginia, but she said, "I'm staying here." So he came home on the weekends. They eventually bought a house in Aberdeen where he was stationed for a while, and then he did a one-year unaccompanied tour in Korea. "Unaccompanied" means the military won't let your family go with you. He did a year at Fort Drum in New York, and, again, she would see him on the weekends.

We never moved out of the house.

I probably got a lot of my independence and my willingness to speak my mind from her. She made it clear to my dad that she considered her career to be as important as his, and she sometimes even earned more money than he did. My parents would discuss things and make decisions together as equal partners. And although it had to be pretty darn miserable to drive six hours home on Friday night from upstate New York to Maryland, and then turn around and do it again on Sunday, my dad understood that my mom needed to work and be successful to feel fulfilled. She had to be more than a wife and a mom.

Sometimes it hurt that my mom worked so much. Because of their work schedules, neither she nor my dad could attend my sporting events, and she had to work a lot on the weekends because the mall was open from 10 a.m. to 9 p.m. But when she was home, she made it fun. She was a master cook, and we spent hours in the kitchen, talking, while she made incredible dinners. My favorite? She would make homemade tortilla chips and incredibly delectable queso dip. It's a wonder that I made the weight requirement to join the Marine Corps.

Mom's career also meant that my sister, Stacy, and I spent a lot of time by ourselves when we were kids. Back in the 1980s, they called us "latchkey kids." It was this "social ill" that made all the big news programs and magazines. We didn't really do after-school programs or childcare then. We definitely didn't do helicopter moms. We just learned to take care of ourselves.

We were independent and resourceful, but we still had to depend on each other. My sister took full advantage of the situation, even though she was only two and a half years older than me. Until we got to her senior year in high school, we went to different schools, and she always got home before I did.

You know where this is going, don't you?

Stacy would get home, grab the key from underneath the doormat, let herself into the house, and then lock the door. She did this because, every single day, I would come running home because I had to pee.

"Stacy! Let me in!" I'd scream.

"What's the hurry?" she'd say. "It's a nice day."

Or, she might just stand in the window and thumb her nose at me.

"Neener-neener."

They'll probably have to replace my bladder when I turn sixty—I'm pretty sure I stretched it beyond capacity, dancing on the porch and begging her to let me in.

But I survived. I came out strong and independent, and I loved my mom and dad and wanted to have a relationship just like theirs when I grew up. No one ever told me I couldn't do or be something because I was a girl. It never even occurred to me that it was a possibility. I mean, my mom believed her career was as important as my dad's. So I grew up thinking that it was normal for women to excel and have career aspirations.

I went to Goucher College, and studied for my bachelor of arts with a history/pre-law double major while working full-time to put myself through school. I maintained a 3.6 grade point average while working forty hours a week at the mall. But when I was a sophomore in college, I attended a graduation at the Naval Academy. As I watched hundreds of white caps soar into the blue sky and then flutter back down, I decided I wanted to be a Navy officer. I immediately fell in love.

Unfortunately, I wasn't competitive for the Naval Academy because of my math score on the SATs.

No big deal. I wasn't going to quit at the first sign of difficulty, so, during my junior year of college, I went to see a Navy recruiter. He gave my SAT scores a cursory glance, and then he told me the same thing the Naval Academy had said: My math score was too low. He said I would never be selected as an officer.

That was the first time in my life I had ever been rejected.

I had been class president all four years of high school. I played four sports. I was voted Miss Popularity and Most Likely to Succeed, which is funny because I'm an introvert. But I was friends with everybody. I wasn't judgmental, and it was easy to be me just because I genuinely liked people. There was nothing cliquey about my world—I floated in and out of every group. It's a good way to be. But it wasn't good enough for the Navy.

I had been in all sorts of clubs, and I took the Advanced Placement classes I knew I would need to go to college. But I'm not super-smart, and I had never excelled at math or science, other than geometry and biology. My older sister? She was incredibly smart, but she lacked some common sense. I was the other way around. I was plenty pragmatic, even as a kid, but it took me a lot of effort to do well in school.

And then the Navy recruiter reinforced that: You're not smart enough.

When I experienced failure at TBS, all of a sudden, everything I thought I knew about myself fluttered away like those white caps. It was the first time I couldn't ace everything I tried. I began to believe that what I had heard about female Marines was true, and it affected how I perceived myself and my potential for service. Nowhere was this more evident than in my chosen job field.

By the end of TBS, I could choose to become a military policeman (MP) or an adjutant (human resource officer) when we graduated. I think if I'd had someone kicking me in the rear end—someone saying, "Hey, Germano, you are better than this. You need to stop doubting yourself and just do it, because it's not rocket science."—I would have been like, "Huh . . . Got it!" I probably would have been a lot more confident, and I would have become an MP.

Instead of pushing me, my captain at TBS tasked me to do the administrative tasks for the unit. Why did he pick me and not one of the many capable male lieutenants? You see it all over the military, even today. Women who are trained in anything but typing somehow find themselves doing the administrative work in their units. There is a perception that women are somehow naturally better at typing and filing than they are at shooting. In fact, when I was at Parris Island twenty years later, I got fed up with my female officers constantly being cherry-picked to take admin jobs at the regiment and depot, even if they had trained in another field. When I questioned the chief of staff, a salty, old colonel, about it, his response was that he thought women were "naturally" better at administration than men. Seriously?

At the end of my time at TBS, my captain completed my final evaluation. He wrote that I was his "little ball of sunshine."

That's exactly what every Marine likes to see on an evaluation. "Follow me, Marines! I'm a little ball of sunshine!" I hear that's what Chesty Puller said just before earning each of his five Navy Crosses.

In some ways, my experience with failure at TBS was good for me. It taught me how to bounce back, even if it took a year or two. But even when I was successful, I felt like an imposter. No matter how good I was at administration or recruiting or just leading Marines, I constantly wrestled with the suspicion that I was only successful because I had taken the easy route. I had convinced myself that I wouldn't succeed at doing anything more challenging than administration, and, therefore, I didn't risk trying.

When I got to my first unit in Twentynine Palms, California, it turned out that low expectations for women Marines were even more pervasive. When I went to my first physical-fitness training session, this reality hit me in the face. As we prepared to go on a group run, we lined up in formation (kind of like Beyoncé at the Super Bowl, but with less snazzy costumes). We formed our square in the battalion parking lot. All of the enlisted Marines lined up in four rows, with the battalion commander in the front to set the pace. When I took my place with the other battalion officers in the rear of the formation, the executive officer, a grizzled, old sucker asked me in front of everyone, "You're not going to fall out, are you?"

Now, I may not be blessed intellectually, but I have a strong body. I can keep the pace. I can set the pace. I can leave men behind. As we started to sing cadence, I groused inside my head: *How dare he?* But about a block into our run—which was more of a slow shuffle—Marines started to pop out of formation. Let me clarify: women began to pop out of formation.

C'mon, ladies.

At that point, I understood why Major Mackey had asked the question.

Because he had seen it time and time again, he assumed it was the norm. I proved him wrong, so I didn't fit the paradigm. As a result, I sought out challenges. I realized I needed to prove him wrong—I enjoyed it. I wanted to be the exception. Hell, I loved being able to prove myself. Soon, I found myself volunteering for the toughest jobs, my challenges at TBS forgotten.

But I also had some incredible bosses who, unlike some other male officers I had encountered, treated me like all of their other Marines.

I had my best experience in the Marine Corps when I deployed to Iraq in 2004 with the 31st Marine Expeditionary Unit during the second battle for Fallujah. As the adjutant, I had to track our deaths and casualties, and ensure notification messages went out correctly and quickly so the families could be notified. It was horrible. I knew somebody had to do it, and I was glad to take the weight off of someone else's shoulders, but it sucked. I don't think I even realized how badly it stressed me out, but that daily processing of casualty messages hit hard, and tallying the numbers to brief my boss, Colonel Walt Miller, every morning drained me. I know it wasn't comparable to what the guys on the ground faced, but that daily grind of sending messages about Marines with catastrophic injuries or those who had died in combat just hurt. I didn't know the injured or killed Marines, but it overwhelmed me to process the reports and then try to work through a useless headquarters back in Okinawa to get combat replacements for them.

Despite his heavy burden of command in combat, Colonel Miller recognized that I struggled with that task, so he started giving me all of this other stuff to do. I had so much respect for him—he was the one who realized the military needed to up-armor Humvees to better protect Marines against IEDs— improvised explosive devices, or roadside bombs. In 2004, when the Marines first deployed to Anbar Province, the threat of IEDs did not yet exist. When my husband was with the 1st Marine Division for the initial invasion in 2003, everyone drove Humvees that had soft-skin doors, like an old Jeep, and floors that a blast would instantly tear apart. Even then, Marines sandbagged their vehicles' floors and hoods to protect themselves from mines, bullets, and rocket-propelled grenades. Soon, our guys were getting slaughtered because the insurgents hid explosives in creative ways, like inside the carcasses of dead donkeys on the side of the road, and because the IEDs grew large enough to destroy a thirty-ton armored Bradley Fighting Vehicle (BFV). Deadly explosively formed penetrators (EFPs)—aerodynamically stable rounds that could tear through armor after being shot from long distances—came in from Iran and other places, and began to appear on the battlefield. Because Colonel Miller knew we had to continue to patrol our area of operations, he directed his Marines to hammer plywood and weld scrap metal to the outside of the vehicles and continue to cover the floor with sandbags. We used to call it "hillbilly armor."

Even as he bore the burden of an impossible mission, Colonel Miller cared enough about me to try to take my mind off of those daily casualty logs. To keep me focused, he let me be on the retrograde cell, to plan our return movement back to our ship when we left al-Asad. He also took me with him when he went to visit his forward-deployed Marines. I felt like such a part of the team, and I loved meeting the people we were supporting. We flew all over Iraq, and I was also allowed to participate in a civil-affairs mission in which we delivered supplies to a school for little girls.

After the second battle for Fallujah ended, the uninjured Marines from the battalion landing team returned to al-Asad to get a little bit of R & R, which was great. Some of them had been wounded in combat, but they returned to their platoons after they recovered. After just a few weeks of recovery time, in January 2005, we were tasked to support the first democratic elections in Iraq by providing security at the polling sites. In the middle of the night, one platoon of Marines loaded up into a CH-53E Super Stallion troop-transport helicopter to head out to the polls near the Jordan border. There was a bad sandstorm, and the helicopter crashed, killing thirty of our Marines and a sailor—a Navy corpsman who served as a medic for the Marines—in one single accident.

I have a hard time even thinking about it. After the victorious return of the Marines to al-Asad following weeks of sustained and brutal hand-to-hand combat, and right before we were supposed to head back to our ships to go home, we lost more Marines in one day than on any other day in the Iraq War.

I learned a lot during that deployment, and I finally felt like a Marine—not a female Marine. I felt like a Marine.

I took a risk for that assignment. In 2001, I was diagnosed with multiple sclerosis. To be fit for duty with the 31st MEU (Marine Expeditionary Unit), I had to stop taking my medication, because the shots I had to give myself had to be refrigerated, and Iraq was a hot, austere environment. Ironically, considering all of the crap we were burning in pits and burn barrels in Iraq, my disease probably had something to do with how the military disposed of waste when I was a kid.

I grew up about six miles from Aberdeen Proving Ground, and there are bad chemicals in the air and soil there. During World War I and World War II, the government manufactured and tested toxic chemicals, including mustard gas, at the ranges on the installation. In the years since, the Environmental Protection Agency has found napalm, white phosphorus, and chemical agents in the ground and water. When scientists conducted groundwater testing, they detected significant levels of heavy metals, volatile organic compounds, and chemical weapons. Not good.

No one knows what causes MS, but I can tell you that drinking that kind of water can't be healthy. As kids, we don't worry about drinking water, but I began to wonder about it when the media showed up at my high school my senior year because base personnel had found containers full of mustard gas buried in the ground. As an adult, I started reading about another site like that, in Spring Valley, a neighborhood near American University in Washington, DC. Spring Valley is a million-dollar residential community now, but it was once where the military tested weapons during World War I. Scientists have found chemicals in the water—lewisite, mustard, arsenic trichloride. Bad, bad stuff. It's the first military Superfund site in a residential area where the Army is still looking for old chemical weapons buried in the ground.

My mom was diagnosed with breast cancer after I was diagnosed with MS, and I always thought I was a one-off because I didn't know anyone else in the family who had MS. But when Mom got sick the first time, we started to put dots on the neighborhood map for people who had gotten cancer. The lady across the street died from a brain tumor. The lady kitty-corner from our house? Brain tumor. Another neighbor, whose driveway lined up with ours, had cancer.

Right before my mom died, my dad, Joe, and I were with my mom in her room at Johns Hopkins. During his rounds, the oncologist asked my dad about her medical history. My dad said, "She has MS." I stared at him. "No shit?" I thought, but I never talked with him about it, because it was too painful. After she died, it was too hard. She had never told me she had MS, too, because she was afraid I would worry about her.

When my mom was first diagnosed with breast cancer, she didn't tell me that, either. Joe and I were stationed in Japan at the time. She waited to call me until she had her double mastectomy. She wanted to know it was going to be okay before she spoke to me about it. I flew home immediately, and it devastated me and my family. Mom was always super-independent and lively and fit and busy, and after her surgery, she slowed down.

A few years shy of her five-years-clean mark, she felt exhausted and had a weird pain in her side. She went to the doctor for an appointment and took my dad with her. As the doctor examined her, he assured her that it was probably just a pulled muscle because she had finally felt well enough to work in the yard. But my dad told me that as soon as the doctor touched her stomach and side, his expression changed. Mom and Dad both knew the news was catastrophic. We lost her two months later. Just before she died, she was so disoriented because of a buildup of calcium in her system that she kept sending me garbled text messages. It was like she was trying so hard to tell me something, but by the time I was able to fly home from California, she couldn't even talk. She couldn't eat—and she was so tiny. All through my life, she had showed by example that no boundaries should exist for me on account of my sex. All through my life, she stayed strong to show me I could also be strong.

All through my life, she had high expectations of me.

When she was alive, I swore I would never let her down. When she died, it became even more important to make her, Joe, and my dad proud. I wasn't going to let MS or anything else keep me from challenging myself.

It wasn't until I started to take on more responsibility that I realized how few women make up the Marine Corps. Only 4 percent of Marine Corps officers are women. By the time you hit major, the numbers begin to drop off dramatically. In 2016, 208 female majors served in the Marine Corps. There were 3,667 male majors. That puts us at about 5 percent of the Marine Corps majors. At lieutenant colonel, I was one of sixty-three women—or about 3 percent of Marine Corps lieutenant colonels. General? Yeah. One out of eighty-three. Seeing a female general in the Marine Corps is akin to seeing Bigfoot riding a unicorn. It's awfully hard to make it into the general-officer ranks without infantry experience.

That may sound absurd, but if you look at the Fortune 500 ranks, you'll see that women make up about 4 percent of the CEO positions. It's the same dynamic with the good old boys and glass ceiling.

So you would think that women would band together to raise each other up, right? Guess what else never occurred to me until I arrived at Parris Island?

There's no mentoring or professional network for women in the Marine Corps. There are so few of us that it's dog-eat-dog. We're all trying so hard to fit in that we're not about to group together. We're trying to be one of the guys. Our buddies are guys. *Is someone having a hard time? That sounds like drama—I'm going to stay away from her.* But that's just it—we shouldn't have to fit in, and we shouldn't think twice about checking in with each other and supporting each other when there is drama. "Drama" in the military is often code for sexual harassment or sexual assault or gender discrimination or being looked down upon because you can't get behind the wheel of a Humvee when you're nine months' pregnant or not being able to pass a physical-fitness test because you're not strong enough. None of those things should qualify as "drama."

When I was at recruiting command the first time, I was one of two female operations officers in the nation. When I took command on recruiting the second time, I was the only female commanding officer. As I was leaving, I reached out to another woman taking command to let her know I was here for her for whatever she needed. I never got a call back. And I know why. You don't want to be that woman—the one who needs another woman's help. The woman who can't manage to hang tough with a bunch of guys, no matter what. It's my biggest regret that I didn't go out of my way to lift other women as I worked my way up the career ladder. But I was that person who thought, "I don't want to associate with her, because people will think I'm weak."

Surprisingly, the expectation that women will fail can be strongest among other women.

Of course, it shouldn't be only women who rally to support other women, but it seems like a pretty good place to start.

Instead, we learn the old-school ways, the way the Marine Corps (or the company or the sports club or the family) has always done it. When I was a recruiting-station commanding officer, I shouldn't have felt like I needed to cuss or I needed to yell. I shouldn't have felt like that's what people do to get a point across, but it's everything I had observed my leaders and counterparts doing. It was just normal. It's the way we were raised in the Marine Corps. But it's a double-edged sword for women to be aggressive leaders.

Let's face it: My yelling comes off completely different from when one of my peers yells. If Major Sam Smith called in one of his Marines and said, "Hey! You need to get your head out of your ass!" Lieutenant Jim Jones would be like, "Oh. Okay. I just got my butt chewed." But if I called someone into my office and said, "Hey! You need to get your head out of your ass!" it's abuse. When I yelled at Marines to hold them accountable for screwing up, they were more likely to complain to my boss that I was mean. And most of my bosses were more likely to feel sorry for them and to lecture me on being nicer rather than to examine the reasons for the counseling to begin with. They would never say this to a guy.

I remember coming home and telling Joe about a counseling session I had with some of my recruiters who hadn't written a single contract in months.

"Well, what did you say?" Joe asked.

"Well, I told these Marines that if they didn't start doing their jobs, I was going to f-ing fire them," I said.

Joe looked at me thoughtfully.

"You know, if I said that, they'd be saying, 'That Plenzler is a tough leader,'" he said. (Plenzler is Joe's last name.) "'Don't get on his bad side.' But because you said it, you're being mean, or just being a bitch."

Sometimes, Joe sees things I don't see, because he knows how men treat each other. I could see him sorting out how to tell me what he thought.

"For most men serving in the Corps," he said, "the thought of a woman as a peer, competitor, or boss is a complete paradigm breaker. They understand women as moms, teachers, sisters, girlfriends, girlfriends that dumped them, and girls they couldn't get, but that's pretty much the extent of it."

Even so, have I mentioned this was the Marine Corps? No matter how you feel about women, you should, as a Marine, have the ability to have your ass chewed. It's almost innate. It shouldn't matter if the ass-chewer is a man or a woman. We are supposed to be rough and tough, and yet my male Marines were given carte blanche to act as they wished, while I was told to smile more and be nicer—no chewings of asses, because the men couldn't handle it.

My experience as the commanding officer of a recruiting station was the second time I had a boss who understood what I was trying to achieve and the obstacles I faced with gender bias. For my first year, a (rare) female general was in charge of the region, and she served as a mentor for my boss. He respected her even though she was a woman, and it caused him to think a little differently. So, if he heard a Marine complain about me, he would offer a different perspective. Further, he had four daughters and a more egalitarian view. If someone said, "Germano's mean," he would say, "Well, is she really mean? Or did she sit you down and do what any officer should do and tell you to get yourself straight because you're worth it? And did she do it any differently from how any other officer would have done?"

But most of my peers had never served with women. Remember, women make up only 8 percent of the Marine Corps, and, until 2015, we weren't allowed into ground-combat units except as support. There are still whole battalions made up completely of men. For my first year and a half in command, I was the only woman out of all of the commanding officers in the nation. I've never had a female boss, and rarely was I assigned to units where I worked directly with other female Marines, particularly officers. For me, that was normal. That's how my whole career had been. But for the men, it was weird to have a female in their ranks.

For instance, when Joe and I met at the Marine Corps Air Ground Combat Center at Twentynine Palms, there were maybe four active-duty female officers on the base. Joe was a platoon commander at 2nd Battalion, 7th Marines at the time, and when I visited him at his company area, it so shocked the Marines to see a female officer that they would stare at me. I felt really uncomfortable. Joe would explain to his Marines in caveman speak that it was okay for me to be there—something like, "Mongo, she woman. Okay. You. Mom. Woman, too. Okay. She no hurt. Be gone soon."

Joe does the caveman impression way better than I do.

In any case, even when I wasn't smiling on the job, we were improving our recruiting numbers and retention rates like crazy. I had specific goals, and everyone knew what he or she needed to do. It ended up being good for the recruiters and their families—their quality of life improved—but I was strict about it. I had high standards for my Marines, as well as for the young men and women we recruited, because I believed we owed it to the Corps to enlist only the highest-caliber kids, to ensure success in battle. And our efforts paid off. Enlisting fewer kids who required waivers due to brushes with the law resulted in fewer kids quitting training. We started winning awards and earning kudos from the leadership. Best of all, we achieved the lowest attrition rate—number of recruits who don't complete boot camp—at the recruit depots, for men and women, in the history of the Marine Corps. My Marines did that, and they made me proud. They still teach things we implemented at the Recruiters' School.

But the commanding officers went to recruiting conferences that rotated around the district, which covered California, Nevada, Utah, Oregon, Hawaii, and Wyoming. At these conferences, each recruiting-station commander gave a formal brief on his or her stats—the good, the bad, and the ugly. I don't think a military mission has gone forward in twenty years without a Death-by-Power-Point session. So, at one of these conferences, I briefed my peers on the incredible things my Marines were accomplishing. Our statistics were off the charts, but instead of my peers congratulating me or asking how we had done it, most of them just pooh-poohed it. I didn't understood that. But, knowing what I know now, I think it was partially because they had a hard time accepting that I could compete. Again, that paradigm breaker.

That was the first time I saw it. Imagine this: You're briefing a room full of your peers, and you're showing all this great stuff, and instead of people saying,

"Hey! Great job. How did you guys do that?" it's almost like they resent it. I now realize that it wasn't because we were doing well so much as because I was different. Female.

At the next conference, one of my peers, the commander from Portland, Oregon, pasted a picture of my face over a picture of a guy doing something athletic with the text, "Shhh! I can't hear you over how awesome I am!" in his brief. I can take a joke—if it's a funny joke at my expense, I'll gladly laugh along with you—but I remember thinking, "That's messed up. I don't feel like I talk about what I'm doing personally, and I don't brag; I make it about what the Marines are doing and how great they are." But as a woman, you're damned if you do, and you're damned if you don't.

My recruiting station was number one when I left. Most of my peers, I think, had a hard time accepting that.

All of us need to work to fix that. Until we change how women are perceived as leaders, there's always going to be a Private Germano, a Captain Germano, a Sergeant Germano, or a Lieutenant Colonel Germano who feels ostracized because she's doing well, but her peers think she's an asshole because women aren't supposed to talk about their accomplishments. When women talk about what they do and how they do it, they are perceived differently from men who do the same thing. Guys don't have that problem. Research shows that, in most instances, men's confidence exceeds their actual abilities, but they don't feel any reticence in faking it until they make it. Why? Because they can't hear you over the sound of how awesome they are.

Oomph.

As I said, I didn't recognize it as gender bias at the time. Part of that is because I love the Marine Corps so incredibly much, and I love most of the people I served with. I would do it again—I can't even imagine doing anything else. There are days and people I'm proud of. But part of it was also that I didn't want to admit that gender bias existed, because admission meant I was complicit in the problem.

Here's the interesting thing: When I finally faced it, and I led the female Marines and recruits at Fourth Battalion, I realized that they needed a strong leader to say, "No, failure isn't acceptable simply because you are women," and, "I expect you to do better, because you ARE better." I know now that certain language can suggest in an unconscious way that women aren't good at some things and shouldn't be expected to excel. I didn't learn until I got to Parris Island that there was a name for this: the Golem effect. The Golem effect is the idea that if you have low expectations for a group of people because of their race, gender, or ethnicity, they will underperform. In the end, failure becomes a self-fulfilling prophecy. I saw this firsthand when I tried to figure out why, for decades, the female recruits had achieved such miserable results on the rifle range:

Everyone knows that girls can't shoot.

CHAPTER 4

DATA GEEK

Kate,

   Let me know if you need anything. I think highly of you, and I know you set and hold Marines to a high standard—for the right reasons. I will gladly help you if I can, and I am happy to chat with you if you need someone to vent to.

   S/F,

   Brian

   LtCol Brian P. Coyne, USMC [a peer CO on recruiting duty]

   Commanding Officer

   2d Bn, 3d Mar, 3d MARDIV

My peers gave me a hard time about not being able to focus on any-thing outside my own awesomeness, but here's a secret: We made obvious, easy changes at the recruiting station.

   It shouldn't have been a big deal. I didn't see anything particularly "awesome" about it, but I was hoping presentations from my district could help everybody else. Stress levels were high; the suicide rate was up; recruit success was down. So, how do we fix those things? Well, we give people more time off, we make sure recruiters have time to take care of themselves, and we pay attention to the standards for new recruits. If we do it right, all of those things will work together.

   While I was commanding officer on Recruiting Station San Diego, we changed the status quo—the way things had always been done. And that set off waves of bulldog hackles up and down the West Coast.

   In the military, the response to an attempt at change is often, "But we've always done it that way."

   I don't believe the Marine Corps is different from most large companies in that respect. When you think about it, if companies had been operating outside the status quo, more women would be CEOs. Management would be more diverse. More products and services would be aimed at women and minorities. And, just as I experienced on recruiting station duty, making those changes would increase the companies' success rates.

This shows up in so many obvious ways: Women, and especially minority women, are paid less. Women talk about making a choice between a career and a family, but—except in rare cases—men would never break down life that way. And women often rely on healthcare and services and products that are geared toward men, not women.

This plays out in doctor's offices; doctors believe that women's heart disease and men's heart disease are, in fact, completely different animals—that they're not even the same disease. Treating them the same could be killing women.

It can play out in seemingly small ways, too.

When I go to buy outdoor gear for my hikes along the Appalachian Trail with Joe, many packs don't fit my frame and my color choices are often limited to pink and purple. (Okay, so I happen to love pink, but still . . .) But think about the woman who likes to fish or hunt, or who works as a firefighter or a service member, and think about the gear limitations. Female service members will tell you that body armor chafes chins, digs into hipbones, and sticks out an inch or two from the body, rubbing against that soft spot on the back of the arm. We manage, but it's not built for us.

Not only is there an obvious fix, but some genius will make a mint marketing toward an already-existing crowd. (Some already are: *Outside* magazine devoted its April 2017 issue entirely to female athletes supported by advertisers marketing women's gear.[1])

And female CEOs? In 2015, Quantopian found that female CEOs in the Fortune 1000 helmed companies with three times the returns of companies led by men.[2]

I suspect that more women in leading roles would also translate to a Marine Corps inspired to new ways of thinking about how to do things.

When I got to my recruiting station in San Diego in June 2007, we used data and analysis to determine if "the way things have always been done" was the best approach. This may or may not surprise you: It was not.

I was excited to take over.

I had been on recruiting duty once before, as one of the first women to be assigned as an operations officer, oddly enough. Basically, that meant that I was in charge of making sure we were on track to make our monthly enlistment and shipping missions for kids (the majority are seventeen years old when they sign up, and then turn eighteen before they graduate from high school and ship off) to go train at boot camp. It's similar to what operations officers do in the civilian world. I didn't know at the time that it was some big deal for a woman to do it, because it just seemed like something anyone could do.

I also learned I wasn't that bad at math, despite hating flash cards as a kid.

At my first job in recruiting, I found I enjoyed collecting data and filtering through it with a stubby pencil to identify trends and warning signs. That experience helped tremendously when I got to San Diego. Most of the recruiters at San Diego were male Marines, of course—it doesn't take a math whiz to figure out those odds. Two male officers worked for me at my headquarters, and then I had thirteen recruiting substations, which were small offices, located throughout a 9,000-square-mile territory that spread from San Diego to Orange County to Las Vegas.

As soon as I got to San Diego, I briefed all of my Marines on my command philosophy, part of which is, "Do the right things for the right reasons." I told them, "We're not going to allow this to be about quantity over quality," because there had been this "shit in, shit out" mentality.

For lack of a better term.

This was at the height of the war in Iraq. The surge—or General David Petraeus's move to flood Iraq with American troops as a show of force, but also to enact his counterinsurgency measures to build trust and hope among the local people—had resulted in some successes. But it had also meant an increase in Americans being killed and injured by homemade bombs. The Marines we sent in had to be good, not only for the sake of military success, but also to keep themselves alive.

And they had to make it through boot camp.

We're always looking for the high school student who's on the sports teams, who's on the honor roll, as opposed to the kid who's coming into your office to avoid going to jail.

Yeah. That's a thing.

So, right from the get-go, from the day I started, I wanted to shift that mind-set. The recruiting station had a lot of potential, but it had become known for recruiting in bulk. It had a reputation for turning out big numbers, rather than focusing on low attrition and sending the right kids to be recruits. Rather than seeing the applicants as real human beings, it was common to call them "bones"—as in "roll them bones." This was inexcusable, particularly since many of these young men and women would see combat just months after they completed recruit training.

"Attrition rate" refers to the percentage of recruits who sign up for a set amount of time—say, four years—but don't make it through their training because of injuries, because they fail their tests, because they're not a good match personality-wise for the Corps, or because they physically can't complete the training.

Before I arrived, the recruiters in San Diego tended to be rewarded based on how many people they could get to sign a contract, and there was a lot of pressure—especially at that time—to get high numbers. There was little scrutiny on waivers across recruiting command. During the biggest buildup for the war years, the military issued waivers to allow people in who normally would not be allowed in. The waivers were for drug use, for being overweight, for not meeting education requirements, for having children as single parents, for having prior mental or physical issues, or for having felonies. I knew from the analysis I had done on my previous recruiting tour that recruits who required waivers had much higher discharge rates for disciplinary and mental-health reasons. In my mind, if we cared about the Marine Corps, we should focus on enlisting kids who would stick around and complete their four-year obligations honorably.

Think about it: Almost as soon as a new recruit gets off the bus, there's a drill instructor screaming about how many recruits won't make it. It's supposed to toughen you up, make you feel proud of your success, build the tradition of the Marine Corps as the elite military branch.

Well, that's a waste of resources. It's a waste of taxpayer money. And, holy crap, it can't be good for the self-esteem of a person who walks around for the rest of his or her life thinking, "I failed."

Let's say you have to sign up ten recruits per month, as a baseline. You sign up your ten, but two don't make it through boot camp. The next month, you have to sign up twelve recruits to make up for the two who didn't make it. Not only have you put hours and hours of work into the two who didn't make it, but you now have to spend hours and hours replacing them—on top of your normal base. Well, if you're now struggling to get twelve recruits, you'll take anyone with a pulse. So how many don't make it to boot camp the next month?

What a waste of time. Many of our recruiters had recently been deployed, so they thought that recruiting duty would be a break from deployments. The reality? The recruiters were so stressed out trying to meet their numbers that, at one point, the rate of military recruiters killing themselves was three times higher than the rest of the military.

In the corporate world, a good CEO would probably look at those issues and work to fix them. But changing that mentality in the Marine Corps was hard. It was so important to me, though, because (1) it was about the quality of the Marine we were making for the institution, and (2) it was about giving quality of life back to our recruiters. (We say "making a Marine" to describe the process a person goes through from a civilian to a fully trained, physically fit, confident Marine.) For every discharge, for every kid who signs up and then decides not to go to boot camp, you have to make that up. You have to sign up another recruit on top of the next month's numbers to make up for the previous month's failure.

There was another problem: Some recruiting stations were doing well, but if the district didn't perform well as a whole, that didn't matter. So the recruiting stations that performed better were trying to bring in extra numbers to make up for the stations that didn't perform well, so they could help the district meet its mission.

Man, were they stuck on those numbers. Everyone was happy if we came up with more warm bodies to help them make mission, but, in the end, the Marine Corps suffered as an institution because the high-risk kids weren't shipping to or graduating from boot camp. We'd hear about it from the drill instructors, and then even further up the chain: A recruit might make it through boot camp, but then he or she might have discipline problems or suffer injuries at the unit level. It's not that some people don't deserve the chance, but a kid who desperately wants to be a Marine will prove it. A kid who never thought about being a Marine before, but had the attitude that, hey, it sounded better than asking Mom for cigarette money and, golly, the uniform looked cool, probably shouldn't be hitting our standard for an "elite" military branch.

Bonkers.

I'm not knocking my predecessor. The Marines loved him because he made each of them feel like a winner every month. But his focus on quantity and not quality meant the very Marines who worshipped him as a commander dug themselves into holes every month trying to make mission. The recruiters were working every single day, without any time off, and we weren't making mission until midnight on the last day of the month, which meant the next day, they had to turn around and start the cycle all over again. Their absence from their home, as well as their stress levels, tore their families apart. My recruiters were drinking. They were getting in fights. They were driving while intoxicated. They were arguing with their spouses. They were getting fat and out of shape. I understood why, and I wanted to fix it. That was my priority.

In any case, we had to shift the focus and the mind-set of the Marine recruiters. It took a lot of persuasion and motivation; it took a little bit of yelling; it took being firm. That was especially tough because these Marines had, in the past, been applauded for getting the big numbers—not laid out for the high attrition rates.

Looking at the data helped me figure out where we needed to focus our efforts not only to change and improve the quality of life for the recruiters but also to improve the caliber of the recruits. We realized it was a leadership issue for the district commander. If you have recruiting stations that aren't making mission, your job is to look at them and hold them accountable, give them training, figure out why they're not making mission, and then help them change that—not rely on one recruiting station to do extra at the expense of discharges and at the expense of quality in the Marine Corps.

A CEO would likely look at those managers and say, "Hey. This needs to get straight, and here's how we're going to do it. And if you can't make mission by selling 602 widgets in six months, then I'll just fire you and find someone who can."

Funny thing about the Marine Corps: A recruit signs the dotted line, saying he or she will give up life or limb for her country, and, in return, the Corps will start them out at about a thousand dollars a month for a salary. With this four-year contract, it's awfully hard to fire someone. In the Marine Corps, your boss gives orders, and you follow them, or you get in trouble.

Conversely, in the Marine Corps, if someone's not performing well, punishment probably isn't the best way to motivate him or her; but you have to do something, because you're sort of stuck with that person. And that person's sort of stuck with you—a Marine can't just not show up for work one day.

And civilian bosses, generally speaking, don't want to train up someone, get to know that person, and then can him or her at the first sign of negligence.

In either case—civilian or military—you shouldn't have to use termination as a motivator.

I've spent a lot of time learning about change management and workplace culture. Some of that training came from the Marine Corps: We have to be able to motivate our troops without threat of punishment. I mean, you can only make a person do so many push-ups and paint so many rocks (Yup. Also a thing. Painted rocks are a well-loved feature of military landscaping.) before your next option is jail.

That seems a little extreme for not agreeing with your boss.

Fortunately, my boss had my back.

I think he realized that I made him look good. He was smart enough to look at the big picture and see how it applied across the board. So, when I had a Marine who disagreed, he backed me up.

But that's not enough. I had to show my subordinates how the changes would benefit them personally. I had to explain to them that, yes, it's going to make your life harder in the short run, but in the long run, this will benefit you and your family because you'll be home more. And you'll be healthier because you'll be working out more.

I'll get to that in a second.

Typically, about 90 percent will buy in to positive change like this. But the remaining 10 percent? That's hard. Sometimes, you just need to work on the education piece. You need to make sure they understand that you're not doing it just to be an asshole. Sometimes, you have to cheer them on. "Yup, it's going to be harder, but I know you're capable. I'll show you how."

And, sometimes, you have to remind them that ultimately, it is the Marine Corps, and you have to do what you're told. We call that "pulling rank."

My boss understood that if we improved recruits, we'd have less attrition. And, as I said, I proposed simple changes—it wasn't exactly a hard sell.

First, no more waivers for kids who were overweight, had committed felonies, or had not graduated from regular high schools. Our data clearly demonstrated attrition links for recruits with waivers for these issues.

I felt like waivers were often an easy way out for recruiters who—whether due to a skill deficit or laziness—weren't doing the work: Go out and find a kid who isn't super motivated but needs a way out, rather than look for a kid who has already proven him- or herself and who wants to excel mentally and physically. I also worried—and the numbers bore me out—that those recruits might not be mentally equipped to deal with what they might see in a war zone. That's the extreme. At the most basic level, if a recruit had already rebelled against institutions such as school or local law enforcement, they might rebel against a drill instructor telling him he had three seconds, exactly three f—ing seconds, to wipe that stupid grin off his face . . .

Or, you know, whatever.

Second, I personally interviewed all female applicants. It wasn't that I singled women out; it was that there were so few of them, and our attrition rate for women was 40 percent. I wanted to know why. And, if they wanted to be Marines, I wanted them to see me—to see the possibilities and to see that there are women in leadership roles. If they were there for other reasons—because they needed to escape abuse at home, for instance—I wanted to talk to them about why the Marine Corps might not be a good, safe zone for them. I knew that women who have been sexually assaulted are 70 percent more likely to be revictimized. Since the Marine Corps has the highest sexual harassment and assault rates of all of the services, I wanted to prevent these women from experiencing sexual trauma ever again. After all, I knew they would not be afforded any good resources for preventing future assaults if they did join. All they would get as Marines is the basic annual sexual assault training that everyone else received. This didn't mean that we didn't allow women with a history of abuse to join, but it did mean that we paid a whole lot more attention to their medical histories and their participation in training with their recruiters before we allowed them to go to recruit training.

I paid the same attention to my male applicants who had been sexually abused.

If a male recruit needed a waiver—for a criminal history or because he was overweight or because he didn't graduate from high school—I did the same thing. I brought him in for a face-to-face interview.

And then, out of spite, I sent them all to the Navy recruiter.

Just kidding.

It was just as important to me that these young adults made good decisions for themselves as it was that we got our attrition rates down. In some cases, these men and women were meant to be Marines, and I proudly sent them on their way. But there were times when, after talking with these kids one-on-one, I wasn't willing to risk their safety.

Third, I instituted a strong physical-fitness program, for both the recruiters and the recruits. There's a tendency for recruiters to lose that leatherneck physique when they're working eighty hours a week trying to make up for those attrition numbers. And there's a tendency for new recruits—particularly female recruits—to show up at boot camp unable to meet the minimum standards for upper-body strength, running, and sit-ups.

Standards for fitness and weight regulations should be no different for recruiting units than they are for anywhere else in the Marine Corps. If you're a military police officer or a clerk, you must be able to do a set number of pushups and run in a set amount of time. That doesn't go away when you become a recruiter. That also applies to recruits who haven't shipped to boot camp yet—or "poolees," in Marine-speak. A Marine Corps regulation required Marines to work out together every week, to build esprit de corps and to ensure that all Marines are fit enough to do what the Corps needed them to do. Some of my Marines did, in fact, hold physical-fitness events for some of their applicants.

Volleyball, anyone?

Seriously. They prepared for the Marine Corps by playing volleyball once a week.

I put a stop to that. It was fine for team-building once in a while, but we needed to keep track and hold recruiters accountable for not just their own fitness but also that of the new recruits.

To make sure those changes were enacted, we modified how we evaluated the performance of my Marines. Rather than letting recruiters get away with saying, "We had an awesome PT session today!" I required them to show me how their fitness plan impacted performance. Give me data: New recruit Chandra Smith started as a new poolee running a seventeen-minute mile-and-a-half run; six months later, she can run the same distance in twelve minutes.

It wasn't rocket science, and when my Marines expressed frustration, my constant refrain was, "Train like you're going to war—like any other Marine Corps, non-recruiting unit." It wasn't like I enjoyed always bearing bad news. It made life miserable. But I knew that to get to where I knew we were capable of going, we had to get through a rough patch. Change is always hard, but I was convinced that if I could get the recruiters to see the WIFM (What's In It For Me), they would eventually come around.

And I was willing to miss mission my first month at San Diego to show how serious I was. I wasn't going to let the recruiters hold me hostage as a commander. At midnight on the last day of the month, I elected not to enlist three applicants who required felony waivers, which meant we missed our mark. For a recruiting station that took pride in not missing mission for years prior to my arrival, it was a warning shot that resonated across the entire district. We never missed mission again.

I wasn't always great at motivating or inspiring people, and I had to learn some hard lessons about why my goals weren't everyone's goals; but, in the end, we were not just squeaking by to make our contracting and shipping missions each month. To improve the quality of life for my recruiters, we started planning our prospecting missions to allow us to make mission the first week of the month, which meant recruiters could take time off with their families or go to college or to military training. By cutting out waivers, increasing our screening ability, and improving the physical-fitness program for our applicants, we achieved the lowest attrition rates in the nation—in the history of the Marine Corps.

My people started earning awards, which not only feels good but also shows up on their performance reviews and in their records for promotion. We became the district's top recruiting station for quality the first year. By the second year, we were the region's top-quality recruiting station, and we took Recruiting Station of the Year in my final year.

It was good for the Marines.

That was my job as commanding officer. I gave quality of life back to my Marines, and we worked together to make them successful. They stopped getting into trouble, and when it was time for them to go to their next duty stations, their families went with them, intact. It wasn't always easy, and it tested my relationships with my recruiters at times.

But when we started tying performance to metrics, things changed. Attrition went down. My recruiters had more time off. And we graduated committed, tougher, faster, stronger Marines.

See? Easy-peasy.

That's the best kind of awesome.

CHAPTER 5

THE REST OF THE STORY

Kate,

    I wanted to let you know how proud I am of you. What you have done bodes well for all service members, not to mention my Army 2d Lt daughter who starts field artillery school today. If you ever need to talk, I am available. Keep your head up high. God Bless you.

    Semper Fi,

    W. Lee Miller, Jr. [my 31st MEU CO, and the best boss I ever had]

    MajGen USMC

    Chief of Staff, USSOCOM

I learned something else at the recruiting station—something that perhaps should have been obvious at several points along my military career, but that I had been blind to.

Now I see it everywhere.

Throughout my career, I believed that if I were tough—if the women within my command were strong—they would be safe. Bad things wouldn't happen to them. They wouldn't be harassed. They wouldn't be assaulted. They wouldn't be belittled.

They wouldn't be raped.

Looking back, that's a great source of shame. I believed this: If you're tough, it won't happen to you. If you're tough, they won't treat you that way. I put that pressure on my female Marines. I feel terrible about that.

It comes, in part, from military training. It's part of our culture; and it encompasses a whole series of issues. The first, and probably largest, is that if you show up at your company and you're one of a handful of women, you already stick out like a Marine in a bunny suit. Chances are, you're going to work hard to fit in by trying to be like one of the guys.

When you are the minority in a hypermasculine culture, it is an almost-impossible task. You try hard to fit in, even if it means denying help to or affinity with those of "your kind." We tend to stay away from those who are known as being "trouble," which can include any woman who makes an accusation of sexual harassment or assault. If a female Marine is known for dating around, we assume she could have avoided bad situations by "behaving better." She's the drunk girl. She's the too-friendly girl.

She's the weak girl.

This is the very definition of victim blaming, right?

It plays out in other ways: If a female Marine is seen as a weak link because she isn't a strong performer or is a "problem," and an accused assailant is well-liked within the company and known for his strong performance, why would a commander go out of his or her way to thoroughly investigate a harassment accusation? In the military, the commander decides whether to investigate allegations.

Here's the thing: If women are trying to fit in and be one of the guys, they're not working to mentor each other. We're not reaching down and lifting up. Part of that is also a matter of numbers—there aren't a lot of us, and certainly not in leadership positions, as I talked about earlier.

But some of it is being blind to a problem if you feel that it hasn't affected you directly, personally.

That's exactly why the #MeToo online campaign hit so hard in late 2017: Women everywhere had assumed they were the only ones who had faced harassment, or that they hadn't, in fact, faced harassment, because being catcalled or asked out by your boss or badmouthed by coworkers is so common that it is seen as normal. #MeToo showed them they were not alone, and that those behaviors are bad and should not be tolerated.

But I had tolerated it. I hadn't called it out when it happened to me, and I didn't look for it to make sure it didn't happen to the women in my command. I am responsible only for me, but I was not the only one who didn't work to beat it down.

In fact, sexual-harassment briefings in the military can be places for jokes or denigration of women. Commonly, the man becomes the victim. "Don't shut the door behind you in an office if you're counseling a woman, because she might accuse you of harassment." "Watch your back with women you're dating: She may later accuse you of rape." Or there's the chestnut about how many he-said/she-said situations are really about a woman later seeking revenge, so she reported the guy she had willingly slept with.

Does it happen? Sure. Occasionally but not usually. And just like "date rape" on college campuses, we shouldn't be putting it all on the woman, blaming the victim. We sure as hell shouldn't believe it's a woman's fault if she is harassed or assaulted, because she drinks or goes to a party or walks by herself or dates. It's the assailant's fault, period.

But most shameful to me as an officer is that senior women in the military do not speak out about this issue. They've either not dealt with it themselves or have not recognized it when they saw it. They wave it off as youthful stupidity. That allows them to not consider it their problem.

At about the time I was headed to Parris Island, our first four-star female general, Ann Dunwoody, came out with a book: *A Higher Standard*, about her time in the Army. Sounds right up my alley, right?

In some ways, it was. She writes about being able to run fast, which meant that she kept up with her commanders, which meant she was invited to participate in physical-fitness sessions, which meant that they got to know her, which meant that she got lots of good advice.

The women in the rear? Not so much. After all, this was the Ann show.

She talked about taking risks to deploy to Kuwait during Desert Storm when she didn't have orders to go. She talked about being one of the first female officers to go to the US Army Airborne School. She talked about reworking the Army's supply system so that the soup-sandwich approach that took place in the 1991 war didn't happen again during the wars in Iraq and Afghanistan.

Pretty badass, right?

She went to Airborne School in 1975, which was when female officers were first allowed to attend. She said the first thing she saw was a poster that said, "Paratrooper: The Last Step to Becoming a Man." She also talked about the first time she jumped out of an airplane, saying one of the Black Hats, or Airborne School instructors, slapped her hard on the butt. "That was the only time that happened to me, and I never saw them do that to anyone else," she wrote.[1] She was a stick leader, which meant she would jump first, because the Black Hats figured if she went first, the men would be too embarrassed to chicken out.

When she arrived at her new duty station of Fort Bragg, she wrote that she felt pushed away, and that the leadership didn't know what to do with her because she was a woman. She was given a job she was overqualified for, and she said that would never have happened to her male friends.

She wrote about the hazing that every officer went through who went to an airborne unit, which included being shocked by officers who used a car battery and two wires, and having to tell an extraordinarily dirty joke to get into "the club." She was angry when people assumed she got a position because she was a woman, rather than because she was qualified for a job.

She dealt with a division commander who refused to allow women to jump out of the same aircraft he was on.

She said in the 1990s, as gender-integrated training began, that it was time to overcome "long-held prejudices and sexist views," especially after the scandal at Aberdeen in 1996, when twelve drill instructors were charged with sex crimes involving female recruits.[2]

"I had been in the service for twenty-one years and had never encountered any direct form of sexual harassment or assault," she wrote. "Although in my early years, I was exposed to questionable language, inappropriate comments and jokes, these were a reflection of the Army in the 1970s. I did believe, in this case, that our junior enlisted women had become the easy targets because they were young and less experienced."[3]

I think of this as willful blindness.

And, yeah, I was exactly there.

Until I wasn't.

It's so hard to get into "the club" if you speak out against it.

Listen: I can and do swear like a sailor (apparently, they're worse than Marines). But should a woman who swears be perceived differently from a man who swears?

Absolutely not.

Should I be okay with someone slapping my ass on the way out of a plane, because I don't want to make a fuss?

Nope.

Should I be afraid to tell my female boss, because I don't think she'll believe me that my co-worker is harassing me?

No.

In fact, my female boss should be mentoring me about sexual harassment and gender-integration and how to move up and how to deal with nonsense. My female boss—and all of the other women within my company or command— should be supporting each other to ensure we're all successful.

It should be the norm. We shouldn't have to be "one of the guys." We should be ourselves.

I recently wrote a piece for the *San Diego Union-Tribune* about the issue of senior women refusing to speak out about sexism in the military. It makes sense that the problem can be ignored by senior women. It's an ugly problem—one that is not commensurate with our values system—so to acknowledge it means having to question other fundamental aspects of our service. It would require these senior women to acknowledge that maybe they really aren't part of the club, despite years of trying to fit in.

But even as senior women like Dunwoody are able to explain away harassment and assault they may have experienced, there is no way to deny that their subordinates are being mistreated daily. As many as one in four female veterans report being sexually harassed or assaulted while in the military.

Have you heard about Marines United? Male Marines and Marine Corps veterans posted to social media pictures of female Marines that they believed would embarrass the women. There were nude shots. There were compromising-position shots. There were unattractive shots. Do you know how many Marines participated? As many as thirty thousand. That was in 2016.

In my case, when I was a junior officer, I heard male Marines talk about women in a derogatory way early in my career, and I did nothing. *Barracks whore.* *WM*, meaning "Walking Mattress." If I had spoken up, I would have been "other." Somehow, I believed that they thought of me differently—that I was extraordinary.

Certainly they didn't talk that way about me.

As you move up the chain of command, there's even more pressure to conform and be part of the tribe. So as we gain power, we tend not to use it to reach back to help other women. There's a mind-set of dues-paying, certainly—I had it rough, so you should, too—but it's also this need not to be seen as a troublemaker.

How horrifying is it that mentoring women in the military could be seen as renegade behavior? Why should it be brave to help women fight those battles?

These younger women are aware of our failures. Like other groups that have gone underground to seek help, they go online. They have secret Facebook groups in which they discuss things like dealing with a groping sergeant or a platoon leader who pushes women to the side in favor of men when it's time to get a job done. They talk about co-workers who call them names or hang offensive posters or form Facebook pages purely to talk about how women do not deserve to serve in the military.

And we, women in leadership positions, we stand to the side.

We violate their trust.

We talk about *honor* and *esprit de corps* and *no man left behind*.

But then we circle the wagons to protect the strong man—the true member of the tribe—and ostracize the woman.

Because senior women haven't spoken out, we've allowed lance corporals to bear the burden and be ashamed in silence. To me, that is the worst travesty of all.

We see it in war zones. You're already one woman out of one hundred men. You add the pressure that there's a chance that your hooch (shelter) won't lock. There are loud generators everywhere. No one can hear you yell. Your schedule is long, and your only opportunity for a shower is in the middle of the night, in a freestanding trailer among hundreds of other trailers.

When something bad does happen, you don't go for help. Why? Because the response may be worse than the assault. Will there be retaliation? Ridicule?

Or nothing?

It makes me so angry.

After writing an article about the problem, I got dozens of emails from captains and majors—lower-ranking officers—and I got an email from one of my recruits who is now a Marine in Okinawa—but I didn't hear from any colonels or general officers, except for one.

Marine Corps Colonel Cynthia Valentin, a previous commander of Fourth Battalion, told the *Union-Tribune*'s Carl Prine that she had been harassed and degraded at every level of her career.[4] But until I wrote that article, I had never heard a peep from her or any other senior woman in the Corps who acknowledged that she had experienced gender bias, sexual assault, or harassment.

I heard from another young woman after I wrote that piece for the *Union-Tribune*.

She called to tell me she was proud of me.

Yeah, that's not ego-tripping. She also told me she felt like I never took her seriously when she was one of my Marines at our recruiting unit. That's a crushing blow—when one of your best sergeants—male or female—feels like you let her down. She was the operations clerk, and she was great. She had it together, and we could always depend on her—and she was fabulous to be around. I loved and respected her.

But she had a problem with a master sergeant.

I was completely oblivious to it.

It wasn't even because he was such a swell Marine. I took him to court-martial for all kinds of fraud before I left San Diego, but until that point, I thought he was fine.

As it turns out, he had also been harassing her the whole time. She wanted to blow the whistle on him, but she didn't. Why? Because she thought that I should have seen it. She thought that she shouldn't have had to turn him in, because it was right in front of my face and I should have had her back. And I simply didn't see it.

When she was just about to turn him in, he came to me and said she was being disrespectful—a pretty classic move for someone who victimizes people. I went to her and said, "Hey. What's going on? How is it possible that you're my best sergeant, and you have all this incredible potential, but I'm being told that you're disrespectful?"

That was it. She shut down. She heard me saying that I believed him and I didn't believe her, and I truly regret that. She thought I should have seen that he was coming on to her and being inappropriate. Even if I didn't see it, I should have allowed her to feel like she could come to me with it—that I was a safe place.

Instead, I talked about the importance of being tough and being strong to, you know, fit into "this man's Marine Corps." She interpreted that as, "It's a point of weakness if you allow yourself to be subjected to this." I have no doubt that's what I conveyed.

Devastating.

My blindness to the problem didn't stop there. Just like General Dunwoody, I had experienced it myself and had still been blind to it.

I once had a boss who told me that he loved working with me because there was no sexual tension.

Wait. What?

He out-ranked me. Was I supposed to say I was disappointed? That I was, in fact, glad that he wasn't attracted to me? How about, "I'll bet you say that to all the girls?"

What would the appropriate response have been?

On recruiting duty, I heard from my peers that they didn't respect the work we were doing. Joe will tell you that I would go home and we used to have these conversations in which I would tell him about my inability to fit in with my peers—that they perceived me as being my boss's favorite. They thought we were winning awards because I was the favorite. I told Joe when I had trouble getting some of my male Marines to do what I was telling them to do. I told him about yelling at Marines for not doing their jobs and then learning that I was being called "bitchy."

And I mentioned the cussing. That's not me. F-bombs every five minutes? I didn't grow up like that. But there's no way to be an authentic female leader in the Marine Corps.

I used to say to my Marines, "You need to be able to turn it off and turn it on."

But why? Why can't you just develop your own leadership style? I felt like I had to have multiple personalities, yelling at one person, smiling as I walked so I wouldn't be accused of "resting bitch face," walking back with my leadership so I didn't come across as aggressive, and so on.

I'd come home and say about one of my Marines, "I don't get it. I've tried everything to help this guy be successful. I've tried educating him. I've tried giving him time off. I've tried yelling at him. I've tried giving him more work. Nothing is working." And Joe would say, "Has he ever worked for a woman before?"

The fact that I was struggling with my peers became clear when I would have to give a brief about our stats at the commander conferences. My peers were so cruel about it. It wasn't mere razzing. They would be assholes about it.

Joe got it. But to me it was a sign of weakness to acknowledge that they perceived me differently because I was a woman. Or acknowledging the difference was a sign that "Maybe I'm not as good as I thought I was. Maybe I am being treated specially because I'm a woman." As a woman in a leadership position, you're always juggling those two thoughts. Imposter syndrome and token syndrome: "I'm not supposed to be here, and they're going to find me out" versus "I'm only here because I'm a woman, and they need to make their numbers."

It all leaves you working harder, running faster. You're never good enough.

If I couldn't see it for myself, I couldn't see it for other women. And, furthermore, I couldn't see the effect my struggles had on everyone who worked for me.

I was recognizing that I went into San Diego being hard as nails because I felt like I had to prove myself. I realized later on how traumatic that was for the Marines. I was trying so hard to fit in, but it was a terrible mistake to overlook gender bias and harassment simply because I wanted to be a part of that group. That's what I learned in San Diego.

I never would have talked about that to my subordinates, including my great female sergeant who was dealing with an abusive master sergeant. I'm not even sure what I would have said, because I didn't have answers to how to deal with it myself.

That's a problem.

I regret that.

I think I could have told her, "You're not the only one who's experiencing this, and I will hold him accountable, and I will look at all the facts, and I don't want you to feel uncomfortable."

I never got a chance to do that, though, because she didn't feel safe coming to me.

I had failed her when she needed me most.

I should have not talked about strength the way I did. I think about this a lot because of the way we talk about mental health in the Marine Corps. Most Marines won't talk about depression, even though everyone's dealing with it, because it's perceived as a sign of weakness. I think I could have re-jiggered how I talked about being mentally strong: Everyone deals with adversity differently, and that's part of being human. But I just wasn't there yet.

I was there by the time I left San Diego. I knew it before I went to Parris Island.

By then, I had a better understanding, and I wanted to be that mentor figure. I wanted to help women with their careers. I wanted to help them be strong so they would feel successful, rather than like someone was going to find them out. I needed for my recruits and Marines to understand that the system was not designed to protect them from being harassed or assaulted. I needed for them to understand the odd power dynamics in the Marine Corps and that there were key things they could do to lessen the chance that they would be targeted for abuse by their counterparts.

But, most importantly, I needed them to please, please look out for themselves and for each other. Lift each other. Mentor. Reach back. Be aggressively themselves.

That's where I was when I arrived at Parris Island.

CHAPTER 6

ESPRIT DE CULT

Ma'am,

I am a former infantry Marine from Kilo 3/3. I feel compelled to write to you and let you know that you have the highest degree of respect and support of the overwhelming majority of all the Marines and former Marines that I know.

Back in my day it was expected that a Recruit Training Battalion Commander should be hard as nails, speak the hard truth regardless of whose feelings it hurt, and keep the training hard in order to form and create young Marines fit and ready to face the mental and physical trials of war.

In my opinion, and in [that of] most others I know, you did exactly what you are supposed to have done to ensure your Marines walking across that parade ground on graduation day were the very best they could be and I would have been honored to have served under your Command. Semper Fi.

Very Respectfully,

Alberto D. Santillan

Perhaps you've seen the commercial: The square jawline. The gleaming saber. The rifle spun by strong male hands.

The few.

The proud.

The Marines.

Even our advertisements boast of our uniqueness.

We don't leave the Marine Corps—ever. Former soldier? Former sailor? Former airman? Yes, yes, and yes. But once a Marine, always a Marine. It's sacrilege to say "former Marine." Wave your flag, wear your emblem, plaster "Semper fi" on your bumper.

Anyone who serves should be proud of his or her service, the willingness to risk life and limb. But have you ever wondered why the Marine Corps beefs up the brand so much? To the point that the other service branches joke that we're a cult?

It's because we should not exist.

After World War II, the United States didn't have a lot left for its military budget. The Army argued that the Marines did the same thing as soldiers and sailors, so why not move things about so the Army could have the Marine Corps' money? That did not go over well, and the Marine Corps generals argued to Congress so full-throatedly that the Marines were ultimately protected by the National Security Act of 1947.

We have not forgotten.

In his book, *First to Fight*, Marine Corps General Victor Krulak argued the importance of continuing the Marine Corps, asserting several times the uniqueness of the Marines: We can fight and we can do it while wet.

That history has led to an eternal fight for relevance.

We're tied to our stories and our accomplishments on the battlefield and our heroes and our nicknames because we can't let you forget our importance. We say our aviation is different. It's not—both the Army and the Air Force have similar operations. We say our amphibious operations are different. Well, the Army does amphibious operations, too. We say our infantry is different and that's why women shouldn't serve in it. We are the only service to maintain segregated boot camp. We say that everything about us is different, but that's not true, and the differences that we do have are not always different in good ways.

But, of course, we don't take ownership of any problems, or someone in Congress might hear us and do away with us. I think it's the fight for relevance that makes us seem a bit cultish.

The fear of a threat to your existence will make you fight harder and dig in your heels harder. When was the last time you heard about a cult admitting to an error?

Our messaging is particularly impressive.

We push this image that Marine infantrymen are the ultimate athletes. Nope. Just like the other branches, we get a bunch of skinny eighteen-year-olds who smoke too many cigarettes, drink way too much beer, and eat Pop Tarts for breakfast. That's okay: Eventually they grow up and they do their jobs. Sometimes they even bulk up. But the point is that we've become so great at telling America what we are—brawny, bulky, leathernecky men—that America believes us.

We're the most trusted service, and we're 'Merica's 911 fighting force. Why would anything need to change?

We're perfect.

I love my Marine Corps, and I've told you why; but, in some ways, we set ourselves up for scandal because we're so afraid that if we acknowledge the truth, the myth might fall.

Joe and I never fit that mold. We always looked at the Marine Corps with one eyebrow up because we knew we weren't as good as everybody thought we were. I think it's healthy to have that kind of skepticism. I think that's how you get better. The State Department emphasizes the need for constructive dissent in its ranks for exactly that reason, and they even give awards for it. It allows them to fix issues before they become disasters, while also making people feel like their voices are heard and respected.

The Marine Corps doesn't have anything like that. To speak ill of the Marine Corps if you're in it means you are "other." *You* become the problem.

Oddly enough, until Parris Island, most of my bosses recognized that I was "other," but they didn't see my squeaky wheel as a problem. This was because they understood that I wanted to make the units I was in better (which, in turn, made my bosses look better, too.)

Parris Island, however, takes cultish behavior to an extreme. After all—this is where we "make Marines." Because young officers fall under drill instructors' command while they train at Officer Candidates School, officers tend to be intimidated by DIs. The campaign hat and the shiny belt buckle evoke images of eating dirt while doing push-ups. This attitude can even be held by those who outrank the DIs. For example, Joe told me that when he ran the DI school at San Diego, his first sergeant trained the officers who would go on to lead recruit units. Lesson number one? "Don't be afraid to step up and correct the DIs. This is no different from the rest of the Marine Corps: You're in charge."

But that is exactly what is different at Parris Island: The enlisted personnel run the cult. The enlisted don't want officers interfering with their business. The enlisted Marines believe they're the ones who make Marines. Nowhere else in the Marine Corps would it be acceptable that officers didn't contribute to the welfare and education and mentoring of their Marines.

You walk onto the base and, as an officer, you don't feel welcome in your own house. You have the sergeants major, the most senior enlisted Marines on the base, contributing to this idea that officers shouldn't be walking around their base; officers shouldn't be in their squad bays. And officers allowed it.

If all of the enlisted Marines had been doing an amazing job, I suppose Parris Island could have been an easy tour for an officer.

They were not.

CHAPTER 7

FOURTH DIMENSION

Good Afternoon Ma'am,

First of all, I hope things are going as well as they can be going for you right now. I never got the chance to officially shake your hand and tell you thank you before my wife and I left. If there was ever an officer that I would want to emulate, it would definitely be you, Ma'am. My wife speaks so highly of you, your ambition, and your character. She loves to say that you and her have the same mentality. Ma'am, I truly appreciate everything you have done for her. She never lost faith in you and the SgtMaj. You were the main driving force that kept her fighting to work harder, be louder, and demand more from everyone than she ever thought she could! Thank you Ma'am! You will never understand just how amazing you really are, but those that truly know you and have your vision are following in your footsteps! I wish you the best blessings in life and whatever path God leads you. No matter what trials and tribulations you endure, remember that God takes care of his people! Semper Fidelis and Ductus Exemplo!!

Respectfully,

SSgt Moffett, Latoya [one of my former DIs]

Platoon Sergeant, 2nd Platoon

If the Marine Corps was a haven of cultish behavior, and Parris Island had a subculture that pushed that cult to the extreme, then Fourth Battalion was like *Lord of the Flies*, with women.

Nobody wants to see that movie.

I officially took over on June 10, 2014. I had spent the week prior talking with the previous commander and learning more about the inner workings of the battalion. I expected "left-seat, right-seat" training, where she would show me the ropes and then observe and advise: Here's my daily routine; this woman's your go-to for getting things done; don't eat the potato salad in the chow hall.

I would have a battalion made up of four companies: three for training—November, Oscar, and Papa—and one for administration, headquarters company. Each company had a company commander and a team of officers and enlisted noncommissioned officers—NCOS—to assist them. Fourth Battalion is the only place in the Marine Corps where enlisted women go to boot camp.

Fourth Battalion fell under the Recruit Training Regiment, which included three other training battalions—boot camp for male recruits—a support battalion, and the Drill Instructor School. My new boss was in charge of the regiment.

I wanted to hear about my predecessor's successes, and I hoped there was a plan to move forward from the ground she had gained.

No ground had been gained.

Instead, she told me about the things she had hoped to accomplish, but had not. When I first met with her, she told me that she wished she had been more engaged with her officers. She wished she had spent more face time with her Marines. She had hoped to spend more time in the squad bays with the recruits, but did not. All of these are normal Marine Corps functions for leaders, but in hindsight she realized she hadn't done enough.

As my predecessor kept talking, I had a hard time believing what I was hearing: She had thought about installing security cameras in her office because she believed her Marines sneaked in in the middle of the night and read documents they should not have. It struck me that she wasn't worried more about transparency. I decided to keep the personnel files in the admin office and leave my office door unlocked. Let the Marines know you trust them, and they should trust you.

I suspect she was really telling me that the job—and the people—had made her paranoid.

She feared the Marines were colluding against her, and against each other. She had had several Marines request masts—help from someone above their commanding officer—because they believed they were being mistreated. She believed that her Marines were setting her up to fail.

She had reason to believe it: Her sergeant major had been pushed from her position for essentially running a shadow command and trying to undermine her.

These were all things I would come to believe, too, but at the time, I thought that what she was telling me was nuts, and I told Joe Fourth Battalion was like Bizzaro World. You know that episode on *Seinfeld* in which everything is exactly the opposite of real life? To have a battalion commander say she didn't feel comfortable walking around in her own squad bays, and that she constantly worried about what her Marines thought of her? Well, who's in charge?

She said she got no help from higher command. She warned me that Colonel Daniel Haas, the regimental commander and my new boss, didn't want anyone to rock the boat. She seemed, rightfully, certain that any trouble would lead to what she referred to as his "tomato face," as she described his habit of pursing his lips and turning bright red when he was angry.

"You need to be careful here," she told me. "It's not like the rest of the Marine Corps."

I guarantee you there's not a single male battalion commander in the entire Marine Corps who's ever said these things to his replacement. But that was normal for Fourth Battalion.

Fourth Battalion seemed to embrace its "Fourth Dimension" nickname, this idea that it was a different world from the rest of the Marine Corps and not necessarily a better one. Unless there was a VIP visit and the regiment wanted a dog and pony show, no one from the outside paid any attention to the battalion or the female recruits. The male battalions already considered the women an afterthought, and, physically, we were almost invisible. Men and women didn't eat together or train together or generally even see each other because our buildings were separated by time and space.

The leadership didn't visit because, "Oh, Lord, what if I walk into a squad bay and the women are undressed?" The female drill instructors were allowed to do whatever they wanted, however they wanted, because no one checked in and no one cared about standards. The women did not focus on making war-fighters. They were too busy abusing each other and being cruel to the recruits, their subordinates. Nowhere else in the Marine Corps would that kind of behavior be tolerated.

The Marine Corps didn't take ownership of this issue: This was just how women were expected to behave. To me, it was immediately apparent that women were seen as "other," and therefore as a problem.

First, we were segregated. The Marine Corps is the only military branch that trains women separately from men in their boot camp or basic training. The leadership liked to say that the training requirements were identical to those for male recruits, and, yes, the training for women was thirteen weeks long just as it was for the men. On paper, the women were required to do all of the same things the men did, like rappelling, swimming, going through the gas chamber, and participating in field training. But because segregation bred a "hands-off" mentality by the senior leadership on the recruit depot, the way the training was conducted was completely different from the men.

Second, for decades, women had underperformed, and no one had ever questioned why or demanded improvement.

And, third, when I worked to improve our standards, I got pushback from some of my peers and from within my battalion: They said I was being too hard on my Marines and recruits because I was trying to make them stronger, to hold them to something above the lowest standard required for women.

In my mind, women were serving in almost every job and every unit within the Marine Corps in some capacity. If we held them to lower standards and continued to allow them to barely pass fitness-test standards or to half-assedly perform training events, it would make the rest of the Marine Corps weaker.

"They already meet the standards," I was told. "What's your problem?"

At Parris Island, if you draw attention to a problem, the problem becomes you.

And the Marine Corps believed women would never be equals anyway, because they would never be strong enough to be in the ground-combat units. So why change anything?

This cult behavior perpetuates sexism and negative stereotypes: *Why would we change the way we train Marines? They're awesome! It's the best service!* But we're the ones with the Marines United scandal. We have extreme misogyny and extreme hypermasculinity, and we allow Fourth Battalion to be seen as the crazy Fourth Dimension.

My predecessor recognized all of this. She did not try to fix anything. The place was run by the enlisted population, with officers serving as tokens. She didn't want to change anything, because she feared her Marines would turn on her.

These women made fraternity hazing cases seem tame. They did not allow the new drill instructors to drink water. They forced the new DIs to use the recruit head, rather than using the drill-instructor bathroom. (That's bad for two reasons: First, as a drill instructor, it's best not to be in a vulnerable position with recruits. And, second, when you have sixty recruits using one bathroom, disease runs rampant.) They called them "NICs"—New In Command—and didn't allow them to wear their drill-instructor covers (in the military, "cover" means "hat"), even though they had earned them after completing Drill Instructor School and it was a big deal to wear one.

Before I got there, some drill instructors forced a new drill instructor to stand duty for several months straight—every day, at the depot, without a single break. There was such a vacuum in leadership that she was essentially tortured, and no one picked up on it. She didn't get a full night's sleep for months, other than between training cycles. This woman sent her daughter away to live with relatives because, as a single parent, she couldn't stand duty every night and take care of her little girl. By the time I got there, she was a mean, mean woman, and she dealt with that abuse by abusing others.

We've also found that drill instructors who abuse recruits are more likely to have been abused themselves. There's a whole host of issues that need to be dealt with there—from self-esteem problems to a tendency not to respect authority to poor self-care concerns—in addition to providing a safe place for our recruits.

When I arrived at Fourth Battalion, officers and staff noncommissioned officers weren't doing the right things, like periodically walking through the squad bays unannounced at night or reviewing the nightly recruit-inspection results to ensure that sick recruits were seen by Medical. Because we were so isolated and there was no accountability, things were allowed to slide. DIs were sleeping with other DIs, as well as with recruits, so we had both fraternization and abuse of authority.

The pressures of work were so bad that some of the drill instructors were beyond depressed and tired. Empathy was in short supply at Fourth Battalion.

The month that I arrived, there had been a court-martial, and a regimental nonjudicial punishment for two former Fourth Battalion drill instructors who were accused of abusing recruits and other DIs. Nonjudicial punishments allow commanders to punish offenders by lowering their paychecks, giving them extra duty, or reducing their rank without going through an actual court-martial.

Two drill instructors from November Company, one of the three training companies that together compose the Fourth Battalion, were in trouble because they had been cruel to the recruits.

They intentionally tried to make the recruits pee their pants through intimidation, and had told the recruits things like, "I wish you were never born" or "Your mother should have had an abortion." They called them derogatory names—terrible, abusive things.

Training should never be personal.

But this was in a company where the first sergeant referred to her drill instructors as "bitches." She had been hazed, and so she allowed her DIs and her recruits to be hazed.

November Company's DIs would get their recruits up in the middle of the night and make them do push-ups and stupid stuff in the squad bays. Yes, that was common in the old days, but now we know that training during the day is much more effective if recruits are awake for it. DIs made the recruits drink so much water that they'd throw up. Or, after making them drink water, they'd make them run laps if they requested to use the bathroom. Request again? Run more laps.

If a recruit didn't respond quickly enough to screamed demands, the DIs would egg on the other recruits to take out their frustrations on them. It was like a blanket party with words. And the more seasoned drill instructors made the lives of the junior drill instructors hell. You would think that all drill instructors would be created equal and be welcomed into the club . . . not so much at Fourth Battalion. The amount of "hat hazing"—DIs are the only ones who wear their special round-billed campaign hats, and "hat hazing" refers to abuse of those who wore the hats—in November Company was legendary, and would have lifelong consequences for not only the drill instructors but also their recruits, many of whom would end up being dropped from training for mental-health reasons. None of the leadership ever reinforced the idea that the abuse had to stop, even when it was highlighted by courts-martial.

It was not a good situation.

It's not legal. And it sure as hell is not humane.

Try changing that dynamic when DIs have learned, over time, that that's the only way to make tough Marines—screaming at them all day, every day, regardless of what the training doctrine says. Because Parris Island is the only place where we make female enlisted Marines (as an officer, I did not go through boot camp at Parris Island), all of the drill instructors had been trained as recruits in the exact same environment and place: Fourth Battalion.

Parris Island almost felt gang-like in how territorial it was. Marines in the battalion were so terrified of Marines from other companies that they avoided their company areas. They told me, "If we need something, we rely on our own company, because with the rest of the battalion, it's us against them."

I know this is how movies portray basic training. I've seen *Full Metal Jacket* and *Platoon*. But such fictional depictions haven't been the reality for years. There are several reasons for that: First, as I explained before, we spend too much money on recruits to break them. Second, we no longer draft recruits; they are volunteers. They shouldn't need to be forced to do a job they signed up for. And, third, we have a professional military, and, therefore, we want to teach servicemen and servicewomen how to act like professionals capable of being ambassadors for America in the outside world.

But there's another reason that's more subtle. If all of the women came in understanding that we design boot camp to break them down as individuals and then build them up into teammates—that it's all essentially a head game—they might be able to live up to that game. But if you add to the mix a group of women who may have been abused as children, or who may have been sexually assaulted (as we know a high number of recruits have been), or who may have gone into the Marine Corps simply because they didn't yet know what they wanted to be when they grew up, you've got a volatile situation. Exposed to this toxicity, some of these young recruits will come out scarred for life, and that's *not* how you make a Marine.

But most of the drill instructors had been brought up through this abusive system themselves, and they believed that that's how they were supposed to behave—like the woman who pulled duty for several months straight. You could probably create a chart showing that for every drill instructor who had been in trouble for recruit abuse or DI abuse, there had been abuse in her unit when she went through boot camp. The thought seemed to be, "It sucked while I was in. Why would I make it easier for you?"

Changing that mentality would be incredibly difficult, particularly considering that I inherited a first sergeant and a company commander in November Company who never bought in to what I hoped to do. They did not enforce the change from the top down and, in fact, were offended that I told them they needed to change tactics. Who was I to interfere in their business?

Oddly enough, November's company commander took over the month before I got there. The investigation into her drill instructors began several months before she got there. She absolutely could have started fresh with a command philosophy that demanded no abuse, but it appears she also bought into the idea of hard-assery over success—or she was simply too intimidated by her enlisted Marines to try something different.

One of my favorite officers said that being in that company was the worst experience she'd ever had, because she understood what they were doing was wrong. When she tried to fix it or prevent it, they ostracized her, and she got zero help from the battalion commander when she tried to blow the whistle. Before I got there, she said there had been no direction—no way to measure success. And, she said, when she tried to make change, the blowback was so fierce that she went to other officers to ask for help. Their advice? "Pretend you're a squad leader." In other words, sit back and let the enlisted Marines handle it.

Even being professional was seen as a sign of weakness.

Fourth Battalion itself did not promote good behavior. They were short-staffed; they were working terrible hours; their families were often far away; they weren't getting enough sleep; they didn't have a social life; and their basic needs were not addressed.

These Marines had been hand-selected for the assignment. It's a special duty. It's a privilege. You have to be impressive to be chosen in the first place. You go through DI school, and you're the greatest thing since green camouflage, and you even get to wear a cool hat (cover). Then you graduate, get to your battalion, and are treated like shit by your peers—because that's just the way it's always been.

At the very top level, no one said, "Hey. Good job. This needs to change—you worked hard to get here, and we're going to make it better for you."

At the very top level, no one said, "Hey. We care about the safety of the recruits and making good, strong Marines. We're going to make it better for them."

Instead, they sent the women off to their "other" corner and ignored them.

CHAPTER 8

IRON LADIES

Hello Lt Col Germano,

What happened to you is such a dismay, know there are so many of us out there supporting you and rooting for you. Continue to fight! I just read the *NY Times* article and though I haven't had the honor of being in such a pivotal position like yours I can relate to your challenges as I've had a boss very similar to yours. I've also had pushback from troops of mine who didn't really want to work.

You are a unicorn in a balloon factory (Seth Godin, *Tribes*) so yes, people won't like it and some won't like you. You are a trailblazer and though it is so unfortunate that the system worked against you (b/c yes it is archaic) in the dismissal, I believe it is a good thing that it is so public. Though I feel for what you are going through and it must be tough to have the world watching; however, know that this is generating a lot of great conversations and I hope this will bring the toxic/sexist tendencies to light.

I cheered when you said [you would not be accused of] "being overly aggressive if I were a male." I was saying the same thing before I read your words. I am also thrilled you pushed back with your own investigation. I'm disappointed in the results, but it actually proves the point that I often try to make that these biased tendencies are so subtle and hard to note. The commander [who], whether consciously or sub-consciously exhibits the sexist/biased behavior, has so much plausible deniability. We must figure out a way of bringing to light those toxic tendencies . . .

You may have many more emails to read so I will stop here. Know that you have ranks of women (and men too I'm sure!) backing you and your leadership style. I love how we are now at a point where it's not enough to show up, we must challenge ourselves to BE and DO more.

Thank you for who you are, what you do, what you represent, and what you are enduring.

V/R,

Mel

Melody H. Mitchell, Maj, USAF

I realized immediately I would have to hold people accountable from top to bottom, both for performance and for safety. We simply couldn't continue the "tears and cupcakes" routine if we were going to be credible. I'd come in hoping for team-building and joint decision-making, but some folks just weren't making the shift. So, I hit hard with my command philosophy, which I began to develop after my first trip to Parris Island before I took command.

I knew that my command philosophy needed to reflect that I expected my Marines to be responsible for their own actions, as well as for the actions of their peers and the recruits. I had also gone to a Marine Corps commanders' conference in May, where they talked about the need to have a command philosophy to define a commander's leadership expectations for his or her Marines and sailors.

It's no different from a performance-management system, really. Without a kneecap-to-kneecap discussion about performance goals, expectations, and metrics for assessment, how could anyone be successful anywhere—in the corporate world and beyond?

So I put together a command philosophy designed to improve accountability in the battalion, while also increasing esprit de corps and morale. My goal was to make the place no different from anywhere else in the Marine Corps. I had three focus points: confidence, accountability, and pride. I knew if I improved the confidence of my Marines and recruits, they would achieve better results and would feel more empowered to do more than just admin and support jobs. I also knew that if I focused them on improving their overall accountability for their actions and those of their subordinates, there would be less drama in the battalion, and they would be more successful individually. If we improved those two key areas, the amount of pride in the battalion and the recruits would increase. For the service that prides itself on having the highest standards of all of the branches of the military, this seemed like common sense.

And, it had worked before, when I was in San Diego.

We already had the essential guideline: The Recruit Training Order, written guidance from the Parris Island commanding officer, laid out how recruits should be trained, what qualified as abuse, and how to address their physical and emotional needs.

This is what I presented as a guideline of my expectations to my Marines:

Confidence: Physical, Mental, Emotional

Confidence: I know and follow the Recruit Training Order to the letter, and understand what to do to protect the safety and well-being of those under my charge at all times.

I can handle anything that comes my way with the help of my brothers and sisters in the command.

I understand how critical getting quality sleep is to my mental, emotional, and physical well-being and ensure that I and those under my charge maximize opportunities to rest: We take care of each other.

No excuses and no drama—"We've got this."

Accountability: For my mission, actions, and attitude

I am responsible for everything I and my subordinates do and fail to do. I will not make excuses.

I understand that my actions and words have a direct impact on the attitudes and feelings of my subordinates, my peers, and my family, and that positive words, thoughts, and deeds are a force multiplier.

I trust the command to treat me fairly if I make a mistake.

I know taking care of and developing my recruits, my Marines, and my family members is my mission, and everything I do will be focused on this effort.

I understand that everyone in the command will be held to the same high standards and challenged to excel.

Pride: In myself, my subordinates, my peers, the command, and the institution.

I know I have one of the most important (and coveted) jobs in the Corps.

I know my command is dedicated to taking care of our Marines and sailors, our recruits, our families, and our resources.

I know I will be properly recognized for our accomplishments.

Everything I say and do is a reflection on my command.

I know my command will do everything possible to allow me to excel (personally and professionally).

I also immediately started spending as much time as I could with my Marines and the recruits. Obviously, I wanted to drill down and figure out how we could improve, but I also needed to better understand whom I was working with, as well as the culture of the three male recruit-training battalions and the training process in general.

I felt that leadership by walking around was important, and I spent a good two-thirds of my day out with my Marines. This had always been my approach to command, but it was very different from the approach of previous Fourth Battalion commanders. It meant I went to the range, observed DIs and recruits during the Crucible, exercised with them on the PT field, and participated in their hikes. I arrived at work every day by 5:30 in the morning and stayed until late in the evenings so that my Marines knew I was committed to the mission and their success.

It wasn't that I didn't trust what they were doing. Rather, I wanted to make sure that they were okay: Did they have what they needed? Did they feel like they were being properly supported? I felt like it was important that my drill instructors saw me when it was cold and when it was hot.

We were in it together.

I also wanted to observe my company officers—the young lieutenants and young captains. I wanted to make sure they were being mentored and trained as leaders. I crafted my schedule to allow time with each company every day, but I spent more time with the platoons about which I had some concerns, because that's part of supervision and that's part of training—especially in a battalion where officers had previously been ignored.

My sergeant major came on deck in July, too, which helped a lot. I had been operating without one because of the unexpected move of the previous sergeant major when she and my predecessor butted heads. I felt like I hit the jackpot because I liked her and trusted her. So, while I was working with the officers, she could work with the drill instructors, and, as a team, we could get a better sense of what we needed to do collectively to improve both training and quality of life. In the military, first sergeants and sergeants major often earn respect and gratitude from officers because they've usually been in the military longer and understand the enlisted culture and the service members so well. She absolutely served as my right hand, and I enjoyed her company and depended on her advice. There wasn't a day that I didn't spend a significant amount of my time with her.

And she knew the deal. She had been a drill instructor and first sergeant at Fourth Battalion, and she had seen good and bad COs come and go. We seemed to share the same goals for the Marines and recruits in the battalion, and I conferred with her for her input and recommendations before I made decisions. In my previous command tour, I had worked with a few sergeants major who weren't great. But I was impressed with her from day one, and I thought we would be a good leadership team. In fact, I made it a point, when talking to the Marines, to always start my sentences with statements like, "Sergeant Major and

I think" or "Sergeant Major and I decided" so they could see there would be no daylight between us and we could model the relationship we expected between the company commanders and their senior enlisted, the first sergeants.

And as we observed our officers and enlisted Marines, we both had some concerns. Most of the problems seemed to stem from November Company, and we realized we needed to start by fixing the issues there.

To start the cultural evolution, I decided my first all-hands training event would be about abuse, tying in what we were seeing at Fourth Battalion with what had happened in Abu Ghraib several years before. Think about it: Abu Ghraib, the horrifying prisoner-abuse scandal we saw early in the war in Iraq, resulted from a lack of leadership and supervision. Soldiers felt pressured to behave in a certain way to fit in with the larger group, and rather than speaking out against something they knew was wrong—terrifying prisoners with dogs; making male prisoners stand naked in front of women; forcing prisoners to stand on buckets, with hoods on their heads while strapped to fake electric wires so that they believed that if they fell, they would be electrocuted—they participated. Apparently, no one there felt there was someone to whom they could go to report the abuse. The power structure there was similar to what we saw at Fourth Battalion, and specifically in November Company. In other words, the leadership was complicit in the abuse.

As I planned that first mandatory professional military-education briefing about a month into my tour, I also had one of my first encounters with the difference between Parris Island and everywhere else in the Marine Corps—and it would come back to haunt me during the investigation into my command.

As is normal, I asked my operations officer to set up the briefing since the training schedule was complex enough to require multiple sessions and a reserved classroom. This was a pretty basic task and exactly what you would expect a battalion commander to ask her operations officer to do.

She didn't do it.

The next morning, as I got ready for PT with the recruits, she came into my office to shoot the breeze. I said, "Hey. I asked you to set this up. Why wasn't it done?"

She told me she had been too busy, so I held her feet to the fire. "You can't say you don't have time when the battalion commander says she wants to do an all-hands, and you're the one who's supposed to facilitate training," I said. I'm sure I wasn't smiling pleasantly, and I'm okay with that. I also explained that if she had been too busy, common courtesy would have required her to let me know she wasn't going to get to it that day, but that she would do it the next day. Had she just said something the day prior, it wouldn't have been a big deal.

But here she was, in my office the day after it was supposed to have been scheduled, just wanting to chat.

I let her know I was not happy about it, and, remarkably, as I was talking, she held out her hand, palm to my face, as in, "Talk to it."

Wow.

She's a captain. I'm a lieutenant colonel. She gave me the hand.

Before I could quite comprehend what had happened, she walked out of my office. She decided she needed to do some pull-ups before she could face me again. She did come back later to apologize to me, and we did have a fairly level relationship after that because I gave her the opportunity to excel in her job and provided regular feedback to her on her performance, good and bad. But, at the time, it was absolutely my prerogative to chew her ass for not doing what she had been tasked to do.

She told me that was the first time anyone had, in fact, held her accountable at Fourth Battalion. My coming to Fourth Battalion and making normal requests of Marines and then holding them to those expectation was the kind of practice that would be normal anywhere else in the Marine Corps. But she said it upset her that I confronted her about it. We were able to have a conversation about it and then function as we should afterward. And, because I knew her a bit better after that conversation, I adjusted the way I worked with her in the future. Rather than confronting her about having not done something, I might go at it a bit sideways: "Can you give me the status on this by tomorrow morning?" or "How's the progress on that thing I asked you to do by Wednesday?"

It was the beginning of the tenuous process of walking on eggshells so as not to offend my Marines as I tried to move the battalion in the right direction.

In any case, we did manage to get the briefing scheduled.

I started the briefing by talking about how important it was to take care of each other.

And then I talked about one of the strongest women I could think of: Margaret Thatcher, who said, "Being powerful is like being a lady: If you have to tell people you are, you aren't." I think Britain's first female prime minister would have made an amazing Marine.

Then I talked about Army Private Lynndie England, of Abu Ghraib notoriety, who for the rest of her life will be known for leading a naked Iraqi detainee on a leash like a dog, among other atrocious behaviors.

In describing to the investigators what the reasons behind her actions were, she said, "They [her peers] were being very persistent about it, so I was like, 'Okay, whatever.'"[1]

England was convicted for maltreatment of detainees and committing indecent acts. Her mother had abused her when she was a child, and she had a speech impediment that affected her self-esteem. In the *Washington Post*, Richard Cohen wrote, "She is the sort of woman who is used by others. Powerless everywhere in life except on her end of a leash."[2]

I told my Marines that the hazing at Abu Ghraib was the same as the hazing at Fourth Battalion: an abuse of power. I told them it did not promote team-building, and Marines can't function without teams. We went through the investigations for Abu Ghraib and the two most recent abuse cases in the battalion, and I explained that abuse could be physical, verbal, or psychological, and that even something as seemingly harmless as calling new drill instructors a "NIC" was a way to express power, to make someone feel inferior. Citing the findings of the investigations, I said not allowing DIs or recruits to drink water or to use the bathroom, or pouring hot sauce on a recruit's food or making hard corrections—for example, jerking a recruit's face to the proper position during a drill—all qualified as physical abuse. Slapping, pinching, and cursing at recruits? Obvious abuse of power. All of these behaviors happened regularly at Fourth Battalion.

"The bottom line is that probably none of the individuals involved in these incidents woke up with the deliberate intention of causing their subordinates physical, verbal, or mental pain," I told them. "Instead, they most likely became desensitized because they believe that such conduct was 'normal,' and therefore acceptable."

To people outside of the culture at Fourth Battalion, this explanation for abuse might sound strange, but I believed the abuse we were seeing had become so institutionalized that many of the women thought that was what was expected of them and didn't question it. This is what they experienced when they went through boot camp as recruits themselves. When they came back to Fourth Battalion as new DIs, it was still that way; and, as a result, it was how they thought they were supposed to act.

They felt powerless to change the system.

To me, there was nothing I could imagine more horrible than one of my recruits being mentally or physically injured—unless it was the possibility of a woman not living up to her potential because someone in my command treated her poorly.

I told them that true leaders were confident and had high self-esteem—there was no need to abuse someone else to feel worthwhile themselves. I also told them that there would be consequences for those who violated the Recruit Training Order and my guidance on how recruits should be treated. I wasn't joking about accountability.

Some of the drill instructors of course interpreted this to mean that I was soft on recruits.

My sergeant major and I then had to make it clear that there would be consequences: Anyone who was cruel, abusive, humiliating, oppressive, demeaning, or harmful would face the Uniform Code of Military Justice, which is the legal code for the military. Any of my Marines and recruits who looked away rather than reporting such behavior would face administrative or judicial punishment as well, for enabling the abuse. We told our Marines that we would investigate all allegations of hazing and misconduct.

We reiterated our expectations for behavior and the treatment of recruits and each other in a battalion policy on hazing: "By treating every recruit and teammate with dignity and respect, we will ensure that the proud legacy of Fourth Battalion lives on," I wrote. "Sergeant Major and I admire you for what you do to make Marines. Stay confident, accountable and proud!"

During those first few months together, my sergeant major and I also heard rumblings about women feeling that both the reward and the punishment systems at Fourth Battalion were implemented inconsistently and unfairly. We conducted a command-climate survey and talked with the Marines about the results during our first-quarter education briefing. We found that they did not trust the command or each other. We determined that if we were fully transparent—if we talked about everything openly within the battalion—things would get better. We also wanted the Marines to know that we were listening to their concerns and were going to try to improve their lives.

We asked our officers at the company level to take responsibility for their Marines and to try to handle issues at the local level before they became problems at the battalion level. We asked them to stand up for their DIs and recruits, and to ensure that they were safe, were getting enough sleep, and were properly trained at all levels—exactly what would have been expected of Marines everywhere else in the Marine Corps.

When I got to Fourth Battalion, I found that none of the company commanders toured the squad bays—where the recruits sleep—at night; consequently, the DIs didn't have to worry about being caught doing bad things to the recruits or to each other. I have no doubt that that this type of neglect by company staff contributed to the cultural problems in the command, particularly in November Company.

The concept of officers and staff noncommissioned officers having a regular presence at the barracks was not new. This was exactly how they were supposed to behave in every other unit in the Marine Corps.

Once again, Fourth Battalion was different.

The good Marines enjoyed having sergeant major and me come by to see how they were doing. It was one-on-one time to joke and laugh and get to know each other. I learned some amazing things about my Marines that way. I wasn't there to judge them. I wasn't there because I was worried that they were doing something wrong. I was there because supervision is, as Marines always say, the most important troop-leading step. That was my job as a battalion commander, and it is exactly what I was trying to teach my company commanders.

I figured I was setting the standard and modeling the behavior I expected, and I began holding my company commanders accountable for ensuring that they and their series commanders and staff noncommissioned officers routinely checked their barracks, unannounced, at night.

Unfortunately, this might have made people feel like they were not trusted. It might also have made the officers and senior staff noncommissioned officers angry, because they now had to make time to tour the squad bays during what they perceived as their "personal time."

But, in my view, and knowing what I knew about the reputation of the battalion, trust wouldn't come for free. If there had been no abuse taking place in the battalion, and if the company and series commanders had already been doing what had been laid out pretty clearly in their job descriptions, there would not have been trust issues in the first place.

I was trying to do the right thing, but it was a change. Some of the Marines blossomed when given greater responsibility and guidance. But some of these folks didn't see the recruits as people who needed good treatment.

With them, you could have cut the resentment with a tactical spork.

CHAPTER 9

GREAT EXPECTATIONS

LtCol Germano,

Not sure if you remember me or not, we went to Command and Staff together. I just wanted to reach out to you to let you know how much I think of you. If you ever need anything, please do not hesitate to contact me. The Marine Corps has made a terrible mistake and I weep for the future of our Corps, especially all the young ladies who would have benefitted from your leadership. Now they will never really know what it means to be a Marine, but rather only what it means to be sub-standard. Truly a shame.

r/

Jules

Julie A. Mattocks

Deputy Chief of Staff

Marine Corps Systems Command

The Marines at Fourth Battalion had plenty of reasons to be disgruntled, and I quickly went after some of the issues I saw as contributing factors.

First, we had to make some improvements in staffing so that my staff could function properly.

Second, we needed to talk to the recruiters about making sure recruits were properly screened and prepared for boot camp.

And, third, I had to stop briefing congressional VIPs with a PowerPoint presentation that I was sure would be the death of me: It argued that women trained better if we kept them separate from the men. The reasoning? A non-scientifically validated theory that the only way we could create confidence in female recruits was through segregated boot camp. Personally, I prefer to provide executive presentations that aren't pure BS.

So I figured I'd follow the road map I used on my two tours on recruiting duty: First rule of change management: Get buy-in. More specifically: Get buy-in from the boss.

Easy, right? The Marine Corps wants well-staffed, high-performing units; the Marine Corps already requires recruiters to send qualified recruits to boot camp; and as for that PowerPoint? Well, I was sure a little bit of logic would win the battle.

It had worked before, so I was hopeful it would again.

In the process, I hoped buy-in from the boss would help me gain buy-in from my Marines.

Heartbreakingly fast, I realized I would not have buy-in from the boss on this tour. Not only that, but he would work behind the scenes to undermine pretty much everything I would attempt, often in ways that I didn't find out about until much later—just as my predecessor had predicted. I hoped that if I could just show him that the changes could bring success and that success would reflect well on the unit, and therefore, on him, he would come around.

I had the magic combo that 99 percent of the leadership at Parris Island didn't have: I was a woman and I had achieved significant success on recruiting duty before making my way to the drill field.

I was awfully naive.

Just as I did on recruiting, I looked at how hard my Marines had to work and how much time they got off. During the thirteen-week training cycle, drill instructors work a lot of long days. But I quickly learned that because of a shortage of female drill instructors, my Marines were working way harder than their male counterparts.

I know. Everybody act surprised.

Let's break down this organization: I was the battalion commander. My battalion had four companies: a headquarters company and three training companies. Captains head up each of the companies, and the expectation is that executive officers—lieutenants or other captains—are there to assist the company commanders with their administrative tasks.

Within those companies, all but Oscar Company had two series, a series being two platoons of recruits that trained together. O Company had recently gained a third series to afford the DIs more time off between their training cycles—or between graduation of the latest Marines and arrival of the new recruits.

Let's break down the numbers: Since each company had two series—except for Oscar, which had three—each company had between 228 and 264 recruits; each series had between 114 and 130 recruits; and each platoon had between 57 and 74 recruits. Each series was led by a series commander—a captain or a lieutenant, and a series chief—usually a staff sergeant. Everyone in my battalion except my logistics officer was a woman.

If you're tracking, that's up to 1,000 people in my battalion at any given time, including drill instructors, staff, and recruits.

For those who are not familiar with how the Marines are ranked, I offer here a super-basic rank primer:

Enlisted:
> E-1 Private
> E-2 Private First Class
> E-3 Lance Corporal
> E-4 Corporal

Non-Commissioned Officers (including the higher-ranking enlisted—drill instructors are NCOs):
> E-5 Sergeant
> E-6 Staff Sergeant
> E-7 Gunnery Sergeant
> E-8 Master Sergeant (First Sergeant)
> E-9 Master Gunnery Sergeant (Sergeant Major)

Commissioned Officers (including platoon leaders, company commanders, me, my boss):
> O-1 Second Lieutenant
> O-2 First Lieutenant
> O-3 Captain
> O-4 Major
> O-5 Lieutenant Colonel (My rank)
> O-6 Colonel
> O-7 Brigadier General
> O-8 Major General
> O-9 Lieutenant General
> O-10 General

If you were a new recruit, I'd make you memorize that.

A drill-instructor tour is a bit different from every other imaginable job: A DI is responsible not only for looking after sixty or so recruits during a 9–5 day but also for essentially babysitting them twenty-four hours a day—to make sure that they're memorizing knowledge and following rules, such as not mixing with the opposite sex, smoking cigarettes, or fighting. There is also a duty drill instructor around at night, to do health and hygiene inspections, conduct training after the regular day has ended, and make sure the recruits are getting enough sleep.

There's always, always supposed to be at least one drill instructor in the barracks prior to the start of the day and after the training schedule is complete for the day. Think about it: There are about sixty people in an open bay, which is basically a large room filled with bunk beds and lockers. The majority of the recruits are younger than twenty-two. There are personality conflicts, bouts of homesickness, and huge levels of stress.

It ain't a slumber party.

But the shortages in female drill instructors and officers made staffing at Fourth Battalion a challenge. We were supposed to have eighteen officers, but we had only fourteen throughout my time at Parris Island.

We were supposed to have seventy-nine drill instructors. We averaged fewer than sixty-four.

Things looked dramatically different between male and female battalions.

For the men, there were generally four or five drill instructors per platoon. That meant that each individual had to fill the twenty-four-hour duty requirements only once every four to five days.

But for the women, we had three teams with three drill instructors per team because we were so short on people. That meant the female drill instructors were standing duty twenty-four-hours-a-day once every other day!

Try to imagine that for a second: Do you remember finals week? When you had to pull all-nighters? Now think about doing it every other day—without the pizza and care packages and light at the end of the tunnel.

I'll bet you never thought you'd feel sorry for a DI.

A good drill instructor can scare the bejesus out of a person while still keeping that person safe and building up that person's physical strength, skills, and confidence level. But it's much harder to do those things without sleep. It's also a lot tougher to control your emotions when you are sleep-deprived, as any new parent knows.

Because we were short officers, none of my companies had executive officers. The company commanders had little relief, and we constantly had to limit time off because of the supervision requirements during the training cycle.

This played out for my Marines' families in ways that were equally as important. I looked at how many of my drill instructors were married with kids or single parents with kids, as well as where those children were living. We had anywhere between twelve and twenty-three single parents who were trying to work those ten-hour days or twenty-four-hour shifts while they took care of their families, or who had shipped their children off to grandparents or other relatives while they worked a three-year tour as a drill instructor.

I can't think of anything more stressful than being a mom who has to send her children away for three years. Can you imagine? That's three years of missed birthdays and baseball games and first days of school. This was generally a pressure the male drill instructors couldn't begin to fathom, because most of them were married to non-Marine, stay-at-home moms. I quickly learned that many of my drill instructors suffered incredible feelings of guilt and regret because of the family sacrifices they made for the Corps. Imagine how it would weigh on you over time, and then couple this stress with a lack of sleep and you can see how bad things can happen.

Technically, you can turn down drill-instructor duty if you are selected, but it doesn't look good. First, it's an honor to be chosen. And, second, when duty calls, you man-up, so to speak. When you get picked for drill-instructor duty, you go.

Every man and woman in the military is required to create a "family plan" that designates exactly what will happen with the kiddos while Mom or Dad is on assignment, whether that's in Iraq or in South Carolina. Since this is a normal requirement everywhere else in the Marine Corps, we know that going in. But because women in the military are more frequently single parents, you can imagine the pressure they feel. They don't want to leave their kids, but they know that there is an expectation that they find a solution to be able to deploy or serve on special duties like the drill field. Otherwise, they wouldn't have the same promotion opportunities.

But my perspective was, "Hey, if there are easy ways around three years of misery—as well as around three years of kids having to live without their mothers—let's figure them out." Otherwise, it feels almost as if someone wants you to fail.

By now you're probably dying to know why we had fewer women drill instructors.

First, the percentage of female Marines is low to begin with. Remember that women make up just under 9 percent of the Marine Corps.

Second, when upper leadership needs administrative positions filled on the recruit depot, they tend to choose women for the jobs.

You know, because "women are better typists."

Most of my DIs had probably never assumed the guy who played on his Apple computer all day was any less capable on a keyboard than a woman. But this is an old tradition: Walk into any military orderly room, and you'll often find female service members who have been trained in fields like signal communications or Humvee mechanics sitting behind a desk, trying to process leave (military parlance for "vacation") and promotion paperwork. Because the perception is they're better typists.

We're talking about filing and typing. I'm pretty sure the fellas had to learn their ABCs in kindergarten, too.

Worse, all of the drill instructors had jobs they'd been trained to do when they joined—admin, supply, intel—just because of the ratio of men to women on the depot, there were way more male Marines who had been trained in admin than there were women. It was sheer numbers. But the senior leaders would always pick the women to be the staff secretary, the protocol officer, or the adjutant. Everyone had signed up for drill-instructor duty, no matter what their job training had been, but, proportionately, more women were pulled for support duty than men were, and more men had been trained to do those jobs in the first place.

Because of this, our captains and drill instructors were frequently whisked away to process paperwork and do protocol tasks, leaving us with fewer people to train recruits and lead the drill instructors. The training battalions were also required to staff the drill-instructor billets for the support battalion. But those drill instructors still counted toward staffing in my battalion, even though they weren't doing the work for the battalion, because they were doing work elsewhere—so they couldn't be replaced.

And, third, when female drill instructors become pregnant, they no longer perform the duties of a drill instructor, but they continue to count against the battalion's personnel structure. That's nine months of pregnancy plus four months of postpartum recovery when no one is doing the drill-instructor duties assigned to that person. By pointing this out, I do not mean to suggest that female Marines should not become pregnant or should not receive adequate maternity leave; rather, I aim to demonstrate that there is an organizational problem with how the Marine Corps operates and accounts for (or, rather, doesn't account for) its pregnant Marines.

So, in attempting to square with these constraints, I tried to implement some common-sense changes to reduce the workload for my Marines. I immediately talked to my boss, Colonel Haas, about reducing the number of duty requirements we had, as well as increasing the number of female drill instructors and officers.

I wasn't asking for more than anybody else had.

I approached him with hard data. I showed him that we had a problem with drill instructors getting pregnant—which made sense, really. Three years is a long time to ask a young person to put off having a family. It's a stressful job, and asking to leave the position would hurt your career. But we also had drill instructors who just didn't want to do the work or be in Fourth Battalion. Getting pregnant was an easy way to be excused from training while still allowing a DI to earn special-duty-assignment pay and get her ribbon.

Instead of doing DI tasks, she would be assigned administrative responsibilities in the battalion. When we crunched the numbers, we found that between eight and ten drill instructors and officers got pregnant each year. These individuals were essentially not able to be assigned to recruit platoons for almost a third of their three-year assignment, but they still counted against my rolls. That meant everyone else had to work harder. It turned into this horrible cycle: There's too much work, so someone will get pregnant, then there is too much work, so someone else will get pregnant, and on and on.

I showed my boss the numbers.

This was my first introduction to the perspective of the regimental leadership and higher-ups: They did not care.

I told Colonel Haas that resolving my staffing shortages was my top concern, and I asked him to help me get some relief from Headquarters Marine Corps, which controls all assignments for the service. I asked for either more female drill instructors or that the leadership reduce the number of duty requirements at the support battalion, the regiment, and the depot headquarters so that some of my women could go back to being drill instructors. He wasn't willing to do either.

So, I went directly to Headquarters Marine Corps. That's what we all do. If your orders for a next job aren't coming through or something's up with a promotion or you need help finding Marines to fill positions in your unit, you go through the monitor at headquarters. Every Marine has a monitor, or career counselor, assigned to him or her, and I figured the easiest way to get to ground zero on why we were so short-staffed was by talking to the man behind the curtain himself. After they figured out they couldn't rely on the regiment for support, my battalion-commander peers also began contacting Headquarters Marine Corps directly. We knew the regimental staff didn't give a hoot about supporting our needs.

I contacted the branch head at Headquarters Marine Corps to explain the battalion's predicament. The colonel was super helpful and explained that we were short in part because of how the depot personnel officer assigned women to units. Headquarters Marine Corps sent enough women to Parris Island to bring my staffing levels up to acceptable levels, he said. But after they checked into the depot, they were reassigned to other places on the base, which was exactly what I had seen. He recommended that I try to fix the problem by going through the depot manpower officer, and he said he would do his best to reinforce my effort.

Having Headquarters Marine Corps help me fix problems caused by the depot manpower officer made some people unhappy. So, of course, someone told Colonel Haas that I had contacted headquarters. And, naturally, Haas reprimanded me for going to the monitor, but he did nothing to help me fix my manpower challenges.

After being reprimanded, I worked on the personnel piece in-house the best I could.

"Look," I told the drill instructors. "If you get pregnant, you will not receive special-duty pay, because you're not doing the duty you're supposed to do." Special-duty pay accounts for jobs that entail extra hours or hardship, such as recruiting or drill field duty. It was about $375 a month—a lot of money for a young enlisted person.

I wrote an information paper explaining that pregnant drill instructors should be moved out of the battalion and assigned to jobs they could perform while pregnant. I also tried to implement a policy that stated that to earn the coveted drill-instructor ribbon at the end of a three-year assignment, they had to serve at least twenty-four months in an actual drill-instructor position. It seemed fair and logical to me and my sergeant major.

Colonel Haas refused to support both options.

He wouldn't help me fix my manpower shortages, nor would he allow me to implement solutions that would stop the bleeding.

It was absolutely maddening. If you had male drill instructors who had mental-health issues—and we did, because a lot of them were coming to Parris Island directly from combat tours—you would never have said, "I'm sorry. I'm not going to administratively send you back to the fleet because you're not physically or mentally ready for this duty. Instead, stay here and do the job." But that's what we do with the pregnant women.

Colonel Haas later told investigators this was when our relationship began to go south.

To me, this was more than a pissing match with my boss. It was a safety issue for my recruits. I was afraid someone was going to get hurt or killed because the drill instructors were exhausted. So, my sergeant major and I tried to work on some issues internally. We created policies for sleep, stepped up the requirements for more eyes-on supervision by the officers to prevent accidents, and we increased the supervisory requirements of the support staff, such as the operations section, so they could help to relieve some of the pressure on the drill instructors.

My sergeant major and I also worked to address the stress levels in the battalion. I hired a yoga instructor to hold class at the battalion once a week on Tuesdays while the recruits were at lunch. It was absolutely hilarious to think about a bunch of hard-ass, scary DIs doing tree pose, but they loved it. The last thirty minutes of class, the yoga instructor would spend time teaching them deep-breathing exercises. But by the end of the class, they'd all be snoring.

It was awesome to see, and you could tell the DIs felt better when they left.

I couldn't convince anyone to pay for the classes, so I paid for them out of pocket.

At the same time, I worked to try to improve the caliber of recruit we got from the recruiting force. Two tours on recruiting duty had taught me that the Marine Corps had long recruited women to lower standards, and sure enough, we still had a large number of female recruits who absolutely could not pass the initial strength test.

To pass the initial strength test (IST), women must perform the flexed-arm hang for twelve seconds (just like you did in school for the presidential fitness test), do forty-four crunches in two minutes, and run one and a half miles in less than fifteen minutes.

By comparison, male recruits must perform three pull-ups, do the same amount of sit-ups, and run one and a half miles in less than thirteen minutes and thirty seconds.

The IST is supposed to be a regularly occurring test while recruits are in the delayed entry program (the time between being recruited and shipping off to boot camp), with recruiters monitoring the improvement of their poolees to ensure they have the fitness and discipline to be successful at recruit training. If you don't pass the test administered by your recruiter, you shouldn't be allowed to ship off to boot camp.

At Parris Island, new recruits take their initial strength test after they've completed their initial processing, which includes things like filling out paperwork, receiving immunizations, or getting their new uniforms. It's the last step in the administrative week before drill instructors pick up the recruits to begin training.

When I got to Parris Island, I was saddened to see how poorly the female recruits performed. The average run time did not meet the requirement. Slow run times and a general lack of awareness of what to expect in training meant that these women were disadvantaged mentally and physically in every way possible. They were more at risk for injuries; they slowed up everybody else; and they were less confident than their peers. That low confidence seeped into other areas of training.

I knew Colonel Haas had seen how poorly our women performed. The only time I ever saw him at my battalion was during the initial strength test and the next day when the drill instructors gave their pick-up speeches to the new recruits. He was well aware that the female recruits had an IST failure rate that was eight times that of the male recruits. And he had seen countless female recruits quit running during the mile and a half run around the track because they were too tired or out of breath to continue.

At the unit level, we want the recruiters to be successful; we want the recruits to be successful; we want the drill instructors to be successful. But the latter two can't happen until the first does.

I was lucky because I had prior experience as a recruiting-station operations and executive officer before I was selected to be a recruiting-station commander a few years later. I knew how to do data analysis to identify trends and implement corrective-action measures. But most of the recruiting-station commanders had never been exposed to this part of the Marine Corps. They wanted to succeed but were often overwhelmed by how different recruiting duty is from any other type of assignment in the Corps. They often just didn't know where to begin. In my view, we needed to team up if we were going to ensure that all Marines were tougher, faster, and stronger, regardless of gender.

Recruiters are supposed to hold the poolees accountable—to make sure they're training before they arrive at boot camp so they can be mentally and physically strong enough to succeed at boot camp. This is key first for the recruit's individual success, but also because if the recruit doesn't make it, the recruiter has to recruit someone else to fill her spot (as I've mentioned earlier).

That spot between being recruited and shipping off would be a fabulous time to download a couch-potato-to-5K running program on a smartphone, or to set up alerts to do push-ups throughout the day.

When I was on recruiting duty, I had my recruiters hold my female applicants to the same standards as my male applicants when it came to physical preparation and progress and learning their basic knowledge. As a result, we achieved the lowest IST failure and boot-camp attrition rates for men and women in the history of the Marine Corps. I knew change was possible.

Based on my experience, I did what felt obvious to me: I started reaching out to the recruiting-station commanders. I said, "Hey, I know what it's like. I've been in your shoes. But there are things you can do that will make your recruits successful and stronger and faster and tougher."

Many of the recruiting-station commanders welcomed the feedback about their recruits. But one of them did not. He went to his district commander, and his district commander complained to my boss three months after I arrived at Parris Island.

This is when things soured like a recruit uniform that hasn't dried properly.

So, my boss found out that I was communicating directly with the commanding officers at recruiting because one of them complained to his boss. Had my boss had my back—or the Marine Corps' back—this still would not have been a problem. When he received the complaint, Colonel Haas could have responded with, "Yeah, that's been a problem. Want to talk to your recruiters?"

He could also have said, "Was there an issue with the tone of the email from Lt. Col. Germano? If there was, I'm happy to talk with her about her approach."

He could have said, "Huh. I didn't know about that. Let me talk to her and find out what's up."

He didn't say any of those things. Instead, he assumed I must have been in the wrong, and he decided to reprimand me.

I can't tell you how frustrated I was. I didn't go to the recruiters and say, "Hey! I know everything there is to know, and you need to fix this!" I said, "Hey, Recruit So-and-So is being dropped today for this reason. In looking at her history and looking at her stats, here's what I found. Here are the trends. Here's what my sergeant major and I can do to help ensure your kids are successful, if you help us do x, y and z."

I'm not stupid, and I had been in the Marine Corps for almost two decades by this point. I was never a know-it-all—especially as a woman. Otherwise, I would have never made it that far. If I had said, "I was a highly successful recruiting-station commander and I know what I'm talking about," they would automatically think I was an asshole. There was no, "The recruits are failing and it's your fault" aspect to my calls, mainly because I was painfully aware of the tightrope I needed to walk to communicate with these guys in an inoffensive way.

When I look at the email objectively, I see a lieutenant colonel emailing a major (a slightly lower-ranking officer) to say, "Hey, we've noticed these trends, and we want to help make it easier for you."

In September, Haas approached me at a meeting and basically said, "I was contacted by one of my peers who is mad because they feel like you're trying to tell his recruiting-station commanders how to do their job. You're being too direct."

Up to that point, I hadn't had a lot of one-on-one interaction with my boss, but I didn't think we had a terrible relationship. It was awkward, but I thought that was because he was a super introvert, not because he thought I was a terrible CO.

It was the first time he said, "You're being too direct; you're being too aggressive; you're being too abrasive."

I made the mistake of blurting out, "If I were a guy, you would never be telling me this."

At that point, it was just him and me standing in the former food court that he now used to give his speeches to the company commanders, staff, and drill instructors prior to each new recruit class.

I watched his face turn red, and so I tried to go with logic.

"Well, sir, correct me if I'm wrong," I said, "but I briefed you when I first got here that I wanted to build a bridge to the recruiters so we could increase the number of recruits that we're graduating. If you read the email, there's no ill intent there."

That was the first time I think I ever made him angry. Before, when I disagreed with him on the duty issue, it was cordial, and he had even told me that he admired me for being willing to disagree. I understood I wasn't going to win, and that was it. But this time, he got mad. He was so passive-aggressive that he wouldn't say anything, I could just tell he was angry: There's not much you can do about the tomato face.

He later said that that was the beginning of the end for me.

Why? He essentially tried to put me in a corner to tell me I wasn't allowed to talk to the recruiting-station commanders.

He *tried*.

But, to me, this was a matter of principle. I told him that when I was selected for the job it was because someone on the selection board had thought my prior recruiting experience would be valuable at Parris Island.

"If you don't allow me to communicate with the recruiting-station commanding officers because you're afraid of what they might say to their colonels," I told him, "we're missing the institutional perspective, and that's wrong."

In other words, don't let little battles stand in the way of the Marine Corps' mission.

By the end of a thirty-minute conversation, he said, "Just make sure you CC me on the emails."

I did. Every single one. I sent probably two hundred of those emails in an eight-month period. He never came back and said, "Maybe you should word it differently," or, "You might want to tone this down." In fact, he never once even responded.

Hold that thought until the investigation. He apparently did.

This conversation was my first inkling that I was perceived differently by Haas because I was a woman. In each previous assignment, I had always dug in and worked hard. All of my performance reviews up to that point in my career had been stellar. I liked my co-workers. I enjoyed my job. I was known as a go-getter, and my opinion had been respected.

This time, I was aware I'd lost a battle. I knew he was not going to be a champion for big change. He was more concerned about having to answer the mail when he got complaints from his peers than in ensuring that all recruits were as tough and as strong as they could be before they got to boot camp. I knew it would be a challenge to work with him.

But I didn't realize I had, in his mind, disobeyed an order not to communicate with the recruiting station COs. He never counseled me. He didn't say, "Don't do that again." Prior to this interaction, I didn't feel like we had a strong partnership or that he had my back, but I didn't feel like I was in trouble, either. I also felt that, because he had explicitly said to copy him on future emails, we had reached an agreement that it was okay to continue communicating with them as long as I kept him in the loop.

I felt like I was doing things for the right reasons. I continued to focus on that.

For example, when I first arrived at Parris Island, I had to brief VIPs when they came to visit. These included members of Congress, educators, journalists, and senior officers. They would come down to Parris Island, get a dog and pony show, and come out going, "I love the Marine Corps." The Marine Corps has always been exceptionally good at the dog and pony show. You know—the cult and all. *Oorah* and stuff.

We did these events called "educator workshops," for which we bring in teachers from all over the nation. And a lot of the teachers are anti-military for their students, or they're sort of borderline. It makes sense, right? They see the kinds of kids who typically serve in our wars. In their view, it's not the rich. It's not the well-educated. It's not kids who have other opportunities.

These teachers have seen years of war with young people dying—their young people. There's a bigger conversation to be had about why we ask the very young, rather than those with life experience or other options, to serve. However—and I believe this with every bit of myself—the military can be a place of great opportunity and great pride for an awful lot of people. And it's honorable. It's a promise we make for the greater good. That's why you see young service members so upset that people can tell you Britney Spears's life story, but they can't find Baghdad or Kandahar on a map.

Ahem. I digress.

Anyway, these teachers come down and see the depot for a week, and by the time they leave, they are converts. Even if they're not, they may have a bit more interest in helping their students who do want to pursue military service to achieve their goals. The same thing happens with the VIP visits: The Marine Corps wines and dines them; they go to receptions at the commander's house; they get squired around by general officers.

It's all ego.

So, I was supposed to give this slide-show presentation that said we needed separate training for women to help generate confidence in their abilities. Most of these VIPs just eat what you feed them. And most of these guys are, in fact, guys, so it didn't seem to occur to anyone to question it—even though most of them had gone to "co-ed" colleges and high schools, and had been through "co-ed" training at their jobs. These guys saw women make it through med school and law school and the police academy without needing to be separated to boost their confidence.

I know there are women who feel more comfortable in an all-women setting. I know that they may be more likely to speak up. I know that they might be less afraid of failure, and therefore may try something new when, otherwise, they might stand back and watch someone else try. I know they may have a greater opportunity to try because they're not dealing with guys who are used to pushing to the front and doing a thing.

But my recruits were training for war.

I gave this brief to one congressional delegation.

And then, after three months, I had seen enough at Parris Island to know this was total horse shit. In fact, my experience showed that segregating the men from the women has the opposite effect. Instead of providing women with genuine confidence borne out of hard work, separating them falsely inflated women's confidence. This was because they were competing only against other women. And, worse, because we had held them to such low standards from the time they were recruited, the women were only competing with average to below-average women. That's not how real confidence and success works—not in the Marine Corps and not in the real world. So we were setting up the women for failure.

Ten days after you graduate from boot camp, you ship off to integrated Marine Combat Training (MCT). After recruits finish boot camp, they are considered Marines—rather than "recruits." They then go to an advanced training—MCT—to learn more basic Marine combat skills before they go on to schools to learn their jobs, such as military police or cook or infantryman. In the other services, men and women train together during basic training (boot camp), and then everyone immediately goes off to their job-training schools, skipping the advanced combat-skills course unless they have infantry-related jobs.

When the women arrive at MCT, all of a sudden, it's like, "Oh my God. I'm not only slow, I'm slower than every male Marine in my platoon." Imagine the psychological havoc played out time and time again in this scenario.

These women suffer a crisis of confidence as their male counterparts watch. Male Marines knew these women had been treated with kid gloves by their recruiters and were never held accountable like they were. Male Marines knew boot camp was different, and somehow easier, for women.

And, because female Marines tend to have more college credits when they enter the service than do the men, they automatically get promoted to Private First Class and outrank their male counterparts when they get to MCT. So, the women are behind on physical training, but they outrank the men. Now place yourself in the male Marines' shoes. How do you respect someone who outranks you but can't keep up on the basics? Clearly we are doing a disservice to both male and female Marines when we train them separately.

I was very honest with VIPs about my perspective on more integrated training. I said, "Look. I'm not talking about integrating the squads. I'm talking about mixed battalions. Three male companies and one female, and they train alongside each other the whole time. Female drill instructors are in charge of females, but they can correct males and vice versa."

I told Colonel Haas that I couldn't brief that PowerPoint presentation anymore, and I changed the slides.

Morally, I couldn't present something I didn't believe.

At the time, he didn't say anything. Again, I was given no guidance. Yet, months later, he chalked it up to just another example of me willfully disregarding his guidance.

CHAPTER 10

SEPARATE BUT NOT EQUAL

Ma'am,

You may or not remember me but I was on the 31st MEU with you 2005/06 time frame, I was the disbursing chief. Not for the reason of the email. . . . Bernie Mac the comedian would start his show by saying "America I say what you want to say but are afraid to say." Ma'am thanks for being our Bernie Mac. Semper Fi!!!!

r/s

Bradley R. Newton

Master Gunnery Sergeant

Finance Chief

United States Marine Corps

Fourth Battalion is, by its very architecture, separate.

But it's not equal.

We were different in every way.

We were isolated.

They called us the "Fourth Dimension."

They talked about "all that drama" at Fourth Battalion.

"Other."

Because the male Marines thought less of us, there was no reason for them to make changes to help us succeed. They expected that we would never match up. In fact, I often heard members of senior leadership say that the female training program had "no value." So, why bother?

As soon as I arrived at Parris Island, the consequences of that attitude and, I would argue, sexual discrimination, played out in everything from training to expectations to the disrespect shown to women from the bottom up.

A reasonable person could believe that men would typically perform better in some training activities, such as running. Others make no sense—unless you're at Parris Island. This underperformance is attributable not only to attitudes about gender but also to the space we inhabited. It affected our performance, and it affected the behavior of our drill instructors and staff.

For example, we've always done worse than the men in drill—marching and turning and moving our rifles in different positions. There's no reason why men should be better at turning left or right than women, and certainly no reason why they should better be able to stay in step. Seriously, if we had them out there line-dancing, whom do you think would win a competition?

But the men practice everywhere they go. Women do not.

The male recruits did not have dining facilities and classrooms on their battalion compounds. Instead, they had to march to the dining hall and to the consolidated academic facility for classes.

But at Fourth Battalion, there were narrow catwalks or passageways between the buildings in Fourth Battalion, so the women didn't have to go outside to get where they needed to go. It was essentially two blocks' worth of buildings, with headquarters and the chow hall in one building, along with clothing and supply. Then there was a courtyard. The barracks were two stories high, with the classrooms upstairs. We had a beauty salon, a clinic, and the squad bays where the recruits slept.

Fourth Battalion's passageways were so narrow that the women couldn't do drill with their weapons as they marched in formation. They could basically walk forward at sling arms—rifle hanging straight down their backs with the strap over their right shoulders—and that's it. The catwalks were just wide enough for four recruits to march four abreast in formation. They couldn't march at port arms with their weapons carried diagonally in front of their chests—a staple of close-order drill, and because the classrooms were on the compound, they only had to walk about five hundred feet in any direction to get there.

The men carried their weapons all day long, practicing drill, and going through Tap, Rack, Bang and other weapons-handling drills as they walked to their classroom. (Tap, Rack, Bang is a drill for quickly figuring out why your weapon has malfunctioned.)

In addition to fine-tuning their drill movements, the difference in the battalion compounds played out in another fundamental way: By the time they went to the range, men were more familiar with their rifles than women were.

The male recruits had to march outside about a half a mile away, several times a day, to get to their classrooms at the consolidated academics facility. It doesn't seem like a long distance, but it was enough time to get a lot of extra practice working on precision movements at the command of the drill instructors, which is exactly what the close-order drill competition was about. My recruits only practiced close-order drill outside when there was time for it on the training schedule—once a week, at best.

Being able to drill on the way to class also helped the male recruits build their upper-body strength. An M16A2 service rifle weighs about nine pounds, and if you're constantly moving it around, you're going to get a workout—especially if the DI has you holding it out in front of you or using it for shoulder presses.

But if you carry it at sling arms while you march in tiny hallways, you're missing out on that upper-body strength training.

And if you're inside, you're not taking your recruits to the sand pit and giving them incentive training, also known as push-ups with sand in their noses.

I'm sure the female recruits didn't mind, but, as it turned out, those little things can make the difference between being first and being last.

All of that indoor marching also added to our invisibility. The making of a female Marine is shrouded in mystery, and I often wondered if the male recruits believed we spent our time knitting and learning to put on makeup (which was an actual class until recently). They definitely believed our training was less rigorous, and they were correct.

Further, we were small—barely noticeable, really. Our compound had been constructed in the 1960s, and I don't believe the male leaders in the Marine Corps thought women would ever comprise more than 6 to 9 percent of the entire service. Instead of thinking ahead and constructing a larger compound to accommodate a larger number of women who would want to serve in the future, they built the squad bays so small that they artificially limited the number of women who could be trained each year to about 3,200. To grow the number of women in the Marines, they needed more bunk beds, more staffing, and more offices, but the leadership has settled since at least the 1980s with what they have. There was no "If you build it, they will come" mentality.

But even though we had fewer recruits to train and supervise, we had to provide the same number of staff members for the same number of hours as did the male battalions.

We were particularly short staff sergeants (E-6s) and gunnery sergeants (E-7s), which was hard, because the only way a sergeant could run a platoon as a senior drill instructor was with the permission of the regimental commander.

Our senior drill instructors needed to have maturity and experience both so they could supervise and so they could teach. The guys weren't as short-staffed. They had issues with having too many sergeants and not enough staff sergeants, or too many staff sergeants and not enough first sergeants, but they were much healthier in terms of their staffing than we were.

Between July and August, I decided to change the duty policy. I'd been there only a month, but it seemed like the most obvious thing to do as battalion commander if I couldn't get help from higher up—and my male peers were already doing it.

So I tried to solve the shortage issue in-house.

The battalion officer of the day had to be on duty for twenty-four hours. The early/late checks person had to be in at 3:30 a.m., before the lights came on, had to be there for lights, and then also had to be there late in the evening. They also had to be at the chow hall to make sure the DIs weren't stressing out the recruits. I consolidated the duties so that the same person did both.

They were sham duties, in a way. It was important to ensure the recruits' safety, but our compound was so small that one person could literally do a tour of the chow hall and the squad bays in a five-minute period. The male battalions did not have their own co-located chow halls. Instead, they were required to march the quarter mile from the classrooms or their squad bay buildings for breakfast, lunch, and dinner.

We were supposed to have one early/late check officer (ELCO) per company every day. That's three officers out of the fourteen I had, and they were also standing other duties in their own company, as well as staffing duty at the battalion. So, I made the battalion officer of the day the early/late checks person, or ELCO.

I thought that was going to be great because the company ELCOs report back to the company commander. The battalion officer of the day reported to me, so the change would allow me to have better oversight on what was going on at the company level and reduce the strain on my companies.

Instead, I got busted.

The inspector general, who we fondly called "the spy on deck," randomly wandered the battalion spaces to see if we were following the recruit training regulations. He would randomly visit the chow halls to make sure we had someone on duty to do the early/late checks.

All three of the male battalions used the same chow hall, so it was harder to know which battalion was sitting where and who was ELCO. I had my own chow hall, so it was a lot more obvious to the inspector general walking around that there weren't as many officers on deck.

He reported it to the regiment. They said, "Why do you think you're qualified to make this decision?" I tried to explain that it was for the good order and discipline and welfare of my Marines. Besides, they were already well aware that I was severely understaffed for officers and staff noncommissioned officers.

But my idea went over like a 4:30 a.m. formation.

The other battalion commanders—the guys in charge of the male recruits—already had made changes to their duty plans, but I wasn't going to squeal on them.

After he found out about it, in the last week of July, Colonel Haas told me to come see him, so I showed up with a proposal. I put together Power-Point slides (have I mentioned how much the military loves PowerPoint slides?) showing that the officers would get better sleep and better supervision by combining the duties, but we'd still meet the Recruit Training Order requirements. More important, the change would allow me to have greater oversight of the process, since the battalion officer of the day reported directly to me, while the ELCOs reported directly to their respective company commanders. For the first time ever, having a small, self-sufficient compound could work in favor of my battalion, since it took only a minute for the ELCO to transit from the chow hall to the squad bays.

Colonel Haas said no.

He would have had to go to the commanding general to get an exception for Fourth Battalion. He refused to do that even though the construction of Fourth Battalion made it a commonsense request, and we needed more people to reduce fatigue and incidents of recruit abuse.

This was particularly true for one company in Fourth Battalion: November Company, whose barracks had been built later and outside the immediate battalion area.

Each of my companies had separate offices for their company staff on the first levels of their buildings. A set of stairs outside led to the individual squad bays—the big rooms where recruits slept.

In Papa and Oscar Companies, there were squad bays on the first deck (or floor, as anyone who doesn't think of a building like a ship would say) and second decks. Each squad bay was split into two halves for the two platoons, with a duty hut—or DI office—in the middle, connecting both squad bays. This meant the drill instructors from either platoon (there were four platoons in Papa

Company and six in Oscar Company) could watch over all of the recruits at night, which reduced the number of Marines required to be on duty at night. Papa and Oscar Companies were situated directly across from each other, with a shared compound for drill and formations outside in the middle. Our medical facility, classrooms, PX (store), and hair salons sat on the first and second floors along the outdoor passageways connecting the two company buildings.

November Company lived in a separate building to the rear of the compound. The building, which was constructed in the 1980s, was connected to the compound by a catwalk, but it was separate and distinct from the rest of the battalion. Unlike in Oscar and Papa Companies, in November's building, the squad bays for each platoon were separate, with a duty hut at the front of each for the platoon's drill instructors. As a result, the drill instructors in November Company had to stand more duty periods than those in the other companies.

I believe the separation of November Company's building from the rest of the battalion created a complex in the minds of the drill instructors: They did not feel like a part of the rest of the battalion. They gained that underdog syndrome, believing that they had to work harder, and believing that they did not have to follow the same rules. The additional duty requirements also created additional stress for the drill instructors due to a lack of sleep. This made for some poorly behaved Marines, and it didn't take long for me to find that November Company had a big problem with recruit and drill-instructor hazing and abuse. In fact, I put a chart together tallying up the number of recruits who were dropped to support battalion for remedial training or were discharged, and who was leading the pack? November Company. It appeared that the drill instructors made it a habit to focus more of their efforts throughout the training cycle on being vindictive so recruits would want to quit than they did actually training and mentoring them.

You'll never guess what happened when I went up my chain of command for help.

Yeah, nada.

No one was willing to take apart the issues and say, "This is why we need more people."

Why? Because it's "all that drama" at Fourth Battalion.

CHAPTER 11

CORSETS KILL CAREERS

Not only are the women separated but they're also treated like children who can't handle basic Marine Corps requirements, such as going on a real hike, correctly adjusting their gear, running an obstacle course, and standing up for longer than five minutes at a time.

Or, you know, eating.

All of it came down to how we were situated apart from the rest of the regiment. The three male battalions ate together, went to class together, and saw each other as they marched and trained.

The women in Fourth Battalion had their own chow hall, a tailor, and a beauty salon. When it was built, it was like, "We'll just make it self-sufficient so the women never have to leave—and we never have to see them."

Fourth Battalion was essentially two squares with courtyard areas in the middle of each. There was a catwalk that connected the command post—or headquarters building—and the chow hall, classrooms, gymnasium, and support offices. The squad bays, beauty salon, recruit store, and medical offices were in the square next door.

Did I mention that the chow hall smelled terrible? It seeped into the squad bays.

But God bless Mr. Terry. Mr. Terry was the chow-hall manager. Nicest guy. After each Crucible (a new recruit's crowning achievement near the end of boot camp), Mister Terry would order up a warrior breakfast and bake a beautiful cake because it was the first time the new female Marines could have sweets.

The female recruit diet was different from the men's because they weren't allowed as many calories. There was no salt and no sugar and no sweets. The men got cookies in their chow hall, but there was none of that for the women.

These were grown women, but rather than teaching them good eating habits, we just made sure there was nothing there to test their discipline—at the same time we were supposed to be teaching them to be disciplined. Because the physical training was not very challenging for many of the women and many showed up to recruit training at their maximum weights by regulation, many recruits lost muscle mass and gained weight in training. Rather than holding recruiters accountable for sending us women who were fit and trim, and rather than making the physical-fitness training at boot camp challenging, we said, "You can't handle the treats!"

So the recruits were supervised in a way that didn't teach them how to take care of themselves after they left boot camp.

Worse, when I got to the Fourth Battalion, the DIs used breakfast, lunch, and dinner as opportunities to harass the recruits.

The drill instructors are not supposed to yell while recruits are eating.

The recruits go in. It's supposed to be silent. They are supposed to get twenty uninterrupted and peaceful minutes to eat, from the time they put their trays on their tables.

The silence? It's so they don't choke. I can't tell you how often recruits had to be given the Heimlich maneuver because they choked on their grub after a DI got up in their faces and forced them to shovel food into their mouths until they simply couldn't breathe. Most of them aren't used to being screamed at by adults while they eat. (Further, this behavior obviously has no training benefit.)

When I arrived, there was very little supervision by the officers. Officers were supposed to walk around making sure the NCOs followed the rules.

The standards were different for the basic daily functions of female recruits, as well as for how they were treated as humans.

They weren't held to the same standards by their recruiters, and then they were shipped to boot camp with the men, who had been forced to show that they can do the work and make improvements to their physical fitness.

In their journey to boot camp at Parris Island, everybody—men and women—is loaded on a bus. Everyone is equally terrified, but the male recruits have been better prepared mentally and physically by their recruiters, so they tend to know more about what's to come. As they sit on the bus, they're dead silent. They all have the same expression on their faces: fear. They're waiting for the DIs to get on the bus and for the yelling to begin.

And begin it does, and it doesn't let up again until after the first phase of training—unless you were in Fourth Battalion, where the screaming never stopped.

When the recruits got off the bus—correction: when they ran off the bus trying not to trip over themselves as the DIs yelled "Move! Move! Move!"—

they saw a formation of yellow footprints painted on the asphalt, and they were ordered to plant their feet in them.

When I was at Parris Island, the drill instructors would order the male recruits to run to the front of the formation, while the female recruits were directed to the rear of the formation.

Immediately after that, after the men saw the women ordered to stand in the back of the formation, the DIs whisked the women away to Fourth Battalion, where they were mysteriously made into Marines.

It's no wonder that there's a lack of respect between male Marines and female Marines that has spanned generations. We cheat the female Marines out of the actual boot-camp experience because we don't think they can take it.

Of course, it didn't stop with the footprints.

But separation allowed standards to slip. Training regulations stipulated that the men and women were required to complete the same training events. But because of a lack of supervision at Fourth Battalion, from the regiment to the series officers and staff, all of the hikes were too short, including the Crucible hike itself. I measured it: We were hiking seven miles instead of nine. Again, there was zero company-commander supervision when I arrived, and the previous battalion commander rarely attended training events except for when she met the recruits at the halfway point of the Crucible hike. Yeah . . . at the halfway point.

When I got to Parris Island, the men and women conducted all of their hikes separately—they rarely even saw each other. They graduated in the same class, but they rarely trained together. They never tested together. For decades, the Marine Corps has considered a company of male recruits standing in their own formation next to a female recruit formation as boot-camp integration.

I will never forget the first time I hiked with the female recruits. It was a five-mile hike—slow as hell. We're talking three miles per hour or less. I mean, city girls do that in three-inch heels, but these women were dropping like they'd been training for a beer-chugging competition rather than combat. They started out with way less than the standard combat load in their packs, because it was supposed to build up their strength, but we still had women dropping out.

We also had women break their hips. The male leadership assumed it was because of a physiological limitation, rather than a combination of a lack of fitness, their poorly fitted packs, and recruits running during the hikes rather than taking short, choppy steps.

Just like everything else at boot camp, hikes were part head game, part physical fitness. A lack of mental preparedness could make five miles seems like a marathon. But some of it was due to a lack of attention by the drill instructors and staff. The hip-injury rate at Fourth Battalion had me wondering if I was training teenagers or octogenarians.

A lot of the problem had to do with how the women wore their packs. They wore their packs too far down, so the hip belts hit the wrong place. So, as they added weight, they hurt themselves. As it turns out, at one time, our athletic trainer had conducted a class with the drill instructors to train them on how to fit the packs for the recruits. But she had given the class to the battalion the year prior, so the new Marines and recruits hadn't gotten the training. Broken hips were the result of a problem that could have been remedied with a simple solution. No one had shown the recruits how to adjust their packs properly.

Literally adding insult to injury, the Marine Corps used that data—the hip-injury rate—as justification for why women should be excluded from ground-combat jobs.

Funny thing about women and their injuries: Research shows that the better shape they're in, the fewer lower-extremity injuries they have. And, as both men and women become more fit, the difference in the injury rate shrinks. In other words, as both groups train, their injury rates equal out.

It has everything to do with fitness and little to do with gender.

The prevailing view by Marine leaders was that by their gender, women were too frail to compete with their male counterparts, which affected how training was conducted at Fourth Battalion. And before they ever got to their permanent duty stations after training, recruits learned that they aren't expected to be as capable with basic Marine skills—and the men learned it, too.

For example, during the Crucible, the culminating event at boot camp a week before graduation, all of the recruits gathered on Page Field for a seventy-two-hour exercise involving a lot of running and problem-solving stations, and little food or sleep. Page Field used to be an airfield, and it still looks like one: Weeds pierce cracked concrete in the shape of a cross with trees and swamp on all sides. Alligators, snakes, and sand fleas love it.

The brainchild of Marine Corps Commandant Victor Krulak in the 1990s, the Crucible was meant to test the mettle of recruits, to make sure that they had the honor, courage, and commitment, as well as the necessary mental and physical wherewithal to be Marines.

Throughout the Crucible, the recruits are always on the move, running from problem-solving station to problem-solving station. There is a night-movement course simulating the combat conditions and a night hike, followed the next night by a 2:00 a.m. wake-up call for the final nine-mile hike back to the parade deck. The recruits are essentially up all night for three days straight.

But, in the Marine Corps tradition of separate-but-not-equal, men performed their tasks on one end of Page Field, and the women went through the motions on the other end. They saw each other in passing, but they didn't work together. They didn't push each other to succeed or see each other being pushed beyond their perceived physical and mental limits.

The women body-sparred; they did martial arts; they went through an obstacle course in a tactical manner—you know, with weapons and looking for potential shooters. They had problem stations they'd visit. So, as a recruit, you got a piece of gear and dummy, and you had to figure out how to get the dummy over an obstacle without hitting booby traps or mines. At each spot, one of the recruits had to take charge, and she was then evaluated on her leadership.

Some of the women did a great job. Some of the women sort of half-assed it. No one, from a leadership perspective, seemed to care how they performed. And they should have, because many, if not most, of the women would graduate and be assigned to units heading to Iraq or Afghanistan. Other than screaming at the recruits to get through the specific problem or obstacle, the drill instructors and black shirts (our tactics teachers) did little to ensure that the women were following proper protocol or using the right techniques.

In addition to seeing the disparities in evaluations of male and female recruits by the DIs and black shirts, I quickly found that the female recruits were not held accountable to perform all of the tasks. By that point in the training, the drill instructors were there not only to observe and evaluate but also to have mentorship discussions with the recruits at the stations.

Yet many of the drill instructors did not make the mental shift from yellers and screamers to coaches and mentors.

Through it all, the male recruits and drill instructors were watching from afar.

Still, by the end of it, the recruits were blistered, mosquito-bitten, and sunburned. They were tired, and they had sand in places they didn't know they had before they joined the military.

In theory, the recruits had gotten some sleep; but, really, it's South Carolina. Sand fleas. All over. Snoring. Hot. Humid. You're either pulling something over you to avoid the sand fleas or throwing something off you to avoid the sweat. Stinky. Oh, man—so stinky. And they've hit that point where they're so tired that they can't quite fall asleep. They're practically hallucinating, but we need them to know just how tough they are. After moving all day for days straight, they've had three Meals Ready to Eat in three days, which amount to about 1,200 calories each—if you eat the creamer and the flavored drink powder, and if you can stomach whatever you happened to get. (Mmm, cold spaghetti and meatballs.)

And just when they thought they couldn't do any more, they had to complete a nine-mile hike. After two or three hours of sleep, we woke the recruits at two in the morning, and they forced their swollen and blistered feet into their boots, and formed up in the dark for the final test of their resolve: a stiff, painful, and blister-filled hike through the woods and swamps and then on hard pavement, carrying packs with fifty pounds of sweaty, stinky gear, as well as their nine-pound weapons, back to the Iwo Jima sculpture on the main parade deck. You know it: There's one in Washington, DC, too. It's based on the famous World War II Associated Press photo of the Marines raising the American flag after they've taken Iwo Jima. It represents everything that's important to Marines.

The hike culminates with the "emblem ceremony," and it's rich in ritual. Back in 1996, the Marine Corps decided that recruits should know what it felt like to be an actual Marine before they left Parris Island, so they didn't keep acting like recruits at their next unit. It was basically a way to integrate them into the Marine Corps. So, they started the emblem ceremony. The emblem, of course, is the Eagle, Globe, and Anchor (EGA)—or that shiny bit of business you see on the collar of a Marine's dress uniform. It means a lot to us.

At the end of the hike, the recruits gather around the Iwo Jima sculpture on the Gray Deck, and they are a mess. They're sweaty. They're hurting. They stink. (I might have mentioned that. Lord.) They're trying to look good, because it's one of the most important moments of their lives so far—straightening each other's uniforms, squaring their shoulders. But they're absolutely bawling. All of them. There's snot everywhere—both the men and the women. As the chaplain leads them in prayer, it's like a wave of sniffles going through the ranks.

It's absolutely gorgeous.

This is where you become a Marine.

After a motivating speech by one of the first sergeants, the recruits take the Oath of Enlistment. We hand them their very own EGAs, and there's more sniffling, and the drill instructors act like proud parents. The new Marines now call the drill instructors by their ranks and names, rather than "sir" or "ma'am." Or, more specifically, "Ma'am, yes, ma'am!" And then, finally, they all join in a rousing rendition of the Marines' Hymn.

The men would be standing chest-out, chin-up at attention during the ceremony.

Sounds motivating, right?

But lined up behind the female formation stood a conspicuous row of chairs. If any of the women, the ones about to become part of the few and the proud, felt tired or light-headed, she was invited to sit.

I'm having a hard time thinking about it even now.

Generally, the women sitting in the chairs were the ones who had gotten into the van that trailed behind the hike to pick up strays because they were "too tired or sore" to continue. They had not gotten into the van because they were pushed past all exertion. Even during the Crucible activities, they weren't being pushed. They were the ones who throughout training had not been held to a higher expectation for performance.

Oh, it was humiliating!

If you don't think the new male Marines weren't looking sideways at the female Marines sitting in those chairs, you would be mistaken. They watched and judged. And, it was heartbreaking. We have whole generations of female Marines who sat in those chairs and will never understand what it feels like to earn their emblems.

Some of them were my drill instructors, who just a few years before had been too tired or sore to stand for the ceremony. And it didn't end there.

A week after the Crucible, the families and friends of the new Marines gathered on Parris Island for the grand finale: graduation. The new Marines wore their dress uniforms, and they looked pretty slick: patent-leather shoes, a brand-new physique, fabulous posture.

We had them out on the parade field, with their families watching from the stands, as we read out the lists of accomplishments while they switched from attention to parade rest to attention, and there was a band and flags and plenty of pomp and lots of circumstance.

And as the female battalion commander, all I could think was, "Please don't fall out. Please don't fall out. Please don't fall out."

If we couldn't expect the female recruits to complete a nine-mile hike without needing a row of chairs to sit down in because they got tired, why would we expect them to not fall out during a parade?

But they always did. Like bowling pins.

There was always a corpsman—a Navy medic—back there with his little go cart to pick them up after they fainted.

My peers would look at me and shake their heads.

Fourth Dimension.

CHAPTER 12

MOVING TARGETS

I came to Parris Island excited about the successes we'd had at my recruiting station. In spite of my initial issues with Colonel Haas, I still hoped we could replicate my previous successes at Fourth Battalion. And to replicate those successes, I knew I had to look at the data.

This time, I wasn't afraid of the math. I wanted pie charts, bar graphs, and Venn diagrams, and I wanted them all to eventually show improvement. I wanted research and documentation and history. I craved statistics.

What I found shocked me.

Even though women had to do less to earn higher scores on the physical-fitness test, they consistently came in after First, Second, and Third battalions—the male battalions. They could run slower and at the time only had to do the flexed arm hang, while the men had to run faster and do pull-ups.

The combat-fitness test, where they also had to perform fewer ammo lifts, low-crawl under fire more slowly, and dash 880 yards less quickly, also showed the women coming in dead last. In drill, where you basically have to know your left foot from your right foot, and turn when the DI says turn, the women typically tied for third. Academics? Last. We had more recruits with a college background, but lower academic scores. Shooting? We always came in last on the rifle range.

In fact, in any given decade, we found that female recruits never performed better at a single graduation requirement than the men—ever.

You might have a month in which the women had better academic scores than the men, but for the year—for the decade—women always underperformed. And no one ever said, "This isn't right."

I couldn't believe how poorly we had been doing for so many decades—in areas that didn't make any sense for us to be doing poorly. Close-order drill?

For heaven's sake. Women have been walking for centuries.

And academics? Well. We have a Marine who will cross that parade deck at graduation, and she's a private first class because she has college credits, so she outranks the majority of the men, but she can't run three miles in less than twenty-six minutes, she barely passed her basic knowledge tests (despite having more college training than the men), and she's terrified of her weapon. And we wonder why male Marines lack respect for female Marines.

In my view, we're doing both genders a disservice. We should have high expectations for the women, and those high expectations should lead to better scores, and those better scores should lead to more respect from the men, more self-confidence for the women, and a better Marine Corps with Marines capable of taking care of each other and doing their jobs to defend the nation's interests.

To me, it was just like recruiting duty: We had to figure out what the problems were, and then, we had to not only communicate that to the Marines but also ask them for ideas. Then, we needed a plan.

I laid it out for my Marines, and, straight-up, they were just as horrified as I was—90 percent couldn't believe that the women had been doing so poorly for so long. They were mortified. No one had shown them the data before.

It wasn't just worse: It was far worse.

In 2014, at least 33 percent of the men qualified expert at the range. For the women, it was 20 percent.

We were last in written tests.

Most of the drill instructors felt that it was a poor reflection on them—and it was. For too long, their priority had been constantly screaming at recruits for thirteen weeks straight, rather than ensuring that when they crossed the parade deck on graduation day, they could compete with the men—their peers.

I came in wondering what was different for the women that would cause them to be last in categories for which gender should make no difference at all.

I talked earlier about how far behind the women were when they arrived because their recruiters didn't hold them accountable for physical fitness. They failed that initial PT test at an average rate eight times greater than the men.

After boot camp, the recruits all head to Marine Combat Training (MCT), if they aren't in ground-combat jobs. Support Marines, who comprise the majority of the Marine Corps, spend twenty-nine days in the field, training in basic combat skills, before they go to their job-training school. The Marines learn how to shoot a grenade launcher and a machine gun, and look for improvised explosive devices (bombs). They learn what to do if bad guys attack a convoy. But they also complete obstacle courses and hike and run.

My colleague Rob Hancock was the commanding officer of MCT, so he'd send me the attrition data for women.

As a recruit, you can basically quit at any point until you graduate from boot camp. After that, you're going to fulfill your contract. If you sign up for four years, and you make it through boot camp, you're doing four years unless you screw up.

So everyone who starts MCT should finish it. But Rob had women quitting and saying they no longer wanted to be Marines.

If the women refused to train, the school would just administratively separate them—clear the decks for more Marines to train.

Holy crap. No.

Occasionally, there were one or two men who didn't make it. But every cycle, women dropped out or were unable to complete the basic requirements.

It was too tough for them.

I think it is important to note that MCT is the first time the men and women are exposed to each other every day in training.

In boot camp, the male recruits rarely saw female recruits in training, so it was rare for them to see the female recruits up close leading tasks, performing physical training, or speaking out in classes. At MCT, the male Marines saw the women refuse to train or consistently come in last during unit PT, obstacle courses, and, of course, hikes. Many of these women were senior in rank because they had been promoted to Private First Class with those fifteen college credits. Yet there they were, last in everything.

Rob also started sending me statistics showing how many female recruits were getting broken in training. There were a lot of injuries because the women were not prepared; they had no idea what they were getting into when they showed up at boot camp, and MCT was tougher. They did poorly on timed hikes and weren't strong enough to climb the ropes on the obstacle course with their gear on. They stressed out and dropped out for mental-health reasons.

At Fourth Battalion, our attrition—or discharge—rate was up to 50 percent higher than the men's, and discharges for mental-health reasons were the majority. Injuries comprised the second-largest group of discharges. Rob was seeing a mirror image for the female Marines of what I saw for female recruits.

The recruits fell out of hikes. They dropped back. They broke.

My sergeant major and I started digging deeper into the why of it, and things just got crazier.

We started working on the rifle range first, because, again, "Every Marine Is a Rifleman." But the female recruits were told that it would be difficult for them to shoot well because the weapons were not built for a woman's body.

Isn't that funny? Consider this: Civilian professional shooters are taught that, because women have a lower center of gravity, they might actually be better shots. And men and women compete against each other all the time.

In fact, Eleanor Roosevelt toured the United States with Lyudmila Pavlichenko, a Soviet sniper with more than three hundred confirmed kills during World War II, to promote the idea of women serving in the military. (The American media focused on whether Pavlichenko's uniform made her look fat. Really.)

And Annie Oakley brought in crowds during the nineteenth century as part of Buffalo Bill's Wild West show.

But female Marines? Allegedly they were too short and their arms made it difficult to assume the right positions to ensure accurate shots.

You know, because men are all the same size. And every single woman is small.

Instead of promoting expert riflery, rifle coaches would tell female recruits that, in the past, women hadn't done well on the range, but the coaches would do the best they could with them. In other words, just pass and earn your marksman badge, and that is enough. So the rifle coaches didn't spend as much time coaching female Marines.

The same was true for the initial-strength-test failure rate. And no one thought about making the fast ones faster, or getting the middle group to do better. It was all just everyone plodding along together, at a pace set by the slowest in the group.

So the recruits who came to Parris Island and passed the initial strength test basically stayed at that same fitness level until the end of the course. They never got better, because, for eight weeks, everyone performed at the level of the lowest person—the one who came in unable to pass that initial strength test. The one who wasn't supposed to be there in the first place.

The first initial strength test is pretty simple, really. But if you've spent your life thus far watching a lot of TV and going to school in a district that wasn't big on gym and extracurricular activities, it could be tough.

To be able to ship to recruit training, the men had to be able to do three pull-ups, and women had to do the flexed-arm hang for twelve seconds. Men and women had to do forty-four sit-ups in two minutes. Then men had to run a mile and a half in about ten and a half minutes, and women had to run a mile in thirteen and a half minutes, which is horrible.

Before any poolee—male or female—ever ships to boot camp, his or her recruiters are supposed to monitor physical-fitness programs and ensure the recruits can pass the initial strength test. Lord knows, if they can't pass it at home when they are well-rested and happy, they're probably not going to pass it on the first day of boot camp.

So the new recruits did their initial processing—filled out the paperwork and so forth—at Parris Island, and then, the day before they were picked up by their drill instructors for training, they'd take the initial strength test. If they passed the test, they went on to training. If they didn't pass the test, company commanders could select some recruits to stay on and dismiss others. Some recruits were close, some showed potential, and some weren't really trying or looked as if they were struggling after three sit-ups. We had some leeway.

But when I got there, they were taking most of the woman who failed. There was no real assessment. All women were dropped straight into training, regardless of their performance or their weight—and with no remedial PT to build them up. This meant the women who failed the IST were at a disadvantage immediately. We knew they couldn't perform well, but we unceremoniously plopped them in with people who could perform well. And then they would break. We had them doing too much, too soon at Parris Island; this was in part because they—and their recruiters—hadn't used the delayed-entry program to prepare for boot camp.

I wasn't necessarily appalled by the new recruits. Instead, I was appalled by the physical-fitness program. The high-school track team stars who whistled as they ran past? They trudged along in formation with those who failed—the slow ones who didn't spark a breeze so much as they seemed weighed down by the Earth's gravitational pull.

Instead of breaking the recruits into ability groups for PT so that each group would be challenged to run faster, we lumped everyone into one category. Instead of getting faster, the track stars ended up getting slower, and the slow recruits never had any incentive to improve. It was a mess.

The fast recruits? We should have encouraged them to outrun the men, but instead they were segregated with no competition.

There's nothing I love more than the smell of kicking a guy's ass in a training run in the morning. (Just ask my husband.) When I was on recruiting and would regularly participate in poolee (ahem, new enlistee) PT sessions, the new male recruits would hear me running up behind them, and they would freak. All of a sudden, they would start sprinting, just so a woman—much less a middle-aged woman—wouldn't beat them. It was hilarious.

It's silly, when you think about it: We group people based on their intelligence and their innate abilities into appropriate jobs. Cool. If you're super-smart, we're going to develop that. Let's see, Sorting Hat says "engineer." But if you were fast or strong, as a woman at Parris Island, you were stuck with the rest of the pack.

The hikes. Good lord, the hikes. My company commanders weren't clocking GPS properly for the routes that we hiked, so they were too short. They weren't weighing the packs to make sure they were properly loaded, so the women weren't properly prepared for the weight of packs and the length of hikes they would do with men in their future units.

And, even so, they were still falling out of hikes that weren't as long as they were supposed to be. Or, they were so overloaded with gear—because no one checked their load—in packs that had not been properly fitted, that they broke.

As I mapped out all of this data and tried to come up with a plan, I would stop and stare at a board that hung on the wall in my office. It listed the names and dates of every previous commander of Fourth Battalion. You don't head up Fourth Battalion if you're not a top performer compared to your peer group. I could go down the list and recite where they were now: General officer. General officer. Senior Executive Service, which is as senior as you can get as a civilian federal employee.

After a while, I started to wonder about their accomplishments, especially in light of what I had seen in the statistics.

I found that commanders at least back to the late 1990s did the same things over and over again, never changing the training to achieve better results.

You can't say you're a good leader and ignore the data. You can't say you're a good leader and ignore that one of your Marines has been on duty for seventy-something days in a row. You can't be a good leader and know that your Marines have sent their kids away so they can do this duty. I just can't reconcile that. You are not a good leader if you ignore the fact that you are sending women who have never been able to shoot their rifles to units that go to Iraq and Afghanistan.

In my mind, it is not okay to know that your Marines are failing and your recruits are failing, and just ignore it.

My approach has always been that I go to my units and I find things to fix. I'll tell you that a lot of women on that list are the exceptions. They've been treated like exceptions the entire time they've been in, because they're a fast runner or knowledgeable about their jobs; and they go to Parris Island because they know that's the next step to move up the ladder.

But the realities of going to war and supporting their fellow Marines make the training all the more important.

My sergeant major and I talked about that reality constantly. We didn't want to get our Marines—or anyone else—killed.

CHAPTER 13

PIZZA BOXES

Before I could do anything, I had to address my own deep secret.

Well, I guess it's not a secret if you wear two badges on your chest proclaiming your inadequacy:

Marksman.

Yeah, I had low scores on the shooting range with my rifle and pistol. In the Marine Corps, we call them "pizza boxes" because the marksman badge is a metal square with three concentric circles inside—pizza in a box.

Badges of shame.

The last badge is marksman. If you shoot below marksman, you don't qualify.

I didn't start out sporting cheese-and-pepperoni. The first time I qualified at the rifle range, I shot expert.

That first time, at the Basic School, I felt great. There was never any expectation that we wouldn't or shouldn't do well.

But my next time at the rifle range, I qualified only as a marksman.

See, my first duty station was with an administrative unit in Twentynine Palms, California, and many admin units in the Marines are exempt from having to qualify. This was during the lull between the Gulf War and the invasion of Iraq. I guess during that time frame, the leadership figured that the only thing admin Marines would fire in combat was a typewriter. Why waste bullets on admin pogues if the grunts really needed them? So, I didn't qualify with the rifle again until six years later. By that time, I'd forgotten all the fundamentals.

And, you know, I was in Okinawa; it was windy; I had a hard time adjusting my windage . . . and I completely lacked confidence. So, yeah, I shot marksman.

I went from shooting expert to having to wear a pizza box for my rifle-qualification badge, and, after that, because I was assigned to exempt units, I never had the opportunity to shoot on the rifle range again. At about the same time, I was promoted to major. When you advance to major, you no longer qualify with the rifle—you qualify only with the pistol; so I never got to qualify with the rifle again.

By the time I qualified with my pistol again, I was a bona fide, shaking-at-the-knees wreck. So for seventeen years, I walked around with the marksman badge for my rifle, but also a marksman badge for my pistol. Double-cheese, please.

In the Marine Corps, we judge new Marines checking into their units on what they look like in their Service Alphas (dress uniforms), with their ribbons and badges. Wearing these two badges was humiliating. No matter what else I achieved in my career, whether running a perfect PT test or being selected for top jobs, the first impression when I arrived at my new unit was always, "Huh . . . another woman with double pizza boxes."

I realized that if I wanted to hold the recruits at Parris Island accountable for shooting well, and I wanted to hold the drill instructors accountable for training them, I needed to start with myself.

Because the first thing any good Marine will do is call you on your BS.

I was nervous and embarrassed, but I had to ask for help. As it turned out, Colonel Gerry Leonard and his Marines at the Weapons and Field Training Battalion, which ran the ranges, were fantastic. I think Colonel Leonard was concerned about the poor performance of the women, and he was enthusiastic that I cared too. He was eager to have his Marines help me change the status quo.

I started going to the pistol electronic range—ISMET—in late October. You've probably done something similar at the county fair or an arcade, if you're old enough to remember arcades. Chuck E. Cheese? At ISMET, you basically pretend like you're shooting a rifle or pistol, using a weapon that's essentially the same as what you would use at the range, including the recoil, but you don't use real bullets. That way, you can shoot as many times as you'd like, but it saves the Marine Corps a mint in ammunition. It saves a lot of time, too.

This one, of course, isn't set up to ensure you don't win the big fluffy bunny, like at Chuck E. Cheese. Instead, you work on your breathing: Breathe in. Breathe out. Hold perfectly still. Gently squeeze the trigger. Caress it, really.

You practice over, and over, and over until the muscle memory's there and the weapon feels like a part of you—rather than a scary, loud thing that recoils and makes everything from your shoulders to your eyeballs clench up.

Because it's the Marine Corps, we even have an acronym for how to do this: BRASS. Breathe, Relax, Aim, Slack, Squeeze.

Every single week from late October until my pistol-qualification week in January, I drove my little golf cart to the range, checked on my recruits on the firing line, and then spent an hour practicing my shooting fundamentals. I made it clear to my Marines and recruits that I was going to shoot expert. And, thanks to the amazing coaches, especially the range chief and his company commander, I got so comfortable shooting at the ISMET that we often competed against each other at the end of my sessions. I shot and shot and shot until I got to the point where I felt confident that I had the fundamentals down.

And then, lo and behold, I shot expert on the pistol for the first time in my life.

If I had stayed for the next year, I would have had the opportunity to try again with the rifle, too. My coaches at the ISMET were going to set it up for me, and it would have been a huge confidence boost.

The best part? Colonel Leonard's willingness to partner with me to improve the scores of my female recruits and drill instructors made it possible to start changing the minds of the male coaches about what women could achieve on the range. I wanted so much to pass on to my Marines not only what I learned from Colonel Leonard and his Marines but also how they made me feel. They expected me to do well, and I didn't want to let them down. And, man, I felt CONFIDENT—like a badass, really.

When we began focusing on improving the performance of my recruits at the range, I said, "Hey. I started with me." I told them I was the worst shot on the planet—that I couldn't hit the broad side of a barn—and I tried to be self-deprecating. I told them I used to spend my time at the range praying that someone else would shoot at my target.

I told them I make mistakes every day. I hoped they would understand that screwing up is part of being human, but so is improving.

The funny thing is, when I got canned, the trolls looked at my official command photo and went absolutely nuts because of my badges. Two pizza boxes. I never had my photo retaken after I got my expert, because it wasn't a big deal to me. I didn't have anything to prove to anyone else—I needed to do it for me and for my Marines and soon-to-be Marines. As long as my Marines knew how hard I had worked for that expert pistol badge, I knew my drill instructors would be more motivated to ensure their recruits did well.

After I was fired, the comments from the online trolls about my command photo made me angry. I would have liked to defend myself.

But my Marines and recruits know. And I know. That's what matters.

CHAPTER 14

PREACHING INTEGRATION

I knew about the Marine Corps Integrated Task Force study—the study looking at how well men and women performed when they trained together in ground-combat settings—when I arrived at Parris Island. It was designed to determine whether women should be allowed in the infantry.

Strike that: It was designed to show women shouldn't be allowed in the infantry.

I desperately wanted to be a part of it, to show that my female recruits and Marines could, in fact, perform at higher levels. And I wanted the senior leaders to know that if the female participants were women who had been poorly trained with low expectations at boot camp, they could never expect them to do well.

I knew my recruits could do better.

In fact, I thought if we integrated the men and the women at Parris Island, that would already serve as a big push toward ensuring our women—and men—perform and behave better. Several RAND studies had already demonstrated that integration not only improved the PT scores of women but also resulted in better scores for men as well.[1]

Did I mention that the Marine Corps is the only service to maintain segregated boot camp?

In my eyes, it wasn't just about ensuring that women were physically and mentally capable of joining the infantry. It was about making women in every job stronger, faster, and tougher. I knew that doing so would make the entire Marine Corps better.

I had been looking at our PT scores, and I brought everyone in together to say, "How do we do this better? Why aren't men and women running together?" And some of my Marines who were serving their second tour at Parris Island or who had gone through boot camp there themselves said, "You know, ma'am? When we were here the first time, that's what we were doing. The men and the women did PT and hiked together."

My reaction? *Holy hell. You're telling me we're moving backward?*

As it turns out, integration itself wasn't new. In fact, people way before me saw integration as a positive, beneficial thing, and it had already been done.

You could feel a history lesson coming on, couldn't you?

With women, there's always a history, and it's never easy.

Nothing in the Marine Corps is easy, and the "Southern Service," so-called because of the high percentage of Southern men who make up the branch, was decidedly against opening doors for women.

Many people don't know that 350,000 women served as pilots and clerks and drivers and medics during World War II. The US Army had the Women's Army Auxiliary Corps—the WAAC, which eventually became the Women's Army Corps (WAC). The US Navy had the Women Accepted for Volunteer Emergency Services—the WAVES. There were lots of restrictions: women could not lead men; they could only fill a limited number of officer slots; and they could not serve in combat. If you had children or a venereal disease—no lie—you couldn't serve.

Women served in the Korean War and the Vietnam War, and then they began joining the military in peacetime during the 1970s.

After the draft ended, the all-volunteer force needed women to fill the ranks.

And it's possible that some people saw women as a necessary addition to a modern military.

According to the RAND Corporation, the services thought that the Equal Rights Amendment would be ratified in the late 1970s. Conservative activist and lawyer Phyllis Schlafly led a successful charge against the ERA, claiming that women would be drafted into the military. Today, that doesn't seem that crazy a proposition. After all, women can vote for war without having any skin in the game.

In any case, because everyone thought the amendment would go through, the Army and Navy wanted to increase the number of women serving by two times, and the Air Force wanted to increase their number by three times. The Marine Corps opted for a one-fifth increase. That was when President Jimmy Carter was in office: During his time, the WAC became part of the regular Army, and the services allowed women to go to their service academies, including West Point and the Air Force Academy. Through the years, more and more positions became open to women, and they were excluded only from combat units or missions that exposed them to risk of "direct combat, hostile fire or capture"—or the Defense Department's Risk Rule—that was higher than what they were already exposed to in support roles.[2]

During Desert Storm, women began to fly combat missions.

(Get some, Martha McSally!)

Then, Congress created a new law reinstating the combat aviation ban they had just repealed. Thank goodness that in 1993, President Bill Clinton ordered the services to let women fly in combat aviation roles.

In the meantime, the Army, Navy, and Air Force started integrating boot camp and basic training.

And then Congress got involved.

The Nancy Kassebaum Baker study took place in 1996 in response to the Aberdeen and Tailhook scandals. In the latter scandal, Navy and Marine Corps officers were at a conference in Vegas in 1991 and, by the end of it, more than one hundred of them were accused of sexually assaulting eighty-something women and a handful of men. Most infamously, women trying to get through a hallway to their hotel rooms were forced to "walk the gauntlet," where they were grabbed and pinched, and worse, by two rows of officers as they walked through them.

And the bosses? The flag officers? They knew and didn't do anything. In fact, they blamed it on the enlisted folks.

Anyway.

Lots of people lost their jobs; President Clinton appointed the first female service secretary; and Congress decided they should look at whether men and women should work together.

My two cents? Yes. They should work together. And everyone should be held accountable to act like adults, just as they are at well-functioning civilian organizations.

What happened at Aberdeen? Twelve male drill sergeants assaulted female recruits at the Army's advanced job-training base in Maryland. Four went to prison, accused of rape and harassment and cruelty. This left Congress wondering if men could be trusted to train and supervise women, instead of asking why there was no supervision to ensure the drill sergeants were acting appropriately.

So the Kassebaum Baker study's "Report of the Federal Advisory Committee on Gender Integrated Training and Related Issues" (catchy, isn't it?), came out, and then Congress had a bunch of hearings. It was as you would expect in the late 1990s: The Republican House disagreed with the Democratic Senate on basically everything. It was also peacetime, for the most part, so the questions arose in a vacuum: How would men and women perform together in a war zone?

(Everyone had, apparently, forgotten the men and women who had fought together in previous foxholes, most recently five years earlier during Desert Storm, in which 40,000 women fought and fifteen were killed.)

Kassebaum Baker, the congressional study, recommended that men and women be segregated during basic training and that they be separated at least at the platoon level in the Army (about forty people), the flight level in the Air Force (an Air Force flight is about the size of an Army or Marine Corps platoon), and the division level in the Navy/Marine Corps during basic. A division is a much larger unit, so while men and women could train in the same small units in the Army and Air Force, they'd be widely separated in the Marine Corps and Navy. Why? Researchers said that integration would promote less unit cohesion and more distraction. But they also found that the units split by separate housing couldn't be as supportive of each other or have as high discipline. So the recommendations were to keep the women together and keep the men together for a couple of months, and then send them off to work and train and serve with each other—and expect them to know how to hold each other accountable and treat each other with respect.

Defense Secretary William Cohen disagreed with the findings of the panel because he had already seen integration work well and, perhaps, realized that separating the men and the women punished all women for the men's bad behavior at Aberdeen and in Vegas. (These perpetrators were adult, high-ranking men. No discipline. Seriously, men, get your act together). He instead called for some changes in training and living quarters. His military chiefs had also opposed segregating basic training.

You caught that, right? Twenty years ago, everybody—except Congress and the Marine Corps—understood that training should not be segregated. Secretary Cohen asked for better security and more accountability—in the Army, the first floor of the barracks might be all women; and the second, third, and fourth floors, all men. Yelling, "Male on the floor!" as one entered a hallway apparently wasn't cutting it, and Cohen asked that there be doors installed where they'd been removed and that people have more privacy.

Cohen and some members of Congress argued that segregating men and women decreased the role of women, and that separating their barracks entirely for training would cost too much—the military's eternal best defense against Congress.

His reasoning wasn't based on gut feeling.

Several studies from the US Army Research Institute led the Army to integrate units because they found that both men and women performed better in integrated units.[3] The women were better shooters, and both men and women did better on their physical-fitness tests. Other researchers, including those from the Defense Equal Opportunity Management Institute (DEOMI), found that integrated training did not negatively impact performance or teamwork, or increase "distraction" levels.[4]

They did find, however, that there needed to be buy-in from the DIs. If DIs disagreed with integration, their units performed more poorly.

Ultimately, the services were told that gender integration was fine. In fact, go with gender integration unless you can come up with a compelling reason not to.

So everybody, except the Marine Corps, continued with gender integration.

So in forty years, other than a few commanders on the recruit depot who were willing to push the envelope by having male and female recruits run PT and hike together, the Marine Corps had consistently refused to integrate recruit training, citing the Kassebaum Baker study.

But when the attention wanes and the intention of Congress and the secretary of defense shifts, people come into leadership roles with different biases.

For example, my boss. Judging from my experience, he was not a fan of integration, either because he was too afraid to ask for changes or he just didn't believe women belonged.

He wasn't alone. As the rest of the services began openly discussing the possibility of integrating combat units and allowing women to serve in infantry roles, the Marine Corps closed ranks against the "other."

In this atmosphere, there was no room for Fourth Battalion to succeed.

In 2015, the secretary of defense announced an end to the ban on women in ground-combat units and roles. He did, however, allow the services to request exceptions to the policy if they had concrete evidence that the change decreased combat effectiveness. At that time, the Marine Corps requested a waiver based on the results of their Integrated Task Force combat integration study, which tested the ability of male and female enlisted Marines in various field exercises. And since the women who participated had graduated from Fourth Battalion before changes to training methods were made, the results were exactly what you'd expect. The Marine Corps found that all-male units could move faster, shoot better, and evacuate casualties more quickly than mixed-gender units could.

I strongly believe the USMC study was flawed from the start since it was conducted in a way that would ensure it reached a preconceived outcome. With that understanding, the study's "findings" were unsurprising.

RAND researched gender integration and found that groups that were openly hostile to gender integration had lower unit cohesion after integration than did those that were open to gender integration.[5]

The services have been working to change attitudes about women in general. Also not surprisingly, RAND found that an average of about 21 percent of women in all branches of the military reported sexual harassment, but the rate of harassment in the Marine Corps was higher than the other services: 27 percent reported sexual harassment at work.[6] And units with higher rates of sexual harassment had lower levels of unit cohesion.[7] As it turns out, this is also true for civilian organizations.

But, contrary to the beliefs of many senior Marines, sexual harassment and gender bias are not female problems. As evidenced by the current reckoning across America, men in the top ranks of the news media, the entertainment industry, and elsewhere are being accused of sexual harassment and assault, and are finally being held accountable for their words and actions.

In fact, in 2017, *Time* Person of the Year was awarded to the silence breakers of the #MeToo movement—women who had bravely stepped into the public view to share their stories of sexual harassment and assault in order to draw attention to the enormity of the problem and promote change.

We are finally recognizing and demanding in America that men need to behave better. "Throwing like a girl" should no longer be an insult, nor should we accept the attitude that "boys will be boys."

CHAPTER 15

SHOOT LIKE A GIRL

I understood that, to make improvements, we weren't going to get any help from the regiment. We were on our own.

Fortunately, we had enough strong, stubborn women at Fourth Battalion to figure out the best way to improve the performance of the female recruits.

Most of my drill instructors didn't need to be convinced to face new challenges head-on, and, man, their enthusiasm kept me coming to work every morning excited about the day.

When we began focusing on improving the performance of our recruits, we started with the rifle range because "Every Marine Is a Rifleman." It's our motto. And we didn't want our new Marines checking in at Marine Combat Training (MCT) wearing pizza boxes on their Service Alpha uniforms. We wanted them to show up to their new units feeling confident and proud, and we wanted the brand-new male Marines to have a high opinion of the female Marines from the start.

For decades, women at Parris Island qualified at a rate of about 67 percent to 72 percent, compared to the male rate of 85 percent to 93 percent. The men had more experts and sharpshooters, too.

First, I gathered the Marines: Talk to me about why we're not qualifying at the same rate as the men are.

They told me what they had been told as new recruits:

"You're too short to fire well."
"Your bodies aren't proportioned right for a rifle. You can't reach the trigger."
"Women fail under stress."
"Women aren't used to being around guns."

After a while, we start to believe what we're told.

And it's nonsense. I was convinced that male drill instructors were not telling short infantrymen that they wouldn't be able to shoot as well. I was convinced that male drill instructors weren't telling their city kids that they wouldn't get used to a rifle.

Worse, when I arrived at Parris Island, the female DIs had a history of hazing the recruits so hard at the rifle range that they peed their pants. Once again, instead of focusing on shooting fundamentals, the female DIs seemed interested only in outdoing each other in toughness and cruelty.

That can't have helped with the recruits' controlled-breathing exercises.

Our Recruit Training Order explicitly states no yelling and screaming on the rifle range. Beyond the obvious effects on a recruit's shooting, you don't necessarily want a recruit with a loaded rifle to be angry at her drill instructor and pushed to the point of snapping.

When we talked to the coaches at the range to further understand their impression of the female drill instructors, they said, "Yeah. They're terrifying."

I remember calling Joe in maybe September of that year. He shoots competitively in club matches with the International Defensive Pistol Association and does cowboy-action shooting at Single Action Shooting Society matches—he's pretty good. But when I told him about how poorly our women were shooting, he was flabbergasted. Women beat him on the range all the time. No one freaked out about some biological reason for why women shouldn't be able to best a dude: He told me they just said, "Good job!"

My sergeant major and I came up with a plan—incorporating what our Marines had told us—and then we asked for help.

The weapons field-training battalion was waiting for us.

Once again, I met with Colonel Leonard. I'm positive that if he had been my commanding officer, rather than Colonel Haas, I'd still be at the regiment and performance and morale at Fourth Battalion would be incredible. He was amazing.

Colonel Leonard and I sat down in July and started just spit-balling and brainstorming and thinking about how we could test the different theories that had been presented over the years to justify why women at Parris Island couldn't shoot above marksman. As we came up with ideas, I would take them back to my Marines. We started crossing barriers off the list as we came up with solutions.

The shooting coaches, 99 percent of whom were men, had become conditioned to believe that women couldn't shoot; and they passed on those opinions to the female recruits. So, we had to deal with some language-expectancy issues first.

Our coaches said things like, "Well, you guys will do okay. Women normally don't do well, but we just need you to qualify." That translated directly into the results we got at the range: Our recruits assumed they'd be lucky to qualify.

But all of the excuses from the coaches fell to the wayside in the summer of 2014 when two rifle-range coaches from San Diego came to Parris Island for a visit. Colonel Leonard wanted to find out how much bias came into play with his coaches, so he asked two coaches from the West Coast who had not been exposed to the gender bias on Parris Island to coach two platoons of women on the range. These guys were used to dealing with male recruits and had no experience coaching women, so they had no preconceived notions about what women could or couldn't do. They came in; they focused on the fundamentals; and they taught our recruits how to focus on their rifle sights, breathe, and gently squeeze the trigger.

Holy crap.

No one shot herself in the foot. Nobody broke down. No one needed assistance reaching the trigger. We qualified at record levels.

And it caused the Parris Island coaches to believe that they had to do better to compete with the West Coast coaches.

Colonel Leonard went with it. He went to his rifle coaches and said, "We're going to change this. We're going to start with how you act with the female recruits and how you teach the female recruits."

Whoa.

Suddenly we were qualifying at a rate of 95 percent.

We didn't tell the recruits shooting would be hard because they were women, and we focused the coaches on eliminating any negative comments in their instruction to the recruits. This was about teaching them shooting fundamentals and expecting excellence. And the women delivered excellence.

As Colonel Leonard worked to change the culture at the range, I focused on the mind-set of the drill instructors and the company commanders to make sure they understood they were responsible for reinforcing weapons-handling safety and shooting fundamentals in the squad bays. The range training would no longer end after the women returned to the barracks. Instead, we encouraged the recruits to use their hour of free time to prepare to shoot as experts on the range. Back in the squad bays after evening chow, they would focus on weapons safety and remedial action, practice getting into shooting positions, and get so used to handling their weapons that there would be no stress on the range.

We wanted the drill instructors and recruits to be calm. And in fact, at night, walking through the barracks, you'd see the recruits lying on their backs on the deck (floor) and working on breathing techniques while their drill instructors led them through stress-reduction drills. The first time my sergeant major walked into the squad bay and saw this, she stopped cold. "If I had seen this ten years ago, I would have had a heart attack," she told me. Between my yogi drill instructors and my deep-breathing recruits, we could have started an ashram.

Okay, that's probably a stretch.

But we wanted them to understand trigger control and the impact of deep breathing on stress control, and we were thinking outside of the box to do it. What we'd been doing before clearly hadn't worked.

I wasn't the first one to push this idea. About a year before I got there, Colonel Leonard brought in a master sergeant who was the top female shooter in the entire Marine Corps, Julia Watson. In 2014, she became the fourth female Marine to become distinguished in both the rifle and the pistol at the Competition-in-Arms Program Western Divisional marksmanship competition on Fort Pendleton in California. She also happened to teach shooting.

At the time, there wasn't a whole lot of buy-in from Fourth Battalion.

But after I arrived, he had it.

Once again, we started talking about how we could have her inspire our women on a regular basis. Well, how about making a video of women hitting the targets like it was no big deal? And how about we play it in the squad bays during free time so the recruits would see it day in and day out and become conditioned to it?

And, just for fun, how about we hang targets in the squad bay so the recruits better understand the scoring system? We brought in shooting barrels, so they could practice focusing in on the targets. The metal barrels had different-sized pictures of the targets painted on them to simulate what the targets would look like at different range distances, so the recruits could practice focusing in on the targets in the different shooting positions.

By the time they got to the range, it was all second nature.

In Fiscal Year 2015, we achieved a 92 percent female initial qualification average.

Boom!

Did you see the heavens open up and hear the angels start to sing? Even though it seemed so obvious, it felt like a miracle to have tangible results.

We had a couple of classes that didn't shoot well. The platoons that didn't shoot well were led by drill instructors who did not buy into the changes we were trying to make. Generally speaking, the problems came from November Company.

But I wasn't about to let them hold back everybody else. It was the first time in the history of the Marine Corps that the female recruits were competitive with the men on the rifle range. And it happened just as the Marine Corps worked to prove women should not serve in the infantry because, among other incorrect assumptions, they couldn't shoot. I thought the Marine Corps leadership would be happy about what we were doing to make our recruits tougher and better shots. I should have known better.

Next, we looked at the physical-training playbook, which contained the PT plan for every single day of boot camp. This was our opportunity to improve scores on the physical-fitness test, as well as to decrease injuries. The bulk of the fitness training at boot camp occurs in the first four weeks, and then the recruits move on to other things, like hikes, the rife range, and field exercises. The subsequent four weeks, they're on the rifle range and they're out in the field.

We knew if we didn't improve their fitness during those first four weeks, we would essentially lose the opportunity to build them up for the rest of their training.

So we looked at the playbook to try to figure out how we could get them into better shape faster without breaking them. We instituted some obvious solutions: We split them into ability groups. The fastest recruits ran with the fastest drill instructors, which made the entire group faster. But the same was true of the other groups. If we needed to couch-potato the slowest group to get them to a point where they could keep up without losing a lung, we could do that without slowing down the fast women.

And good runners cross-train and sprint and go fast or do slow recovery runs or do interval training. We could do all of those things.

So we did. And it worked.

We also started tracking lower-extremity injury rates because I wanted to know how we could improve training to avoid these issues. The stronger you are, the less likely you are to have a lower-extremity injury.

But that's not what the women learned at boot camp. During their first week of training, the athletic trainer in each battalion taught the recruits how to stretch and pace themselves and strength-train to avoid injury. In fact, each platoon had a box of stretching bands and foam rollers for the recruits to use during their free time in the squad bays. But when I arrived at Fourth Battalion, those footlockers had a layer of dust on them that indicated that the rollers and bands had not been used for some time. Lower-extremity injuries, the leading cause for training drops in the female battalion behind mental-health reasons, were preventable with the use of proper stretching and recovery. But a lack of supervision at all levels allowed the drill instructors to deviate from the advice of the physical trainers.

We worked to change that:

We performed stretching exercises in the squad bay.

We started enforcing the use of the stretching kits during free time.

We kept track of the injury rates by company and started seeing incredible improvement.

We encouraged recruits to say something when they hurt. Knee problem? Maybe we can do some physical therapy. Or maybe you're overpronating and we should switch out your shoes. Prior to my tenure with the Fourth Battalion, reporting an injury was seen as an excuse to get out of training or a mark of shame. You joined the "sick, lame, and lazy" for "sick call"—a visit to the clinic.

We concluded that perhaps that way of thinking had caused recruits to hide injuries, which had contributed to our injury rate.

I had two investigations going that showed the recruits from November Company weren't being sent to the clinic when they complained of pain. As my other companies improved, November Company had the highest number of recruits with lower-extremity injuries and the highest number of drops from training.

They weren't referring their recruits to the athletic trainer at the first sign of injury. They didn't ensure their recruits did stretching exercises in the squad bays during free time. Why? Because the drill instructors were convinced that the only way to make recruits tough was by screaming at them.

At night in the squad bay, the drill instructors were supposed to go down the line: Raise your arms. Put them down parallel to the deck. Flip your hands over. It's to check hygiene—disease spreads quickly through a room with fifty beds— but also to see if anyone has an injury. November Company didn't bother to do anything more than cursory inspections. If someone complained that she had an injury, she was told to "suck it up." When I reviewed their hygiene-inspection log-books, there were no notes to show that they kept track of bruises, illnesses, or injuries, much less that they referred recruits to the athletic trainer or Medical.

Just as an aside, because you might be wondering about this: When a bat-talion commander tells you to do something, you do it. You might be able to offer input. You may even talk your commander out of an action. But, ulti-mately, she's the boss and you do what you're told.

November Company did not.

We'll get there.

As soon as we started focusing on the basics, we started seeing huge improvements.

After the first four-week phase of training ended, we encouraged the drill instructors and recruits to use their spare time to continue physical training. After the second phase of training began, we had less opportunity for PT throughout the day, so we asked the drill instructors to allow the recruits to use the elliptical trainers and pull-up bars during free time and between training events.

Previously, we had also been taking buses to the rifle range instead of hiking. My drill instructors and I recognized that hiking that short distance to the range would not only improve the fitness levels of the recruits but also would give them the mental space they needed to prepare for shooting on the range. We started marching. We wore light day packs and carried our rifles, and we did a nicely paced administrative move, without yelling by the drill instructors.

In the third phase of training, we better prepared for the Crucible hike. In addition to making sure that the recruits were fit enough to complete the hike, we also had to address the issue of packing their rucksacks. This is because packing it properly can make all the difference in how your back feels during a hike.

Therefore, my athletic trainer developed a presentation to familiarize the DIs with exactly what the recruits were supposed to carry and how they should be carrying it. She also walked the drill instructors through how to properly fit the packs to the recruits' bodies and increased their awareness of how taking long strides and running with packs increased lower-extremity injury rates.

What she taught certainly wasn't rocket science. It was no different from what Marines all over the Marine Corps are expected to do. But Fourth Battalion had always been different.

We also worked on the mental aspect of hiking.

When I first arrived at Parris Island, despite our hike routes being shorter than they should have been, we still had women getting into the van at the halfway mark—at incredibly high rates. This is because we let them. Hell, we expected them to.

To combat this, we started having the medical teams evaluate the women who fell out of the hikes. When they weren't found to be injured, we told them they had to keep going. You know what happened? They finished the hike, and they were mentally tougher for it.

Cultivating this sense of a need to complete a task was important. It's what motivated the recruits to keep moving forward when the going got tough.

However, there was one incident that I will not forget. I had a young woman who took it too far. Actually, it was terrible; I was horrified at the risk she took. She finished the Crucible on the parade field right before the emblem ceremony—with a temperature of 107°. She had not displayed any heat-casualty symptoms. She got all the way to the parade deck, and then she turned as white as a sheet and her eyes rolled back. That may have been the worst moment in my life so far, I was so worried about her. Her life and my career flashed before my eyes, but she had refused to quit. Thankfully, she was fine after she received something like five IVs. She just didn't want to quit, even though I know she must have felt like hell the whole time.

This kid was probably three feet tall. She was the tiniest recruit, and her pack was as big as she was. She was amazing, and, man, did she want that Eagle, Globe, and Anchor.

Did I mention that row of chairs set up for the emblem ceremony?

We took those away in August.

When I removed the chairs, the only problem I faced was fear in the eyes of my boss. He looked at me like it was going to be the most catastrophic event ever at Parris Island.

But as when we told uninjured recruits that quitting was not an option during hikes, when we removed the chairs from behind the female formation, the women stood taller. They were proud to have pushed past their physical and mental perceived limits to earn those Eagle, Globe, and Anchor devices, and, man, was I proud of them.

We had another big success: I had asked Colonel Haas to integrate the Crucible, explaining that it made no sense to have men and women marching separate routes only to end up at the parade deck at the same time for the same ceremony. Everywhere else in the Corps, men and women hike together. Amazingly, Colonel Haas concurred, as long as I worked it out with my male battalion commander peers. We did our first integrated Crucible hike in November with great results—shockingly great, especially since we were expected to fail.

Pre-work—the conditioning and proper training—and the changes to our PT plans had paid off, and we saw significant improvement in the ability of the female recruits to complete the hikes along with the men at the same doctrinal three-mile-per-hour rate of march, and carrying the same sixty-five-pound pack load.

The biggest challenge? Figuring out the logistics of having only one set of heads (bathrooms).

Over time, as we improved everything else, the female recruits' confidence grew. If you're running with the fastest, you're feeling pretty badass. If you're running with the slowest but you're getting faster, you're feeling like you've accomplished something you didn't know you could do. If you're shooting expert, you're beginning to believe you can actually do this whole Marine thing.

Eventually, fewer women fell out of hikes and out of graduation ceremonies.

Even better, fewer women fell out of hikes at MCT.

We had also seen lower academic scores for the female recruits. This made no sense to me, first, because the women tended to have more college experience than the men, but also because academics is another area—like drill and ceremony—where there shouldn't be a difference between the sexes. But, as we started digging in, it began to make more sense.

We knew the male DIs were more likely to have tactical combat experience than were the female DIs. Many of the male drill instructors had recently returned from multiple tours in serious ground-combat situations. They reinforced their lessons with things they'd learned in combat or stories that emphasized the need to do something a certain way. Perhaps more important, they taught with the enthusiasm that comes with wanting to make sure you keep your recruits alive.

Most of our female DIs came from supply or other administrative backgrounds, and they simply didn't have that knowledge. They taught the classes by the book. The learning experience is different when your instructor has been in a live situation with rounds coming down-range and his or her pals being shot at.

Even within our own battalion, there were difficulties. Because different drill instructors gave some of the classes in their squad bays, instruction wasn't standardized. It was hard to know who did a good job, and who did a half-assed job. In a big classroom, you're more likely to get more enthusiasm from the instructor.

I would have liked to have had all of our classes with the men. I would have liked to put a female platoon next to a male platoon on the rifle range. I would have liked to have integrated our physical-fitness training—or, at least, the physical-fitness test. It would have not only brought more knowledge to my women but also created a level of competition and respect between the male and female recruits. And it would have shown the men that the women were, in fact, doing the work.

As we changed the way we trained the female recruits, I recognized that probably 90 percent of my Marines were incredibly motivated. They were excited to make changes and see improvement.

But November Company continued to lag behind the other companies. Probably a third of the drill instructors in November Company just weren't happy. Most of them were on the third year of their tours, and they'd already been told, because no one had looked at the stats, that they were amazing and doing incredible things. So when I came in and changed things up, and everything improved, it made those amazing and incredible things look small.

I wasn't prepared for that—for people who wouldn't support proven good results—but also for leaders who wouldn't get behind me. I was met with the typical, "But we've always . . ." And, in November Company, they simply didn't make the changes, and then they claimed that the changes didn't work. Personally, I would have been so embarrassed to lead the only company that did not show improvement; and, honestly, it was so much fun—the excitement in the platoons that saw success was amazing. But November Company was behaving like the kid who stands in the corner, pouting about something everyone else has forgotten, while everyone else is having fun playing kickball.

One particular sergeant in November Company gave me the hardest time about everything. Prior to my arrival, she had been selected to be a senior drill instructor because everyone thought she was an amazing leader, despite what her recruit graduation scores indicated. When I talked about bias and about expectations and about women not being too short to fire a weapon, she simply said I was wrong.

"I've never had this problem," she told me. "I don't believe any bias exists."

I told her that was fine, but I was showing them in black and white the test results of men and women compared through of years of training.

"If you can show me that your way is better, we can do it your way," I told her. "But you have to show me."

I'm still waiting.

So, what did the recruits think about the changes?

Heh.

The recruits didn't know any better. Recruits arrive at boot camp as blank slates never having faced anything like the training they receive at Parris Island. So, they only know what they're taught. I know that sounds like common sense, but sometimes you forget that they don't know what status quo looks like.

The recruits needed to know only that I expected them to max the fitness test and fire expert on the range so they could compete with their male counterparts.

Easy-peasy.

CHAPTER 16

TRAIN LIKE A GIRL

I started thinking about why military women—whether officers, enlisted service members, recruits—had such low expectations of themselves. You would think that women who join the Marine Corps wouldn't be benchwarmers. Ideally, they are women with some taste for adventure, some capacity for risk, and some need to prove themselves. So why, when they finally had the opportunity to prove themselves, would they settle for the bare minimum?

We can blame the men all day long for holding us back, but we're still *letting* them hold us back. We're 51 percent of the population. It sure seems as if we should be able to recognize in ourselves and in each other what we're capable of and what we're worth—from equal pay to equal numbers of expert qualifications at the rifle range.

In 2014–2015, the timing seemed good to change things at Fourth Battalion. We were starting to see some civilian advertisements and marketing aimed at women—at strong women. That whole thing about a missed market in sports equipment and fitness clothes? People were starting to think about it. And companies that traditionally marketed to women, like the manufacturers of lipstick and tampons and dresses? They too have finally started picking up on this need to be recognized as both strong *and* beautiful.

Part of the change in popular opinion about women comes from sports: Soccer heroes and ballet heroes, like Mia Hamm and Misty Copeland, have emerged as marketing forces, with women responding to commercials featuring muscles as objects of beauty.

And part of this change comes from us: Women who have been serving in large numbers in war for the past fifteen years. We've seen women who show up on the screen in body armor and carrying weapons, or women who earn awards for dragging men to safety and treating their injuries, or women who run for

Congress after serving, one after losing both legs when the helicopter she piloted was hit by a rocket-propelled grenade, so the image of ourselves should be fierce.

Of course we're strong.

So when did it become an insult to train like a girl?

You still hear it—on football fields from fathers with sons, and on the training field from drill instructors with male recruits: *C'mon, ladies, get it together. You look like a bunch of women. You throw like a girl.* My drill instructors and I regularly heard these things, and, worse, yelled to the male recruits when they came in last on a run or showed the least bit of emotion.

This brings to mind that brilliant Super Bowl commercial, "Run Like a Girl," which was created by the brand Always. In that commercial, adult women were asked to demonstrate how to run like a girl. They did: arms flailing, giggling, legs at odd angles. When asked the same question, a bunch of little girls ran as fast and as hard as they could. They did this with no expectation that they should do anything but their best. They ran to win.

My recruits should have embodied that expectation as well. They had joined the Marine Corps. They had to have some idea of what that meant, some personal goal or need to be the strongest of women.

Instead, in the Marine Corps, we separated the women, talked about them as being part of the "Fourth Dimension," and told them that their bodies aren't appropriate for shooting weapons.

This was no meritocracy based on abilities. This was an organization that held women back, based on the institution's misguided expectations of them, starting with Marine recruiters. Generally speaking, the recruiters didn't expect their female applicants to show up for physical-fitness training before boot camp; the women didn't hold leadership positions in the poolee platoons; and, worse, female recruits were allowed to ship to boot camp having made no progress at all in terms of their mental and physical preparation.

We expected nothing of them.

Just as an aside, the first Marine Corps commercial to spotlight a female Marine aired in 2017, and only after the Marines United naked-photo-sharing scandal broke in the news and caused the Marine Corps a ton of embarrassment. Most Marines think it was only released as a PR stunt to try to win back public favor.

By the time male recruits arrived at Parris Island, their expectations of female recruits were already low, as a result of the double standards they witnessed in their recruiting offices. At boot camp, they rarely saw the women—just at church on Sundays and for some training in large classrooms where they weren't allowed to interact—so there was this mystery about how female Marines are made, and even a pervasive idea that they do less than their male counterparts.

Women do follow the same training schedule and regulations as the men, but the women have always been held to lower expectations for performance.

I quickly learned that when you hold women to higher standards, they meet them. If we want to change the way female Marines think about themselves, we have to demand more of them as soon as they walk through the recruiter's door.

In 2015, I decided to make "Train Like a Girl" our battalion mantra.

I had been showing that Always commercial to my drill instructors, working it into my classes with the recruits who were just getting to Parris Island, and showing it to those who were graduating.

I told them there was no reason for us not to perform at the same levels as the men. I told them it was okay to be proud of being women. It's okay to be different—we add something to the fight. We needed to work to convince the Marine Corps of our worth; but, first, we needed to believe it ourselves.

I reminded my recruits and new Marines that they had already kicked ass on the rifle range, and we needed to use that success to build momentum for achievement in our other areas.

How?

We compete.

We hold each other accountable.

We hold recruits accountable.

We strive for better.

And we challenge ourselves and each other.

We should be proud to shoot like girls, fight like girls, train like girls, and win battles like girls.

CHAPTER 17

MEAN GIRLS AND MOBBING

Mean Girls syndrome is a real thing.

The Marine Corps is the last place I expected to encounter it. But it's not just a millennial problem that shows up in movies with Lindsay Lohan. If I had Tina Fey onboard, I'm pretty sure all of my problems would have been solved.

As it turns out, the only way that you can combat Mean Girls syndrome is if the entire chain of command understands that it is a problem, and they are determined to fix it. Basically, Mean Girls or Queen Bee syndrome is when a woman in charge treats women who work for her worse than she treats men. At Parris Island, you could see it in how some women were unwilling to help other women get ahead. Worse, they bullied other women because they believed that bullying is a more masculine trait that would help them fit in with men. I saw it play out every day, particularly in November and Papa Companies.

The Queen Bee was often a senior drill instructor or company first sergeant. For the women who were subordinate to the Queen Bee, life was miserable. The women favored by the Queen Bee existed on tenterhooks, afraid that, at any time, their status could change. The women who were on the Queen Bee's shit list were hazed, shamed, and ostracized.

So much of it was nonsense.

One of my company commanders told me that before I arrived, several Marines stopped using their chain of command to address problems. All of them had several disciplinary violations, and all of them tended to request mast (i.e., to make counter-complaints to someone higher in the chain of command) or file complaints with the inspector general when they were about to get in trouble or when they were asked to do more work or to report something properly. In other words, they filed a complaint rather than deal with their own bad work ethics.

For example, Marine A was upset that Marine B was allowed time to take care of her child if the child were sick or got out of school for an emergency or any of the normal childcare issues. But Marine A also had a child, and she was allowed off every Wednesday to address the particular needs of her child. Other Marines then had to cover for Marine A, which was fine, except it often included Marine B, whom Marine A resented for being allowed to take care of her own child.

Yes. It's convoluted.

That's mostly because it makes no sense.

In any case, Marine A filed several complaints against Marine B for things she didn't like and that weren't based on fact or reason, but the company's leadership essentially ignored the problem. At the same time, Marine A came up with excuses not to work herself, and she barely did her job when she did work. No one did anything to correct this behavior, because they feared retaliation from a small group of Marines in the company. Peak Mean Girls syndrome.

At one point, Marine A overslept and missed a movement (march) out to the rifle range, leaving the company scrambling to find another drill instructor to supervise the platoon at the last minute. But rather than owning up to oversleeping, Marine A said that she had to take her daughter to an appointment that she hadn't told anyone about in advance.

When Marine A returned to work the same day, she made snide remarks about Marine B. When they got back from the range, the new company commander called Marine A into her office. The company commander asked the Marine why she had missed the movement to the rifle range, and Marine A said she had "no excuse." The CO tried to see if there were other problems but couldn't get the Marine to talk. The CO tried to see if there were underlying problems, but again she couldn't get an answer. So the CO and her first sergeant counseled Marine A to stop making snide remarks and to let them know how they could help. Marine A said she understood.

It should have ended there.

Instead, Marine A said someone else was gossiping about her and causing the company commander to dislike her.

She simply had not been held accountable before. The CO told me that Marine A and some other Marines did not like being held accountable when I came in as battalion commander, either. "Now some Marines are using request mast and IG complaints as a way to get revenge," the CO told me. I should have paid more attention to this warning.

Because we saw how this destructive behavior (not being held accountable, not accepting responsibility, and generally falling prey to Mean Girls syndrome) negatively impacted the battalion and the mental health of the drill instructors, we put together a training day for all of my officers. We taught classes about Mean Girl and Queen Bee syndromes, and also asked some career recruiters to provide training on active listening, as well as how to ask open-ended questions to get to the root causes of problems within their companies.

I gave a class on behavior modification and supplied my officers with some tools they could use to ensure that they recognized and rewarded great performance and held their Marines accountable when they didn't meet standards. I asked that they handle problems at the local level. This could mean encouraging recruits to talk to their buddies about things that were causing issues, such as poor personal hygiene or needing to practice push-ups to do well on the fitness test. It could also involve a company commander having direct talks with her Marines about bullying before this behavior resulted in complaints at my level.

During the off-site training, we also talked about relational aggression, which is when you try to affect how other people see someone. You might spread rumors, make fun of someone, or expound upon a person's faults. We talked about cyber-bullying—harassing someone online—because some of my DIs were notorious for bashing members of the battalion on social media.

We conducted these classes in April because I worried about the cases of bullying and abuse that existed before I arrived. But we did this also because, in the five or six months since I had arrived, I had seen how it had played out in November and Papa Companies.

Our changes were coming along and evolving and growing, but it's hard to change the culture overnight. I wanted commanders to be able to quickly identify bad behavior so they could take more of a leadership role to address it at their levels before things exploded and I had to step in. Pretty much everyone needed to have a clear idea of what Mean Girls syndrome looked like: The DIs were abusing recruits. The DIs were abusing each other. The recruits were abusing recruits.

I didn't know what Mean Girls syndrome was until I arrived at Parris Island. Prior to my tour at Fourth Battalion, I had mostly worked with men. Until I started doing research, I didn't realize there was a name for it—I just knew what it felt like. As I worked with my company commanders, I saw firsthand how individual leader personalities could shape the dynamic in their units. Papa Company had an overly aggressive first sergeant who tended to ride roughshod over the company commander. In her view, a drill instructor who said she was sick or injured was weak. The same was true for November Company. Without a strong company commander who took full ownership of her role as the leader of the unit, strong enlisted Marines took over. This didn't always spell disaster, but when the leadership influence was negative, we ended up with suicidal drill instructors locked up in the mental ward of Beaufort Memorial. This is not hyperbole. It is something that had recently happened, and I was devastated about it.

Mean Girls syndrome had been a problem in Fourth Battalion for years.

But rather than being addressed by regimental command, the men just assumed that women can't get along. They assumed that this was only what could be expected of women.

Mean Girls syndrome is not an easy thing to fix—or even to recognize, especially if you've never worked in an all-women staff before. Sixth-grade teachers can spot it instantly, but I never would have expected to see Mean Girls or Queen Bee syndrome in grown-ups.

In my case, I had several things working against my battalion.

First, we had this culture of enlisted Marines running roughshod over officers, so there was no oversight.

Second, we had both officers and enlisted Marines who didn't want change. Some of the officers resented the change because it meant more work for them. Some of the senior enlisted Marines resented the change because it represented a loss of power or status for them.

Third, I had some problem company commanders: One never wanted to be at Fourth Battalion to begin with, and another wanted to go to her soccer practices and games at 4:30 every afternoon and spend her day planning her wedding to an officer in one of the male training battalions.

Fourth, I had an executive officer who encouraged my Marines to complain about me to her, after I counseled her about not doing her job. (I learned this secondhand at the time, and then through statements from the Marines during the investigation.)

And, fifth, my boss appeared to encourage all of the disgruntled folks to bypass the chain of command and go directly to him to complain about me.

That last issue was, of course, the most important. Everything else could, and should, have been addressed immediately, simply by virtue of how the Marine Corps works. We have a rank structure. When an officer who outranks you tells you to do something, you do it. You don't smart off, you don't give the CO the hand before rushing out to do pull-ups, and you don't encourage the people who serve under you to mouth off about their direct boss.

In the military, the chain of command is sacred. You don't jump over it; you go step-by-step through it. When you're having an issue, you go to the person in charge of you, unless they are the perceived problem. But, even then, there are tools like request mast to ensure that complaints can be heard and remedied within the chain of command.

My boss should have had my back on this, even if he didn't like me. People lose rank for talking back to higher-ranking officers. People get written up for going outside their chains of command. Can you imagine how not operating that way could affect unit performance in a combat zone? That's what good order and discipline are for: survival and success.

But that was exactly what was wrong with the battalion when I arrived: No one was held accountable, let alone required to use the chain of command.

So as we were swimming along, doing great things on the range and working to improve physical-fitness scores and our ability to hike, some of my companies did great.

But November Company, which had the most problems with rank structure and Mean Girl syndrome, continued to lag behind the rest of the battalion in every graduation category.

It makes sense, on some level. As a drill instructor, if you've been told for two-thirds of your tour that you're amazing, you're doing everything right, and you're the cream of the crop, and then somebody comes in with no drill-instructor experience and says, "Please don't use foul language" or "You shouldn't be physical with the recruits," you're going to think (or say), "Who the eff are you to tell me what to do?"

Many of the drill instructors and officers in November Company, probably 20–30 percent, even if they disagreed, still changed. Honestly, it would have been stupid for them not to come along, because the majority of the battalion was moving in that direction. But the majority of November stayed stuck. In some ways, it was almost like Stockholm syndrome. The officers had been marginalized, and the drill instructors had been abused as recruits themselves, and/or abused as drill instructors when they showed up at Parris Island. Now they respected or felt protective of the methods that had diminished the status of the officers and had resulted in physical and mental trauma for the DIs.

When I arrived at Parris Island, I had two weak company commanders— for November and Papa Companies. Generally, my other officers were either onboard and enthusiastic, or they were onboard and sort of biding their time before their tours ended. My battalion executive officer (XO) was a problem. That's three of the eleven officers I had on staff, and it made a huge difference. They were a trifecta of negative influence.

Unknown to me, my boss, Colonel Haas, was nursing a grudge because I continued to send out those emails to the recruiting commanders, even though I copied him on each one. To my knowledge, he never said, "Because I'm concerned about Kate's leadership, I should probably spend more time with her and see for myself what is happening in her battalion." He did not counsel me, he did not call me, and he did not spend time watching our training.

There was no way for me to improve my relationship with him.

I later realized that Colonel Haas and the trifecta had set the stage for all of the follow-on discussion at the highest levels of the Marine Corps about me being a problem. I didn't know it then, but that's what "mobbing" is: It's presenting the squeaky wheel as the suspect—making them the problem.

Other.

Outside of the Marine Corps, you might see it this way: You point out some problems with the structure of your organization or some policies and procedures that aren't working to everyone's benefit. Because they feel threatened by the idea of change, your co-workers gang up on you to spread rumors about you, intimidate you, humiliate you, discredit you, or isolate you. This is all done with the intent to try to force you out.

Because such behavior is so far outside the realm of normal, mobbing is hard to respond to or address at first. Mobbing seems petty and silly, and like something that should be easily fixed. When it takes the shape of gossip, as it often does, it's hard to even know that it is going on at all; this is because mobbing is, by design, invisible. As time went on and these mobbing behaviors became more blatant, I thought someone above me would see what was happening and take action to remedy the situation. I thought everyone could see what was happening. In fact, our commanding general told me he knew what was going on. Further, I didn't realize that Colonel Haas was trying to oust me—I thought he simply didn't like me. We've all worked with someone we simply didn't like on a personal level. But that doesn't mean that we push that person out. Working with someone you don't like really stinks, but it happens. You deal with it. After years of stellar work reviews, I thought people could see my merits, too. Not just the gossip and mobbing.

Because I was so unfamiliar with what was happening, I did exactly the opposite of what experts say you should do in that situation: I fought back. I showed them statistics. I argued my case. I tried to address the mobbing directly, with educational briefings and on-site corrections.

But I failed to recognize that it was too late—now it looked like I was the problem. They could present me as a bad leader, push me out, and go back to their poor behaviors.

By the time I realized they were trying to push me out, I was an absolute stress case. I started to second-guess myself. *Am I bad a person? A bad leader?*

By the time I left Parris Island, I thought I was losing my mind.

CHAPTER 18

WHEN THERE'S NO ONE LEFT TO BLAME

When I got to Parris Island, November Company's CO had just taken command.

She wasn't great.

When I first started, I'd have the company commanders come to my office once a week for round-table discussions. We'd do activities such as reading an article about leadership or change management, and then talking about it together. These weekly meetings presented an opportunity to talk about issues within the companies and how best to address them, offered me the chance to mentor based on my own experiences, and allowed us all to get to know each other's leadership styles better. They could toss around ideas and provide solutions for each other. But if I put November Company's CO on the spot by asking her to brief an article—as all of the officers were asked to do—she would cry.

So, that stood out.

She was a college-educated officer in charge of Marines serving as drill instructors at boot camp, and she cried in front of her peers over having to describe what she had read.

Beyond that, the problems between her and her first sergeant were immediate and constant. Every day, all day, for three months, they hen-pecked and defied each other and behaved like children. I finally said, "You can't do this anymore."

But they continued to squabble.

One day, the company commander came into my office and demanded to quit. And then her first sergeant went into the regimental sergeant major's office and demanded to quit.

I bet you were under the impression that you can't quit the Marine Corps.

Once again, Parris Island proved to be different from anywhere else in the Marine Corps. In the rest of the service, having command is considered the greatest privilege there is. You would never, ever hear of a commander marching into her CO's office and demanding reassignment. It was unheard-of.

And just to clear things up: They didn't want to quit because of me. They wanted to quit because they couldn't get along with each other.

The company commander and several of my drill instructors told me and my sergeant major that the first sergeant actively plotted against the CO: "Don't listen to her," she would allegedly tell her DIs. "I know what we should be doing."

I think I mentioned that when I arrived at Fourth Battalion, I discovered that many of the enlisted Marines believed they ran the show. And my predecessor's sergeant major had been pushed out for essentially trying to, as the most senior enlisted Marine in the battalion, usurp authority from the battalion commander. November's first sergeant definitely fell into the the-enlisted-should-run-the-show camp.

The CO was so weak that she never seemed to step in and say, "Bullshit. I'm the person in charge. I have command responsibility." While she was happy to complain about her drill sergeants, it was easier for her to sit back and not do anything—to just let them run the show.

It seemed like she should have had enough experience at that point to assert herself, but, as I said earlier, the DIs can be intimidating. They get special-duty pay for it.

We started meeting the second time she said she wanted to quit. She was crying and saying things like, "I can't take it anymore." I was sincerely concerned for her.

I decided to take her under my wing. To me, that's what good leaders do. I said, "Look, for thirty days straight, we're going to meet and talk through leadership challenges, read articles on leadership, and discuss philosophy, because I want you to be successful."

We plotted out her day to make sure she properly supervised her Marines, as well as to make sure she was visible to them. We developed her command philosophy to make it more positive—to make sure her Marines felt appreciated.

But it felt like she came into every meeting kicking and screaming.

I get it. You don't want your boss all up in your business, micromanaging you. But if you're not doing your job, there should be an expectation that your boss will, in fact, be all up in your business. My hope was that we could do this face-to-face mentoring for a little bit, and then she would learn from it and be able to mentor her own Marines in a similar way in the future. In the immediate future, I hoped she would be a better company commander.

At first, that seemed to be happening. For about three weeks, she implemented strategies we talked about, and I started to see the morale in her company change for the better.

But then she stopped doing the things we agreed she should do. When she faced her first major command challenge, she acted like a five-year-old child being made to eat broccoli: She stuffed my directions in her cheek and then spit them out when I wasn't looking.

It happened when one of her DIs stepped over the line after the Marine Corps birthday ball. Rather than seeing a proud tradition to further celebrate unit cohesion, we saw a blatant example of a Marine left to fend for herself.

Every year, the Marine Corps has birthday celebrations on or around November 10, which is considered the birthday of the Corps. If you aren't deployed or in the field on a training exercise, the celebrations are pretty elaborate affairs with fancy outfits and food and lots of booze, and it's a chance to schmooze with your co-workers and celebrate your bond as teammates.

Well, on her way home from the ball, one of the CO's Marines got a DUI. Any time a service member gets in trouble with the law, his or her company commander finds out about it, and then the company commander can impose a punishment, such as extra duty or a reduction in rank. But getting in trouble can also be a sign of bad morale; generally, Marines who care about their careers don't risk them, and leaders who pay attention to their Marines can usually figure out if a problem is brewing before it happens. And certainly, before the ball, everyone gets a talking-to (a "safety briefing") about the consequences of drinking and driving, as well as a plea to be safe. We don't want to lose any Marines on the battlefield, and we certainly don't want to lose them behind the wheel.

When I asked the CO about the DUI and what might have been going on with the Marine, she basically fell apart. When I continued to probe about how she had briefed her Marines about drinking and driving prior to the event, she dug in her heels and refused to have a conversation. Later in the discussion, when I said it appeared that she was no longer applying the changes we had agreed to, she said, "Well, I started to make the changes, and then I just quit."

I just quit.

It took everything I had to keep it together.

I still have the notes from that day, because I remember thinking, "Holy cow. When I go to my boss with these notes and the documentation from this meeting, he's going to say, 'Okay, you've done everything you need to do as a leader. She needs to be fired.'"

That's what I was thinking.

"I don't understand why it is we can't seem to connect," I said, struggling to stay calm. "For a while, it was going well, and then everything stopped and we're back to square one. I can't have that in the battalion."

"I don't know what it is," she said. "You just rub me the wrong way."

Note: this is a captain. This is a captain talking to a lieutenant colonel.

You've all seen enough movies to know that this is not how one speaks to someone who outranks her. If this single conversation doesn't give you some perspective on the mind-set of that battalion, I don't know what else would.

During our meeting, as I was writing this down, I was thinking, "You just blew my mind." If I ever said anything like that to a colonel, I would be fired.

I told her I would bring her back into my office to resume the conversation after I had decided what the next step should be.

After she left my office, I told my sergeant major about this conversation because she and I were close, and I trusted her advice, but also because she needed to sort out how the CO's behavior affected her NCOs in November Company.

I was also worried for the CO. I thought she was a horrible company commander; but I didn't think she was a bad human. And, as a good battalion commander, it was my job to make her successful. If I didn't care, I wouldn't have spent so much time with her one-on-one, observing her and mentoring her and giving her resources to improve her leadership and herself. I did those things because that's what I thought leaders do.

Before we started with our mentoring meetings, I had laid it out for her. I counseled her. I wrote her a non-punitive letter of caution. It said: You need to do better, and for the next thirty days, we're going to work together to get you there. But if you don't improve at the end of thirty days, I'm going to relieve you of your command.

By mid-December, we had been doing the one-on-one mentoring meetings every day for thirty days. The day I counseled the CO about the Marine with the DUI, Colonel Haas came to my battalion area for an end-of-cycle meeting—the only time he came to visit my battalion.

"Sir, I just want you to know I need to relieve [the CO]," I said. I explained to him why, and I said, "Look, I've got counseling statements three inches thick. I can provide all of that to you, but it's to the point now where she's belligerent with me. I'm worried about her health. She cries every time she speaks publicly. She's crying in front of her Marines."

For the record, all along, I had notified Colonel Haas about my concerns with this CO. I had previously told him that she had tried to quit twice, and her first sergeant had also quit.

"I can't have this," I said. "It's affecting my other Marines."

It was terrible, and I needed him to understand why.

"Well, what are you going to do with her?" he asked.

Because I was short female officers and didn't have a spare captain lying around to replace her, I told him I could make her a platoon commander again. That is a demotion, but it would take her out of the company commander position. That way, I could promote a better-qualified person from platoon commander to the company commander position. That's all that I could do. He knew that I didn't have any XOs at the company level, and we were in desperate need of more officers.

"Let me see what I can do," he said.

That's exactly what he said.

So I was thinking, "Sweet. I've got his support." I was left with the impression that he would go back to support command to try to find a female officer who could backfill the platoon-commander position so I could fleet up the best qualified officer to be the new CO. That way, rather than demoting the old CO to be a platoon commander again, she could go somewhere else on the recruit depot, and I would get a better commander.

I didn't hear, "Don't fire her." I heard, "I'll work with you to figure out a replacement."

I would later find out that his interpretation of "Let me see what I can do" was entirely different.

After he left, the CO was standing outside my office, waiting for me to fire her. He saw her there. He and I had just had this conversation. Typically, you don't wait for a replacement to fire someone who needs to not be in command anymore. Just as the Marine Corps left my job vacant for four months after I was fired, you make do with what you have until you get the replacement.

Forty minutes later, I came back to my office from a training event, and I had an email from Colonel Haas: "Just in case I wasn't clear: I'm expressly forbidding you to fire [the CO]."

My stomach felt heavy.

I immediately picked up the phone and called Colonel Haas.

"I'm really sorry, sir," I said. "I don't understand. I didn't hear that from you at all. I've already fired her."

He refused to talk to me on the phone.

I asked if I could set up a meeting with him for the next day. Right after graduation, I was supposed make the eight-hour drive to spend Christmas with Joe, so I wanted to do it before I left. Colonel Haas refused.

Instead, the next day, Fourth Battalion conducted the initial strength test for a new class of recruits before we headed to a graduation ceremony. I was supposed to give a speech at graduation, so I was getting ready to go to my office to shower and prepare. I walked up to Colonel Haas and said, "Once again, sir, I'm really sorry that it seemed like I disobeyed you. That was not my intention. I would never do that, obviously, and I misunderstood the intent of your words. Is there a time today when we can talk about it?"

He started yelling at me in front of all of my Marines about how I disobeyed an order.

Because all of my Marines and recruits were within earshot of the conversation, I tried walking away from the formation with him. He walked with me a couple of paces and he said, "When you get back from leave, expect paperwork for you to sign."

Oh, God. I'm going to be fired.

I went home for Christmas break, knowing that, when I returned, I would lose my career.

This was the beginning of the end.

I was gone for five days.

I had been going home every three months, and that was my only chance to see Joe. He was working at the Pentagon and going full-tilt, and neither of us had much off-time. It was miserable and lonely. But I knew my Marines were dealing with the same thing—I just had the added stress of feeling like I was going to get canned even though I thought I was doing good work.

The whole time I was home for Christmas, I agonized over it.

That's when Joe and I started talking about what I should do if I got fired.

It still seemed so unlikely—I hadn't been counseled. This is a big deal: In the military, Marines who get into trouble get counseled verbally or in writing for everything. There's basically a three-strikes-you're-out rule. They spend way too much money training Marines; and, as I said before, you can't just quit, and they can't just get rid of you, so it's important to document behavior and performance problems. I had never been counseled by Colonel Haas.

He had verbally told me I couldn't switch the duty roster. Okay. And he had gotten on my case about emailing the recruiting officers, but I thought we had resolved that.

When I left Joe to return to Parris Island, I was devastated, positive I was going to be fired.

But Colonel Haas took his time about it.

The day after I returned, I went to a training event with November Company at the confidence course, still thinking Colonel Haas was going to fire me. It was freezing. The recruits were sweating because they were sliding down ropes and going over monkey bars and climbing giant ladders made of telephone poles. But I just stood there, pretending like I didn't feel it—because, you know, *Marine*.

Brigadier General Terry Williams showed up. He was Colonel Haas's boss. From the time he took command in July, I don't think I had ever seen him at a training event—not because of a lack of interest on his part, but because he was busy. He was in charge of recruiting for the East Coast and spent most of the week traveling to the recruiting stations. But that day, he made time to see me.

He knew me from a previous assignment when we had worked together. He knew I wasn't crazy. And I think he supported what we were trying to do at Fourth Battalion.

He and his sergeant major sought me out on the course.

"How are things going?" he asked.

"Fine," I lied. "Everything's good. The Marines are doing incredible things. We've had unprecedented success on the rifle range."

"No, really," he said. "How are things going?"

Oh.

"To be honest, things aren't going well," I told him.

I wanted to pick my words carefully, so I didn't appear disloyal or like I was bad-mouthing Colonel Haas. But I didn't need to say anything else.

"Got it," he said. "Your boss told me. Keep doing what you're doing—it's my job to mentor colonels."

I realized at that point that Colonel Haas had met with the general to discuss firing me.

But I came away from talking with Brigadier General Williams thinking, "Thank God. Somebody finally gets it."

And I thought I was good.

Later that day, Colonel Haas finally called me into his office.

He acted as if things were perfectly normal—small talk and "how were the holidays" and "how's Joe." I'm thinking, "Just. Get. It. Over. With."

"You know, I'm sorry about the way I reacted at the initial strength test," he said. "I was very angry. I need for you to make sure you're doing a better job of listening to me."

I'll see what I can do. I'll try to figure you out, because, clearly, I don't get you.
"Okay," I said. "I've got it."

He had nothing for me to sign.

I again explained to him exactly what documentation I had regarding the November Company CO. I informed him that she spent much of her time complaining about me to my XO, which was inappropriate.

"Give me what you have," he said.

I gave it to him.

He told me that until he had reviewed the documentation and made a decision, I needed to hire back the CO, which can't have been good for her state of mind, and it certainly wasn't good for my authority within the battalion.

I walked back to my office and I debriefed Sergeant Major. I told her everything. I thought she and I were really tight. We went everywhere together, planned everything, and dealt with problems—and I just adored her.

I told her I didn't understand. Our morale in the battalion had improved; we had fewer disciplinary issues; the Marines were saying they were happier; the recruits weren't being abused; we were improving training; we were even doing yoga and making sure everyone got enough sleep.

What's not to like?

Sergeant Major helped me through it—she let me know that I wasn't crazy and that we were doing good work and that things were getting better.

And, she told me that I needed to document every interaction I had with Colonel Haas. After our meeting, I felt like he still planned to try to fire me, but I knew I had a battalion to lead and that I needed to focus.

I decided not to be negative about it.

"Okay, this is progress," I thought. "Maybe the general has already begun mentoring him."

In hindsight, I realize the general may also have questioned Colonel Haas's lack of documentation about my performance and attitude. It's hard to fire a lieutenant colonel without backing yourself up with paperwork.

Looking back, I think Colonel Haas was even angrier that he lost the fight with the general to fire me.

In the middle of January, he called me about November Company's CO.

"Okay," he said. "You can fire her."

CHAPTER 19

FISTICUFFS

I had three recruit training companies in my battalion, and Oscar Company went gangbusters with the new training goals. They blew off the roof with their numbers. They bought into the program, had good leaders in key positions, and understood what it would mean for all Marine Corps women if our female recruits were to excel in boot camp.

After Colonel Haas finally allowed me to fire the old company commander in January, November Company also started making progress under the leadership of the new company commander, although we still had some abuse issues to sort out. Some of the old commander's DIs were not happy about her relief, so I was waiting it out until, one by one, they transferred to a new duty station and we could change the culture in that company. I hand-selected the new company commander—a strong and engaged leader—and I knew her enthusiasm and positive mental attitude would be good for her Marines.

Overall, I felt like things were going pretty well.

However, Papa Company had a first sergeant who compensated for being a female Marine by being super-aggressive and tough as nails. Earlier in my career, I had also fallen prey to the idea that I needed to compensate for a lack of testosterone by being harder and tougher than my peers. Fortunately, after my recruiting-command tour, I realized I needed to focus on being comfortable in my own skin. Unfortunately, Papa Company's first sergeant had never matured to that point. As I said, she controlled her CO and made it clear to the enlisted Marines that the company commander wasn't really in charge.

You would think that the company commander would have been embarrassed by her lack of authority, but she cared more about being liked. She planned to marry a company commander from one of the male battalions, and she spent more time planning her wedding than supervising her Marines. During intramural soccer season, she regularly rushed off early to make it in time to practices and games.

Apparently, the soccer team needed her more than her Marines did.

So her first sergeant took over for her, running Papa Company.

I started working with them both to hold them accountable for improving the climate within their company. Because the first sergeant was so harsh, recruits didn't benefit from some of the new battalion changes. She showed no empathy. If a recruit said she was sick, the interaction with her first sergeant would leave her believing she was weak. If a recruit said she was sore from PT, she got no stretching tips. She instead learned that she was weak. If a recruit struggled learning to zero her rifle . . . You guessed it: Weak.

The same went for Papa Company's DIs.

It was so bad that one of their Marines was admitted to a psychiatric ward. She said that she was so distraught about how she was treated within her company that she wanted to drink herself to death.

Members of Papa Company also struggled to make progress with their numbers.

Still, I didn't think their company commander was failing. I just thought she needed to be taught and mentored. It never occurred to me that she wouldn't finish her tour successfully in May. But I would have been wrong to look the other way at the problems in her company.

Especially after the fistfight.

A sergeant punched a staff sergeant.

Punching other Marines at work is frowned upon. Punching Marines who outrank you can end your career.

To compensate for the lack of staff sergeants assigned to Fourth Battalion, we had several sergeants serving as senior drill instructors. When I took command of the battalion, I wanted to ensure that the strongest leaders were assigned to key leadership positions like the senior drill-instructor billet. The senior DIs, who wore black patent-leather belts, rather than green belts, to signify their leadership status, played a critical quality-control role in that they were not only there to lead, mentor, and train their drill-instructor team, but also to ensure the recruits had a person they felt comfortable going to regarding inappropriate conduct in the platoon—by other recruits or by drill instructors.

I wanted to make sure we chose only the most trustworthy leaders for the role, so we implemented a board-selection process. Candidates went through an oral examination in front of a group of more senior and experienced officers and enlisted members of the battalion. The board members asked basic knowledge questions about recruit-training regulations, but they might also ask how a person would deal with a specific situation or leadership challenge.

Our career-progression boards helped to ensure that only the best NCOs filled those senior DI slots, no matter their rank. We had some good sergeants do a great job in senior positions. It also allowed us some relief from our shortage of staff sergeants since we had plenty of sergeants in the battalion.

But that didn't last. A few sergeants who had been placed in senior DI positions in the male battalions got in some trouble, so the regiment developed a policy that prohibited sergeants from serving as senior DIs if there were staff sergeants available. So, if we had a poorly performing staff sergeant and a great sergeant, the staff sergeant was assigned the gig.

That meant we put people in charge based on rank, and not because they were the best and the brightest. This didn't seem right to me, because when you're training young recruits and there are so many things that can go wrong—including people violating positions of authority—choosing the best and the brightest for leadership roles seems key.

And, of course, I tried to convince Colonel Haas about how this policy would further compound Fourth Battalion's personnel problems. As usual, I received no support. There was some good news: The policy would allow sergeants who previously had served as senior DIs to continue in that role, as long as we provided justification and asked for permission prior to each new training cycle.

Prior to my arrival at Parris Island, an experienced sergeant was selected to be a senior drill instructor in Papa Company—she was a great Marine and one of my most trusted advisers. I knew she would continue to excel as a leader, so I supported her continuing as a senior DI.

Each platoon had a senior DI, and there were two platoons per series. A few months before I was relieved, it became clear that the new policy was going to cause problems. A staff sergeant was selected as the senior DI for Papa Company's second platoon. She went through the board process to ensure she was bare-bones qualified, and she was selected "with reservation." This meant, "Watch this woman. She's a little green around the edges." She needed training and mentoring from company staff to help her develop strong leadership skills. We didn't have any other staff sergeants to take her place, but we hoped more experienced DIs would help her learn. Ultimately, the company commander and first sergeant supervised, trained, and evaluated senior DIs.

This staff sergeant was not a leader. She had been an administrative Marine who had never been in charge of anyone before she got to Parris Island. She came across as passive and disengaged. She seemed to believe the senior DI's role was to scream at recruits, rather than to mentor and den-mom them and her DIs. It's not as if she was supposed to give out cookies and pizza, but the recruits were supposed to be able to go to her and say, "Hey. I saw this happen. The drill instructor touched this recruit inappropriately." She never understood that, and it may be because her first sergeant also didn't get it.

She also liked to remind other drill instructors that she outranked them—she did not seem to understand that rank did not a leader make.

Sergeant Major and I went back to the CO and informed her that the staff sergeant "has been selected 'with reservation.' You need to make sure you keep an eye on her: Mentor her, train her, catch her mistakes, and reprimand her. She's had issues in the past."

Soon after a new group of recruits showed up for training, however, I saw that that wasn't happening. Instead, the CO carried on with her wedding-planning duties and soccer. The first sergeant continued to rate her senior DIs based on how tough she perceived them to be, rather than by the career-progression checklist my sergeant major and I had implemented.

Even though the sergeant who had been carried over as a senior DI in spite of the new policy was doing a good job, the combination of her leadership not properly monitoring the situation and the staff sergeant being too big for her boots soon forced an explosion.

The sergeant was frustrated because she wasn't getting the rest she needed: She was in charge of her platoon, but she also had to constantly watch over the other senior DI. The staff sergeant was not receptive to advice from the sergeant, even though she had never managed anyone before. Because the company commander and first sergeant never got around to training the staff sergeant, the sergeant had to do the staff sergeant's work.

About a week after the new recruits had been picked up—when all of the drill instructors were tired and impatient—the sergeant lost her temper. The staff sergeant was also hitting the sergeant with some "I'm the staff sergeant you have to do what I tell you" BS. When the platoons came back to the squad bays after morning PT to shower and change, the staff sergeant and sergeant argued over who needed to perform a task. After being told she needed to do the task because she was junior to the staff sergeant, the sergeant lost it, and—in front of the drill instructors and recruits—she punched the daylights out of the staff sergeant.

It was just about the worst thing for the recruits to see—especially from a senior DI. The sergeant, who had incredible potential, immediately felt destroyed because she understood the enormity of what she had done. The recruits and other DIs were distraught because they loved and respected the sergeant as their senior DI, and they knew that her action could destroy her career.

And the staff sergeant? Well, she knew she had technically done nothing wrong, and that her career was safe.

Everyone in the company knew tension had been building between the two senior DIs. But no one stepped in. They said it was "just a female thing," "just an enlisted Marine thing."

This happened in January. We did an investigation in February.

I said, "Look. I don't have a choice here: One's a staff sergeant; one's a sergeant. The sergeant punched a staff sergeant. I have to hold her accountable."

If I had looked the other way, I was going to be the same kind of person my Marines had complained about in the previous year's equal-opportunity survey when they said nobody held anybody accountable.

So we brought the sergeant into my office for nonjudicial punishment. I told the sergeant that the nonjudicial punishment itself was on her record, and I gave her a counseling letter that would remain in her file. I didn't want to reduce her in rank or fine her. I knew the act of going to nonjudicial punishment and being removed from her senior DI billet were more than enough punishment. I wrote the endorsement on the investigation and sent it to the regiment after the nonjudicial punishment, because I didn't want Colonel Haas to come back and say I had to take her to a court-martial.

Here's why: The lack of supervision and the lack of training of the staff sergeant by the company commander and first sergeant led to the sergeant not getting enough sleep and the staff sergeant not being properly trained and held accountable. The sergeant shouldn't have punched the staff sergeant, obviously, but I think the situation was the direct result of a lack of engagement by the company staff—all despite my direct guidance.

"You don't get it," I had told the company commander many times. "You need to be walking the decks, making sure your drill instructors aren't falling out of their shoes because they're so tired. You need to make sure that the recruits aren't being abused."

I tried to work with the commander, and I could see she wasn't happy about it. But I was not mean to her. I did not yell at her.

Roll my eyes? Maybe. I was definitely frustrated. "Frustrated" is probably the wrong word. We're Marines. When we're told to do a job, we do it. We don't mouth off. We don't ignore the direction. We might offer feedback—just like with any other job—but we sure as hell don't ignore the instruction.

I had specifically directed her and her first sergeant to train and monitor their DIs to prevent situations like this one.

At the same time, I could see that the company commander wasn't the one making decisions in her company. The company commander would come into my office and brief "her" decisions, and I would ask her questions:

"Why are you doing this?"

"Have you thought about this?"

"How are you implementing this?"

She didn't have the answers.

That was between February and April.

In the meantime, the officer directly in charge of the sergeant who punched the staff sergeant was angry because I held her feet to the fire, too. She complained to the company commander, who, of course, complained to my executive officer.

Eventually, the staff sergeant completed her tour but did not receive a performance award before she left. The sergeant, who went back to being a regular DI, finished her tour successfully, and I gave her an end-of-tour award. The first sergeant was too busy being tough to notice. After I was relieved, I also sent a letter to the sergeant's command, recommending that her nonjudicial punishment be stricken from her record so she could be considered for promotion with her peers. I wanted her to know I understood what had happened.

The company commander had her change of command coming up in May. She was obviously just biding her time—planning her wedding, playing soccer, counting days. (This is not to suggest, of course, that Marines cannot plan their weddings or have interests and commitments outside of the Marines. However, when those commitments interfere with the completion of their duties, we obviously have a problem.)

But before the CO could escape, one of her Marines requested mast because the other DIs harassed her so relentlessly.

The DI came to me and said, "I can't do this anymore."

The DI said she could no longer work in Papa Company.

During the request mast, the DI, who was brand-new to the drill field, was denied the ability to go to Medical when she was sick. She was also being forced to do all of the menial tasks in her platoon and was not being taught how to lead recruits. She said she felt she was being set up to fail and that she wanted a transfer to another company. When I reviewed the new DI's training record jacket, I found the series commander and staff were not doing what they needed to do to certify the DI and train her based on my requirements.

I had just conducted the Mean Girls syndrome training in April with the company officers. We had talked about performance improvement and engaged listening. I gave them all the tools. They were fully aware of all of the expectations to which they would be held accountable. But the company commander didn't care. She was leaving in May.

I moved her DI—the one who requested mast—to November Company, under the leadership of my new company commander, and she began to do well. I told the Papa Company commander that it was unacceptable that she hadn't bothered to ask the right questions to find out what was going on in her battalion so she could hold her Marines accountable.

"If your Marines are being mean to her and not allowing her to go to Medical when she says she's sick, that shouldn't be something only I can figure out by asking a few questions," I told her.

The CO, of course, complained to Colonel Haas. He later told me that she believed I was too hard on her.

I learned from the investigation that she said she was afraid of reprisal—that she wasn't going to receive her end-of-tour award.

I had already approved her award—she just didn't know it.

CHAPTER 20

WHILE THE CAT IS AWAY

When I arrived at Fourth Battalion, I realized that we had some serious maintenance issues. When things broke, they simply didn't get fixed for many months on end.

When the air-conditioning goes out in South Carolina, it is, in fact, a problem. By the time I arrived at work every day between 5 and 6 a.m., the heat already felt like a steamy blanket. By noon, we were all soaked. My recruits and Marines desperately needed respite—there was no sleeping in that heat without some AC.

At first, I thought the problem was the maintenance people. As it turned out, my executive officer simply wasn't doing her job.

The XO serves as a commander's right hand: She handles the administrative, keeping-things-moving stuff, while the lieutenant colonel figures out the "people" stuff. A good XO can be a fine sounding board, as well as functioning as the in-between for the company commanders and the battalion commander.

Again, she hadn't been held accountable in the past, and, again, she didn't much like it when I came in and laid out my expectations.

She was a major, so one rank below me. We did not see eye-to-eye on any leadership issues. None. And, as XO, she did not keep me updated about the budget or ensure that maintenance problems were resolved. As with XOs in the rest of the Marine Corps, when she talked to my Marines, I expected her to echo my command philosophy.

I laid out my expectations. She ignored them. We didn't have a friendly relationship, because I did not respect her. I thought she was a terrible officer. And she clearly hated me.

Still, we tried to be professional—at least, face-to-face.

It was harder to control what she did when I wasn't standing there.

At first, I just thought she was odd. I knew some of my Marines saw her as unprofessional and almost comical—but not in a she-makes-me-laugh-over-a-beer way. For example, she once asked the recruits during an inspection, "If you could be any animal, what would you be?" Most officers would go with questions about training or what might the recruit like about Fourth Battalion or what is the recruit's biggest challenge—questions that are relevant to a recruit's time at Parris Island, not flippant questions that make both the role of the XO and the training seem trite.

Because of her demeanor and lack of communication skills, the regimental staff did not permit her to escort official visitors to the depot for the first six months she was at Parris Island.

I could work with that—we all have our tics.

But I absolutely could not abide her going behind my back.

Unfortunately, she developed a pattern of going to the regimental XO and CO to complain about me—a fact I learned later from both the investigation and conversations with Colonel Haas.

I believe she spearheaded the effort to discredit my leadership.[1] If Colonel Haas thought I had been a poor leader, he certainly could have sat me down and told me so. He could have done as I did with my officers, and worked to mentor me. Instead, I found that he fostered a culture of gossip and back-stabbing.[2]

This kind of behavior was what my predecessor had warned me about. I should have paid heed.

In this sense, my XO acted as the catalyst by encouraging people to talk about me.[3] The company commanders from both Papa and November Companies would go to her to complain, and, instead of asking them if they were doing what they needed to do to lead their companies, my XO would say something like, "I know she's mean. I don't agree with how she leads."

I think she was more concerned with being liked than with being an XO.

Are you sensing a trend?

There were so many ways she could have handled this. She could have said, "You know, there might be some validity to your concerns. I'll talk with her about what I'm hearing."

She could have said, "You know, that's what commanding officers do—they demand hard work. And our numbers are improving, and that's something to be excited about."

She could have said, "You know, let's see what we can do on your end so that you feel you're better meeting her requirements. Then, you might not feel so much stress, and you might not feel like she's being mean to you."

But she simply did not do the job of an XO—or anything else, as far as I could tell.

I never would have told my company commanders that the XO dropped the ball pretty regularly in her duties or that she failed tasks. I see now that my inability to talk about her failures with my captains made it easier for her to present herself as a good officer open-heartedly listening to their complaints. But genuinely good officers don't address complaints the way she did—even if they think their higher-ups could be doing a better job.

Ultimately, it hurt the people she purportedly tried to help.

As I mentored November Company's first CO (the one whom I ultimately fired) to improve the culture within her company and help her become a stronger leader, my XO invited her into her office to talk—but not, it would seem, to support her by backing up the mentoring work we had done.[4]

As I see it, the XO was like a snake hissing in the ears of those she identified as people she could influence and sway to her side. As I pushed to meet new standards and worked with my Marines to try to bring about accountability, I simply didn't see what she was up to. I didn't expect it, and I was much more excited about the things that were going well.

When she began to feel the heat for not supervising her Marines, Papa Company's commander also began to vent to the XO about me. She and the XO would compare notes about how mean I was. Papa Company's CO claimed that I had treated her unfairly. This all came out in the command investigation about my leadership. In her statement, the XO said she was working with the officers in my battalion to help them better manage my mood swings and unpredictability.

I was not displaying mood swings and behaving unpredictability. I was setting expectations and demanding accountability: Meet this standard. Do your job.

The major (XO) should have understood her role as second-in-command and mentor. Instead, both she and the Papa Company CO were mad because I had asked them to do more work after the fistfight between the sergeant and the staff sergeant. I asked for training logs and counseling statements for the staff sergeant. There were none. I held them accountable.

Ergo, I'm "mean."

In the meantime, the tide was starting to turn in November Company because of the new company commander and new first sergeant. But Papa Company kept me up at night because I worried about the culture in the company. I spent more time with the company commander; then the company commander spent more time with the XO. As indicated in the investigation later on, the XO would then provide Colonel Haas the latest gossip. She alleged that I was mean and that all of my officers hated me.

Let's step back for just a second.

This was Marine Corps boot camp.

Here's the kicker: When I went home for Christmas after firing November Company's CO, the XO had taken the initiative to conduct a survey of my officers and Marines to find out how many of them hated me. She was my second-in-command, and while I was gone, she served as acting commander. She walked around with a notebook and interviewed people about my leadership.[5]

Believe it or not, that really happened. I learned about it from others on staff at the depot, and it was also revealed in the investigative report.

When Sergeant Major called me on leave and told me what the XO had done, I didn't know what to think. When I returned, I tried to talk to the XO about it to figure out what her rationale was and to try to reach consensus on a way ahead. She refused to see how her actions undermined my leadership. The conversation went nowhere, and I knew I wasn't going to change her. So, I restricted the XO to staff-officer duties and told her to stay away from my other officers and Marines. I also told Colonel Haas about her conduct, thinking that surely he would agree that it had been inappropriate for the XO to do her own investigation about my leadership.

This was not the *Bounty*, and I wasn't going to make her walk the plank, but I certainly wasn't about to let her sow dissonance within my command.

But, as usual, I didn't get anywhere with Colonel Haas. In fact, I later learned that, without me knowing, Colonel Haas wrote a letter of recommendation for her to serve as a vice presidential aide-de-camp—or personal assistant to the vice president—at the White House.

A month after I had informed him of the XO's actions, he asked her—in front of me—if his letter of recommendation had been sufficient.

Wow.

CHAPTER 21

THUMPIN' THIRD

Everyone called Third Battalion "Thumpin' Third" because they were known for being physical with their recruits. The drill instructors wore the title like a badge of honor—they were tough, manly men, and they believed that being physical with their recruits made for better Marines.

The first training session I did with my Marines—after I gave my command-philosophy brief—was a comparison of the history of the recruit and drill-instructor abuse at Fourth Battalion to what happened at Abu Ghraib with the abuse of detainees. The training was meant to highlight the need for the drill instructors to step up and do the right thing when it came to the treatment and training of the recruits. But Lieutenant Colonel Joshua Kissoon's drill instructors in Thumpin' Third had a rep for beating up recruits, as was later reported in *Esquire* magazine.[1]

In the Marine Corps, it's absolutely fine to be tough. In some cases, this is encouraged—particularly during training. We aren't training people to work at the Post Office: We're training them to go to war.

However, it is against Marine Corps doctrine to be physical with recruits—or anyone in the Marine Corps, for that matter—and it's against doctrine to mentally abuse them. Tear them down? Yes. Terrorize them? No. There's a difference. When a recruit is led to fear for his or her life, that's abuse. When a drill instructor touches a recruit for any reason other than to correct a position or to keep them from getting hurt, it's against Marine Corps rules.

You might have seen Kissoon's name in the news: By the summer of 2017, he had been relieved of command after a Muslim recruit who, according to witnesses, had been abused by his drill instructors, leaped to his death from a Third Battalion stairwell.[2] It turned out that Kissoon had allowed a DI who was being investigated for another hazing incident involving a Muslim recruit to continue to train recruits.

176 FIGHT LIKE A GIRL

But even before the death of the recruit, Kissoon had been investigated by the Marine Corps for whistle-blower retaliation, making a false official statement, failing to obey a lawful order, willful dereliction of duty, and conduct unbecoming of an officer.[3]

Yet Colonel Haas seemed fixated on my "abrasive" behavior.

When Colonel Haas made his statement for my equal-opportunity investigation, he said that none of my peers liked me and that I thought Kissoon was "the devil," as he wrote in the investigation.

I did think that. The recruit abuse we all knew was happening was just a piece of my opinion. But Kissoon had also made derogatory statements about my battalion and women recruits, and it infuriated me.

Kissoon had been a company commander at Parris Island, so he knew his way around. He'd been there before. Kissoon was also prior-service, which meant he'd done some time as an enlisted man. The rest of us, as battalion commanders, were brand-new to the duty. This caused Kissoon to act like he was superior to us in every way. Honestly, this could have been great. I'm all about it; there's nothing I love more than a good mentor.

But he wasn't a good mentor. He was the most condescending individual I have ever encountered. After the staff meetings with Colonel Haas every Monday, he would offer his fellow battalion commanders tips about how to be successful. But they weren't particularly novel tips. They were leadership tactics any officer who had been a leader and screened for command would already know. From my interactions with them, it was clear to me that my peers from First and Second Battalions agreed with me that Kissoon was super cheesy and sucking up to Colonel Haas.

The battalion commanders had all arrived at Parris Island within just a few weeks of each other, but we spent our first three months essentially listening to Kissoon tell us to remember to brush our teeth at the end of each staff meeting with Colonel Haas. And then it got worse.

In September, I talked with Colonel Haas about why I thought integrating the Crucible hikes was necessary, and I explained that I thought it could be a simple change to the training. I didn't go to my peers first. The Marine Corps is not a democracy. I went to Colonel Haas, who was the only person who could make the decision and direct the battalion commanders to comply.

For whatever reason, Haas supported me in this and agreed to integrate the Crucible hike. But instead of announcing the change himself and requiring the other battalions to comply, he told me I should tell them myself. So, I sent my peers at the other battalions an email saying something to the effect of, "Hey, just wanted to let you know what's up and why it's important."

In an email back to me, not copying the other battalion commanders, Kissoon said something like, "Yup. I'm all for it. Let's do it."

Then, about twenty minutes later, he sent me another email, this time copying the COs for First and Second Battalions, basically saying, "We're not doing this. This is crap. If you think this is worth doing, then, as a commander, you owe it to us to tell us why before the decision is made."

I don't know what changed in the space of twenty minutes, but rather than letting me know directly, he acted as if he hadn't just said that the integrated hikes were a good idea, and instead he laid me out for not asking for his permission—even though we were equals and his "permission" was not at all required.

That was my second run-in with this guy. I let Colonel Haas know about the problems I had with Kissoon, but he didn't help me.

But we did the hikes. I think First and Second Battalions were first in the chute with us. We worked out the logistical kinks, and everything was good. And it did make a difference in the way the female recruits and drill instructors were perceived by their peers. The male recruits had the opportunity to see the women gutting out this final, painful movement back to the parade deck for the emblem ceremony, and it ensured that they knew the women had earned the title just like they had.

In fact, after we worked out the initial logistical requirements, the hikes with First and Second Battalions seemed to run like clockwork. I couldn't say the same for the hikes with Third Battalion. They would intentionally do things to distance the male recruits from the women, like placing ambulances between the male and female formations, when, normally, the ambulances followed the last group of hikers. Third Battalion would also take off earlier than scheduled after bathroom breaks, and they were notorious for making their recruits run—rather than hiking according to the three-mile-per-hour doctrinal hike pace—just to make it look as if the women couldn't keep up with the men.

And then three months into our integrated hikes, Kissoon sent Colonel Haas and all of the battalion commanders an email with an after-action review. (After training exercises and missions, the military looks at what went well and what didn't: after-action review.)

"I have determined no value has been added to the training of recruits by executing the final Crucible foot march concurrently with Fourth Battalion compared to the prescribed execution described in the Crucible Order," he wrote. "In fact, it creates a distraction and collectively we have proven that values based training works to bridge any perceived gender gaps as a result of single gender training at Parris Island."

According to Kissoon, the classes that the recruits received about sexual harassment and assault were so effective that no gender integration was necessary. I found his perspective interesting since, despite being the smallest service, the Marine Corps' rate of sexual misconduct is higher than any other service in the Department of Defense.

It's the unequal high-school dress code issue all over again: "Females" are a distraction. Like my recruits were out there wearing bikinis.

In reality, they'd spent three days in the field with no showers.

And even if they had been wearing bikinis—and if they had bathed—our male recruits should know how to act around their peers, regardless of gender.

This wasn't leadership by committee. Colonel Haas had made the decision to integrate the hikes, but apparently Kissoon felt like he could question Haas's decision by popping off the after-action email.

Haas didn't respond to the emails, nor did he bring it up during our staff meeting with all of the COs.

So, first, Colonel Haas didn't have my back on this. He didn't respond to all of us to explain how integrating the hikes positively impacted the credibility of the female recruits.

And, second, he allowed a lieutenant colonel to publicly question his decision and didn't say anything.

For Marines, it's considered a cardinal sin to call out your commanding officer publicly this way. Think about it—how can a CO ensure good order and discipline and that his or her Marines will do what they are supposed to do when ordered to do it, if we allow subordinates to question decisions in this way?

Yet he said nothing.

He could have said, "Hey, you probably owe Kate an apology. Her Marines and recruits are pushing themselves hard."

Because they were. They kept up with the male recruits, and they deserved to keep their places in the integrated hikes.

Instead, Haas met Kissoon with silence, which led Kissoon to believe he could question the integrated hikes again. And he did. Every time we hiked, there was some nonsense he broadcasted to Colonel Haas as a reason Fourth Battalion should be relegated to seclusion on another part of the base.

By sending the email to all of the battalion commanders and Colonel Haas, Kissoon publicly said he disagreed with a decision Colonel Haas himself had made. In comparison, I privately said behind closed doors that I'd like to talk about changing something, and I was labeled as a troublemaker and someone who consistently disobeyed Haas's orders.

In the meantime, I marched along with my recruits for every single Crucible hike. In fact, because of our training cycle, I ended up doing the Crucible hike every two weeks, hiking from start to finish, because that's my job as a commander. The male battalion commanders only had to do the hike once a month. Had he actually participated in training events, Colonel Haas would have seen that the battalion commanders from First and Second Battalions had no issue with the integrated hikes.

Anywhere else in the Marine Corps, it would have been expected for a regimental commander to participate in training events regularly. We are raised to believe that leaders set the example for their Marines to follow, so participation is critical. As a regimental commander, he never did a Crucible hike with his subordinate commanders, until the month before he had his change of command.

If he had hiked with us, he would have seen how Kissoon treated his subordinates, and how those subordinates treated their recruits.

If he had hiked with us, he would have seen how Kissoon treated me in public.

It was a long hike, so we had rest stops where the recruits could get a piece of fruit and some water or Gatorade. The commanders would gather to chat. Josh wouldn't acknowledge me—wouldn't say hello, particularly if his Marines were there. Imagine if you were one of his recruits: You've got your male commander who won't recognize a female commander in front of his men. What do you think those men thought?

This certainly wasn't the first problem I had with Kissoon.

Three months into my tour, Colonel Haas went on leave. His executive officer was unavailable, so he had Kissoon fill in for him while he was gone. Normally in the Marine Corps, the most senior officer automatically fills in as the acting CO. Kissoon totally had him fooled. Another commander, whom I liked a lot, was also prior-service and had arrived on the depot before Kissoon.

But Haas picked Kissoon to be acting regimental commander. We clashed for the first time during a "pick-up brief" before new recruits arrived at our battalions.

Before every class of recruits was picked up for training, the DIs and officers were required to complete refresher training on the Recruit Training Order and safety requirements and procedures. At the end of the refresher training, the regimental commander told us his expectations during what was called his pick-up brief. Not every graduating class at Parris Island had female recruits, but Kissoon had been assigned as the acting CO when one of my female classes was getting picked up for training, which meant that he gave the pick-up brief comments to the drill instructors and company staff members for Colonel Haas.

About twenty minutes after the pick-up brief, I got a phone call from one of my company commanders who I thought was amazing—she'll be a general officer one day if she stays in. She led Oscar Company.

"I just wanted to let you know that, after you left, I had a really weird run-in with Lieutenant Colonel Kissoon," she said.

She said she was standing in a passageway with Kissoon after he made his comments for the colonel, and he was joking with her and another Marine.

She told me that he had made comments about how everyone knows how it is at Fourth Battalion, with all that drama. In other words, the women couldn't get along with each other and were too emotional to be able to train properly—like we were all PMSing and, therefore, couldn't be expected to excel with a rifle or on a ruck march. This attitude reverberated throughout the regiment: Why bother with proper guidance or have high expectations if the women's hormonal imbalances can't be overcome? She told me, "I didn't really feel like I could say anything."

I wish she had said something to defend the female recruits and staff, but I could see why she was uncomfortable. "All that drama" is passive-aggressive and hard to define, so it's hard to respond to. I find the best way to combat passive-aggressiveness is directly: "You should come see our training. Our women are kicking ass," or, "I think you'll find that, with proper training and leadership, there's no more drama in Fourth Battalion than in any other battalion," or, "Gosh, sir. Our marksmanship scores last cycle were record-level. What were yours?" Instead, she said, she laughed it off. And that makes sense, too, but, as a result of her laughter, he thought it was okay to talk that way. Still, I was glad she told me about what had happened, and I told her I would give him a call.

I can't say I looked forward to it. But I called him.

"Hey, I just had a call from one of my commanders," I said to him. "I wanted to clear the air on something so we don't have any issues as we move forward."

I told him about everything we had been working on, and that the company commander he had spoken with after the brief had been part of it and had had incredible integrity. I told him that despite Oscar being the largest company in the battalion, she was leading Fourth Battalion's top-performing company. I told him I was doing everything I could to improve the training and performance of my female recruits, to make the Marine Corps stronger. Part of that change, I said, had to be eliminating the perception on the depot that Fourth Battalion was the

Fourth Dimension and that because we were all women, that there was a lot of drama. Out of nowhere, he started yelling at me, cussing.

I remember taking a deep breath and saying calmly, "I'm sorry you feel that way. But we're all focused on making our recruits the strongest they can be, and I need for you to understand how negatively it affects my Marines to hear the battalion talked about as if it's some kind of sideshow."

He went into a ten-minute tirade, all the while denying he had said anything of the sort and essentially implying that the company commander had lied. To try to smooth things over, I invited him to lunch to talk about it. I didn't want to have lunch with him. I didn't like him.

But I didn't want to just hang up and leave the situation unresolved, either.

"I've got to go," he said. "Have a nice f—ing day."

And then he hung up on me.

He was the acting regimental commander, and he had just yelled at me and hung up.

I thought for a bit about what to do to remedy the situation. The goal wasn't to antagonize him: The goal was to get some respect for my Marines and build a bridge with one of my peers.

So, I sent him an email saying something like, "Gosh. I don't know what happened. I think we got disconnected?" And I repeated my lunch invitation.

He never got back to me.

I didn't say anything about the disagreement to Colonel Haas. I'm a big girl—I can handle such conversations. I figured that if Kissoon was a rational person, he would figure it out and would want to have a good relationship with all of his peers, including me.

This was in September, which was also when I had my first run-in with Colonel Haas. I hadn't said anything to him about the phone call with Josh, but apparently Kissoon had. During his lecture about the emails I was sending to the recruiting-station commanders, Haas said, "People think you can't get along with anyone." My internal reaction was, *What the hell? I've been getting along with everyone on the depot. Everyone except Kissoon.*

I have always been known as a direct person, a quality that male officers were applauded for having. If there was ever an issue, I'd pick up the phone, or I would go see the involved parties in person to try to massage things. Some people see that as confrontational, but how else do you get things done? Last I checked, that was what collaboration was about—open communication.

But Colonel Haas's perception seemed to be that Kissoon was easier to get along with, so if Kissoon said I was "abrasive" and couldn't get along with anyone, then that's what Colonel Haas believed.

The battalion commanders were all privy to any drill-instructor misconduct that was going on in the depot, because we got together once a month with the regimental staff, Marine Corps Community Services, and a psychologist to talk about what we were doing to mitigate potential misconduct and mental-health issues with at-risk Marines in our battalions. The perception was that the problems with the male battalions were not immediately assumed to be related to people not getting along; rather, the problems were perceived as being related to financial stressors, post-traumatic stress, or family issues. These were the root causes of misconduct and mental-health problems everywhere in the Marine Corps. But for the women of Fourth Battalion, problems were blamed on personality issues, gossiping, and whining because women can't get along.

A male DI abuses a recruit? Boys will be boys. A male battalion commander yells a profanity and hangs up on his female peer? He was just mad. A female battalion commander rolls her eyes in front of her Marines or peers? She's mean and can't get along with anyone.

From our weekly regimental staff meetings, it was apparent to everyone on that depot that Third Battalion had a recruit-abuse problem. It was common knowledge that Third Battalion drill instructors prided themselves on using force against recruits to make them tougher. The regulations say that training staff can't come within an arm's length of a recruit, ever, unless he or she is doing it to make a correction to the recruit's position or uniform, or to prevent accident or injury. So, if someone is holding her weapon wrong, you can gently guide the recruit's rifle into the right position.

But Kissoon's DIs were notorious for making hard corrections. I saw such behaviors, at first, with my own DIs. The female recruits were marching, and the DI yelled, "Eyes right!"—which means you smartly snap your head to the right. If a recruit didn't move quickly enough, a DI would yank the recruit's chin to the right. That's totally inappropriate and wrong, and I eliminated those types of violations after I took command. But in Kissoon's battalion, this type of conduct was encouraged and was disguised as incentive training.

Incentive training, or the use of physical exercise to reprimand a recruit for poor performance, only authorized specific exercises to be performed by recruits. Additionally, the DI supervising the incentive-training session was required to limit—and record—the time for each event and possess a card listing the only permissible exercises. For example, you can make a recruit do push-ups, but during their first weeks at Parris Island, you can't make them do more than twenty push-ups at a time. You can then move on to another exercise, such as jumping jacks, but no more than fifty at a time during the first few weeks of training. You also can't push them past the point of physical exertion; you must make sure that they are safe; and you must make sure that they have enough water and are not suffering from heat exhaustion. After the recruit from Third Battalion died in March 2016, investigations revealed that drill instructors often conducted illegal incentive training for extended periods of time in places where officers couldn't see it happening. These sessions also involved the drill instructors slapping and choking recruits, and slamming them against walls.[4]

According to *Marine Corps Times*, one drill instructor is alleged to have poked holes in a recruit's face with a pen; a drill instructor allegedly forced a recruit to do the DI's college homework for him; a drill instructor forced a recruit to give the DI his Facebook login information, which the DI used to harass a female friend of the recruit; and a drill instructor also allegedly stomped on the back of a recruit while the recruit did push-ups.[5]

Kissoon had more DIs relieved for cause for abuse than any of us did, combined, in my time as a commander at Parris Island. None of my DIs were relieved for abusing recruits. If I caught even a whiff of abuse, I did a thorough investigation, which was just as much to protect the DIs from false allegations as it was to protect the recruits. We could be aggressive and demand better performance, and we should have been able to do that without abusing recruits and losing our jobs.

But Kissoon? Nobody ever raised an eyebrow about his "abrasiveness."

He's a guy. There's a perception that boot camp is supposed to be hard. There are people at the senior-leadership level who went through boot camp in the 1970s and 1980s, and none of what they were hearing about Third Battalion sounded different from what they went through. But boot camp has evolved since the days of disco, and for good reason.

There's no evidence to prove that beating up Marines makes them better. It doesn't make them better warriors; it doesn't make them better in battle.

Yet nothing happened to change the behavior or the culture of Third Battalion. Instead, Colonel Haas thought I was a bad commander who abused my Marines.

After I was relieved of command, Haas's replacement, Colonel Paul Cucinotta, told investigators that he had directed Kissoon to bench three DIs who were under investigation for abuse until the end of the investigation.[6] Instead, without telling Colonel Cucinotta, Kissoon assigned one of the DIs to a senior DI position with a new platoon, according to *Marine Corps Times*.

After the death of the Muslim recruit Raheel Siddiqui, Kissoon later justi-fied this action by saying that he had been short DIs.

While the Marine Corps maintains that Siddiqui's death was a suicide, his family wonders if the fall was the direct result of the mental and physical abuse he suffered at the hands of his drill instructors. Witnesses claimed that Siddiqui was sick, and that his senior DI allegedly had him run sprints in the barracks, according to witness statements from the Marine Corps investigation. The recruit fell as he ran, witnesses said. According to the witnesses, the senior DI allegedly slapped Siddiqui, who appeared to be passed out. According to *Marine Corps Times*, soon after, Siddiqui ran through the squad bay, ran outside, and then jumped from the stairwell of the third floor to his death.[7]

As the scandal grew, reports of Third Battalion DIs choking and slap-ping recruits came out. But this wasn't news to anyone under Colonel Haas's command.

After Kissoon and Cucinotta—Cucinotta for not properly supervising Kissoon—as well as their sergeants major were relieved of their commands, the *Washington Post* reported that another recruit had needed skin grafts after being forced to exercise on a floor covered in bleach and having to wear his wet pants for hours, which resulted in second- and third-degree burns.[8] When he finally reported his injuries to another DI, he was told he would not be able to graduate with his class if he sought medical attention.

The same DI who administered the bleach punishment was taken off duty for three days after he grabbed a recruit around the neck, according to the *Washington Post*, and he was convicted of recruit abuse at a court-martial in 2014.[9]

While I was being investigated for being "too abrasive," Kissoon's battalion was knocking recruits around.

I'm not saying, "But look what they did."

I'm saying that the Marine Corps fired a female battalion commander for being "too abrasive" when she tried to end abuse and hazing within her battalion while enforcing high standards and expectations to ensure her female recruits and Marines reached their full potential. I'm saying that this was done con-currently with the Corps lifting up a male battalion commander who allowed blatant abuse within his units.

It's a head-scratcher.

No, it's more than that.

It's wrong.

CHAPTER 22

GOOD NEWS TRAVELS FAST

My Marines continued to make improvements, and I was so proud of them. I knew they could do it—I knew the recruits could do it, and I knew my Marines could get them there. People started asking the kinds of questions that I was more than happy to answer: "How are you guys achieving success?" and "How did you improve scores on the rifle range?"

But I also worried. After I fired November Company's commanding officer in December, and Colonel Haas made it clear that he was keeping a list of my "transgressions," I feared that all of the progress we had made would disappear. Would any of the gains we made endure if I were fired? We made such great progress, but if no one acknowledged that things needed to be fixed in the first place, it didn't seem likely the forward momentum would continue. The improvements would all be driven by personality rather than a recognized need for change, which meant when I left the battalion, it would soon return to the status quo.

At this point, everything my Marines and I had talked about seemed so obvious. We set high expectations. We clearly communicated them to the recruits. We instilled confidence. And you know what? The young women rose to the challenge. Tell the recruits they can succeed, and they will. We had made a significant difference in just one recruit cycle because we essentially started from scratch. The recruits didn't know any better. They were clean slates. They had never been subjected to the old mind-set of low expectations for women in the Marine Corps, so we didn't need to change their attitudes. We had to change our own attitudes.

But if there's no one at the top saying, "Hey, this is a good idea. We need to keep doing this," then it's as if you're operating in a dark corner. Organizational change takes leadership, commitment, and tenacity. As a leader, you have to will change into existence. You have to be indefatigable and unrelenting. It is exhausting, but it is the right thing to do.

So, in February, I wrote an article for the *Marine Corps Gazette*, boasting about the great progress my women accomplished. I titled it, "When Did It Become an Insult to Train Like a Girl?" The *Marine Corps Gazette* is basically the Marine Corps' professional journal, so the audience consisted of my peers and the senior leadership of both the depot and the Marine Corps' Training and Recruiting Commands.

In my article, I wrote that for decades, women had scored worse than the men in every recruit boot-camp graduation criteria category except the fitness test, and that was only because the requirements were lower for women than they were for men. No one would have been surprised by this. In fact, they assumed it. It was a given. But I also wrote that no one had ever asked the world's most dangerous question, "Why?" And because the notion that women's performance was inferior to men was never challenged, it became the norm.

I dug into that norm with hammers and tongs: Why, if the only thing scored differently was the fitness test, were women performing so much worse than the men?

That's it. That question consumed my hours from the time I woke up to the time I went to bed. This simple question haunted me. It was with me at every turn, and I was determined to do the analysis and find the root causes. I told you I was a data geek.

But I wrote that the repercussions of that performance put both men and women at risk in war zones. It meant that men served under women who outranked them simply because they entered the military with more college courses.

I talked about segregation and silly notions about rifles not being suitable for women's bodies and chairs after the Crucible hike and how women perform just as poorly at MCT as they do at Fourth Battalion.

And I talked about how much ass my female recruits kicked when we held them to higher standards.

I wrote that women underperformed men on the rifle range by a delta of thirty percentage points. For decades, the female pass rate for rifle qualification was between 67 and 78 percent, and the male pass rate was 85 to 93 percent.

I wrote that in a matter of months we were able to bring female passing scores up to the same rate as the men through increased expectations, convincing the mostly male coaches to first assume "chicks CAN shoot" (shocker), and by lowering DI-induced stress at the range.

In one year, Fiscal Year 2015, our rates fell in line with the men's.

I wrote that the same high standards should be expected in every recruit graduation category for all Marines. After all, isn't this exactly what male

Marines had complained about when they said that women shouldn't serve in infantry roles? That the women couldn't meet the same standards?

They can.

Tell them they must meet the standards, and they will.

I sent that steaming-hot, well-crafted article off to the *Gazette*, and you know what? The *Gazette*'s editor, retired Colonel John Keenan, emailed me back and said that he'd publish it in the September edition.

I hated the long lead time for magazine publishing, but I was excited! My thoughts would get an audience in the Corps' professional journal. I described a systemic problem in recruiting and training women, discussed it, and made rock-solid recommendations for improvement.

I was sure that by September I would have plenty more to brag about. Naively, I thought everyone else would be bragging, too.

Boy, was I wrong.

I also provided the sergeant major at Parris Island with a courtesy copy so she could brief the general. I didn't want to go around Brigadier General Williams, and I knew the sergeant major at Parris Island supported what we were doing.

After I gave it to our sergeant major, the Sergeant Major of the Marine Corps (the head enlisted adviser to the Commandant of the Marine Corps) visited Parris Island, and our sergeant major gave him a copy. He took it back to Washington, DC.

That was in March.

At first, I thought that was great. It seemed like a positive thing because I thought he was going to take it back to the commandant. The story of Fourth Battalion was going straight to the top of the chain of command—to the "King Grunt." I had such hopes that with my article, the scales would fall from his eyes. The commandant will see the great work we were doing, as well as what needs to be fixed, and implement my recommendations for improvement. You'd occasionally see solid *Gazette* articles change Marine Corps policy after senior leadership read them.

Boom!

Mic drop!

Voilà!

I'll bet it never occurred to you that Pollyanna joined the Marine Corps when she grew up?

General Joseph Dunford had just taken over as commandant in October.

Dunford did not want women in the infantry, and the chorus of retired general officers vehemently did not want women to join their club. In September 2015, Dunford recommended that women be banned from some infantry jobs, according to *Marine Corps Times*.[1] The Army, Navy, and Air Force were moving forward, but, as usual, the Marine Corps was going to buck anything that hadn't been in place for at least a century. The Corps has always been the boat anchor historically dragging behind the other services when it comes to social change: desegregation following WWII, the opening of aviation to women, and the repeal of "Don't Ask Don't Tell."

But the Sergeant Major of the Marine Corps took my article to the executive off-site or EOS—a quarterly board meeting of all of the three- and four-star generals. These meetings are a big deal: It's like when the cardinals come together to elect a pope. So what I didn't tell you is that Joe keeps a strong information network. His contacts reported back to him that during this EOS in April 2015, the Sergeant Major of the Marine Corps briefed the contents of my article to all of the three- and four-stars present.

The sergeant major didn't read the entire article to the generals. Instead, he threw out points about how, for decades, women have underperformed and been held to a lower standard. And he talked about the great progress we've made. The sergeant major seemed to be completely onboard. He may not have known his boss, General Dunford, was not.

And that's when the wind changed and the weather sock began to point at me. I didn't know it at the time—the breeze takes a while to go from the Navy Yard in Washington, DC, to Beaufort, South Carolina.

The three- and four-stars were outraged. They did not create the ground-combat integration study just to learn that women were making progress elsewhere.

I'm positive, based on feedback that Joe and I received, that the commandant was alarmed with Fourth Battalion's results, especially on the rifle range. Those results would shoot holes in the multi-million-dollar study, the Marine Corps Gender Integration Task Force study, the study that showed that women couldn't perform infantry tasks as well as men.

I'm sure General Dunford wondered how much Fourth Battalion's success would affect the integrity of the study.

Our success weakened his argument against integrating women.

Fortunately for him, my XO said I rolled my eyes.[2]

CHAPTER 23

LIKE A (BAD) BOSS

So, by April 2015, I understood fully that Colonel Haas wanted me out.

You may have figured this out a few chapters back, but I didn't realize what was happening right under my nose until after the fact.

That's how mobbing works. It's insidious.

Still, I figured that Colonel Haas was leaving in July, and that was only a few more months away. I thought I could bide my time until then by avoiding contact with him, celebrating the good stuff, and practicing daily affirmations in the office mirror: "I like myself, and I can do this."

And I had Joe, my sergeant major, and Mister Fitzwizzle, who wrapped himself around me the instant I got home each night like a furry security blanket.

In one way, it wasn't that difficult: Colonel Haas never showed up to observe any training. He never visited me, unless it was for the initial strength test and pick-up or end-of-cycle debriefs. He never came to see what we were doing out in the field, and he never, ever came to see what we were doing on the rifle range. I had never had a commander who spent less time with his subordinate commanders.

But my peers thought his leadership through neglect was awesome. They were away from the flagpole, doing what they wanted to do with no interference from the "boss."

After our encounter in January at the confidence course, General Williams came to visit me on two more occasions to tell me he thought I was doing good things.

"Sir, I think I've got my finger on the pulse of this battalion," I told him. "I know there's a disgruntled group of folks here, and I know that my problems will be mainly solved after two of them move on."

And he encouraged me, telling me that he knew what was going on and that I just needed to wait it out.

So we kept on, working hard to improve the statistics, with me trying not to cross Colonel Haas's path. In February, I made the mistake of trying to talk to him about something that seemed obvious.

I sent him an email with our weekly training report.

"Improving the stats will be critical to improving the credibility of our female recruits," I said, regarding the work we were doing to improve our PT, rifle range, and academic results.

He emailed back.

"I don't understand why you think this impacts credibility," he said. "I'd be very interested in talking to you about it, so let me know when you're available."

Uh-oh.

But, again, I decided to be positive about it. Maybe he was onboard.

I immediately emailed back and told him I would really love the opportunity to talk with him about why I thought improving the stats was so important. I asked for a meeting at his earliest availability.

He never got back to me.

Silence.

My takeaway? He didn't want to encourage change. He didn't want the friction that comes with forcing change. Organizational change is hard.

Still, how could he not understand how performance affects the credibility of the female recruits and DIs? I needed to explain it to him. It wasn't simply a matter of Kate proving a point to her boss: This man would likely move on to command other Marines—female Marines. He needed to understand.

Even though I didn't hear back from him, I continued to try to get through to him. But I hit a brick wall. I don't think that it was just a matter of him not liking me, although that was pretty apparent. I think that no matter who their commander was, he would not have been interested in how the female recruits were performing.

I was left with the sense that if I couldn't get from here to there with Colonel Haas, I needed to do something different.

That's when I wrote the article for the *Marine Corps Gazette*.

And, at that point, some things were going great for Fourth Battalion.

After November Company's first sergeant quit—for the second time—because she couldn't get along with her old company commander, we sent her home on terminal leave before she retired. When you're in the military, you get thirty days of leave—or vacation—a year, give or take, for special circumstances. If you don't use all of your leave, it adds up. So, when you leave the military, you can basically take vacation for the time up until your actual last day in the military. That vacation time is called "terminal leave." She simply went home.

The new first sergeant came in and started changing things with the new CO. They were both amazing, and upbeat, and they were a strong leadership team. The change was palpable when you walked into the company headquarters.

In the meantime, I told Colonel Haas I would not recommend the previous first sergeant for an end-of-tour award. He knew all of the problems—I know he did, because he had to sign off on the investigations into her drill instructors' bad behavior. He knew she fought with her company commander, quit twice, and couldn't function well enough to serve in a leadership position. Not only that, the stats for the company during her tour as the first sergeant were below average.

Despite all of this, without talking to me about it, Colonel Haas gave her an award. She retired with full honors and a ceremony.

In my opinion, she should have been sent home with nothing but her discharge certificate; but that would have required him to acknowledge that what I was saying was true.

In any case, after the new first sergeant and new company commander arrived, we saw progress in November Company. The old drill instructors still had some control, and those who liked the previous first sergeant didn't much like me or the changes I made. When you've had someone in charge of you for two and a half years, and they told you to be hard on the recruits and to show them who's boss, it's hard to change your habits and mind-set. I pretty much had to wait until they left. But as new drill instructors replaced the old, things improved exponentially, and the new company leadership team was a resounding success.

I continued to wait it out. The bad apples would leave. Colonel Haas would leave. Most of my Marines were doing great work. I had one more year before I retired to make significant progress.

And, there had been signs that, despite some negativity, my Marines' morale was high and they enjoyed working with me.

One morning in early March, as I moved between pride in my Marines for all they had accomplished and a sense of dread about Colonel Haas's desire to fire me, I walked into my office and almost fell over laughing. My Marines had filled my office with crepe-paper decorations and "Happy Birthday" messages. But the best part? Some of my Marines had placed about a hundred plastic cups full of water all the way from my desk to my door so I had to go through an obstacle course to get to my desk. I was rolling—just laughing so hard, like someone had released a pressure gauge. That was my forty-third birthday.

A week or two later, Brigadier General Williams had a reception at the Marine museum on base. I mentioned I had just had a birthday, and he asked how old I was. I told him I was forty-three. He started joking with me about my age, and I showed him a picture of the ocean of cups in my office and told him how fun some of my Marines were to work with.

"See?" he said. "I knew your Marines didn't hate you."

Whaaat?

Although the birthday prank had taken my mind off of my worries about Colonel Haas, I now knew better than to relax.

Even though I had been avoiding Colonel Haas, I had apparently been on his mind.

In March, shortly after the reception, my battalion—and only my battalion—was notified that we would be inspected by the Commanding General's Inspection Program team, led by the depot inspector general. This was a highly unusual occurrence, since for at least the previous decade, no training battalions had been required to participate in the inspection program. They were essentially exempt. And now, all of a sudden, we were given forty-eight hours' notice that we would face an onslaught of inspections of all of our administrative and training programs.

It might not seem like a big deal, but it switches up your whole world—throws your training off and changes the mood of the battalion to something resembling pure panic. Everyone knew something was up in Fourth Battalion. Why else would we be selected for this type of invasive, all-out inspection?

At the time, I didn't think it was too weird that we were the only battalion inspected. I figured it was possible that the regiment had been notified by the depot inspector general that they needed to choose a training battalion to inspect, and we had been picked out of a hat. Anything is possible.

And, fortunately, even though we had so little notice, we were ready. When I had arrived at the battalion in June 2014, I made my officers go back to their inspection checklists for their respective areas of responsibility to learn what they needed to know and ensure we were following regulations by the book. I figured that if we were following regulations and everyone knew the regulations applicable to her daily tasks, whether related to safety, administration, supply, or training, we would better serve the personnel in the battalion. That is a Marine value—brilliance in the basics.

I think Brigadier General Williams just wanted everything to go away at that point: He wanted Colonel Haas to leave. He wanted the new guy to come in. He wanted to conduct the inspection and disprove Colonel Haas's suspicions that things were screwed up at Fourth Battalion.

We passed the inspection with a 93 percent, which is really good for a training battalion. We shocked them. Unfortunately, it also seemed to anger Colonel Haas. I believe that he had selected us for a reason: If we had failed the inspection, he could have said, "She's a terrible leader. Not only is she mean to her Marines, she can't even pass an inspection."

In other words, I think this inspection was a way for him to justify firing me.

Just as I started to think I was losing my mind, the inspector general who conducted the inspection for General Williams told me, "Keep doing the things you're doing because I hear good things from your Marines."

Once again, just like the birthday water cups, it showed that most of my Marines were thriving. If you're a crappy leader, your Marines will ensure that you fail. Further, if everybody hated me and thought I was a terrible commander, we also would never have made any progress on the rifle range. The Marines would have dug in their heels and refused to change. I know that. In my heart, I know that. But talk about cognitive dissonance—on one hand, we were achieving historically high training results and most of my Marines were telling me things were good in the battalion. But Colonel Haas was saying I was a terrible leader and that my Marines didn't like me.

There's so much irony there. I taught my Marines that our recruits would believe what we told them about being able to shoot well and run fast and drill perfectly. And here I was trying not to believe what people were saying when they said I was a bad leader.

After the inspection, the inspection team briefed me and my staff on the results of the inspection. The inspector general, a colonel, had been talking to Marines throughout the battalion as he conducted the inspection. I had told him, "This place is yours: Talk to anyone you want to."

But who do you suppose sought out the IG? The same people who sought out Colonel Haas. The IG was great—he came into my office at the end of the day and back-briefed me for the three days they were there.

"You've got detractors," he told me, "but you've got a lot of Marines who like what you're doing and who are very happy with things."

Unfortunately, that comment never made it into his report.

Even though we did well, it was clear to me that Colonel Haas wanted me relieved of my command. And, unknown to me, one of my Marines filed an anonymous complaint against me on April 10, 2015.

So, in April, the general decided to do a command-climate investigation to see what my Marines thought of me.

CHAPTER 24

CLIMATE CHANGE

A command-climate survey should give a taste of the morale of a unit and provide insight on where improvements need to be made. Sergeant Major and I had briefed the results of the previous survey to everyone, in order to be transparent and to show them that we were committed to changing the battalion for the better.

But filling out the survey is not mandatory for the battalion staff, and ours was online, which meant that everyone used the exact same password to complete it. That meant people outside the battalion could complete it. It also meant the same people could take it more than once. Also, the regiment tailored the essay questions in a way that would ensure that they got the information they wanted from the participants. The essay questions for my battalion had a completely different flavor from those of the other training battalions. Good researchers avoid this when they develop surveys: confirmation bias. In other words, be careful how you ask questions, unless you want to ensure that you reach a preconceived conclusion.

You can probably imagine how the survey went for us.

Well before I arrived, Fourth Battalion had a history of negative command-climate surveys. Think about it: You're asking a bunch of people in a high-stress situation at boot camp to talk about how happy they are—folks who don't get enough sleep or time off and who are fairly grumpy anyway.

Commanders are required to administer a survey within ninety days of taking command. When I administered mine, I looked for issues related to trust and accountability that we could address. But I didn't simply assume that all of Fourth Battalion was a miserable place to be, based on the comments, because I knew that the Marines who tend to fill out the surveys are those who have complaints. Again, it's not mandatory to fill out the surveys.

In the survey they took when I assumed command, the Marines complained that people hadn't been held accountable for things like driving drunk, having inappropriate relationships with other drill instructors in the unit, and sleeping with recruits. The second-biggest complaint was that no one understood why certain Marines were selected for senior drill-instructor positions. The third-biggest complaint was that no one in the chain of command—from the battalion up to the depot level—seemed to care about staff shortages and exhaustion.

After receiving the survey results, I looked for indications of drill-instructor and recruit abuse, and I sought ways to improve the command climate, starting by making sure our Marines knew why we made decisions about punishments, assignments, and rewards. Increased accountability required first laying out expectations for performance and behavior, and then holding feet to the fire when Marines legitimately screwed up. We implemented monthly award formations, increased the number of awards given to Marines who excelled, and started sending positive feedback to the company leadership when Sergeant Major and I saw good things happening during training.

We also took every opportunity to increase transparency by debriefing our teams about investigation findings for alleged DI misconduct, as well as requiring that one observer from each company be present at any nonjudicial punishment hearing. I hoped the Marines would see that I took the command philosophy of "Confidence, Accountability, and Pride" seriously.

But, in addition to rewarding my Marines, accountability also meant I had to make corrections, counsel Marines when they underperformed, and, worst-case, fire those who couldn't meet my standards. The command-climate survey from 2014 demonstrated that the Marines wanted accountability, and we used the results to constructively plan for improvement.

But in April 2015, I knew the survey directed by Colonel Haas would not be used for constructive purposes. As soon as I read the essay questions, I was well aware that the results would be used to bolster Colonel Haas's assertions about my leadership.

When I read the investigation after my relief, it confirmed what I suspected about the command-climate survey: Because the password was the same for all Marines, and you could take it from the same computer multiple times, it was no surprise that the investigation also revealed this to be the case. At least one Marine confirmed that the survey link and password were forwarded to Marines who were no longer in the battalion. Shoot, even at least one Marine from another battalion took the survey—he even said so in his comments.

When I read the survey results, I found that a few Marines claimed that I didn't salute them when they saluted me, which is absolutely crazy in such a high traditions and customs and courtesies environment. I can't imagine a time when I would have not saluted someone back—it's automatic. It's not even something you think about after almost twenty years. You just do it.

And they said I rolled my eyes.

Yup. I admit it. Sew a red letter "R" to my uniform: I rolled my eyes.

When people offer me excuses, or when I know they're not telling the truth, I have a habit of rolling my eyes.

The survey showed nothing consistent, just general statements of "She's mean," or "She hurts my feelings," or "She's disrespectful to her officers"—but no specific examples.

Did it look bad?

Yes. And it was horrifying to read, because I knew from conversations with my Marines every day that the results did not reflect the positive things that were happening in the rest of the battalion.

But the survey results were not that far off from previous command-climate survey results for Fourth Battalion, including the one I had administered right after I took command in 2014. And the way the survey was executed was neither fair nor remotely scientific.

The Marines completed the Defense Equal Opportunity Management Institute command-climate survey on April 22, 2015. About 75 percent of the battalion took the survey, including forty-five noncommissioned officers, six staff noncommissioned officers, ten junior officers, and two senior officers, including me. However, the "75 percent" didn't take into account people taking it twice or people who were outside the unit but still took it.

The survey found that there were eight reported incidents of discrimination, two reported incidents of racial discrimination, and two incidents of gender discrimination.

Two Marines asserted that their claims of gender discrimination would not be taken seriously if reported (I was one of the Marines who said that), and three reported that they feared reprisal if they reported their complaints. (Marines could check more than one box, so the same people who believed their cases would not be taken seriously may have said that they feared reprisal.) There were no reported cases of sexual assault. No one filed formal complaints about sexual harassment.

We were near service averages for feeling safe and for feelings of having command support. We were above average for restricted reporting knowledge—so the Marines and recruits knew how to report a sexual assault or harassment anonymously. Recommendations for our unit were general, including this one: "Many interactions that lead to sexual assault begin in social settings and often involve alcohol. Such policies should promote responsible alcohol use, encourage all involved to be on the lookout for situations at risk for sexual assault, and outline how to safely address inappropriate behavior."

This struck me as ironic, considering that later in the same report, I was also accused of "victim-blaming" when I told my Marines and recruits to be careful about putting themselves into situations—such as becoming intoxicated—that could make them more vulnerable to an attack.

The survey asked if we promoted a climate based on trust and respect; thirty-five said yes and twenty-nine said no. Fifty-two said they would feel comfortable reporting sexual assault, and twelve said they would not. Eight said we would not take a report seriously; thirteen said we wouldn't keep it confidential; eight said the report would be sent to people other than investigators; ten said we might not help the person making the report feel safe; and nine said we wouldn't support the person making the report. Twenty-four said we would label the person making the report a troublemaker, and twenty-five said there would be retaliation.

We were at the lower end of "near service average" for organizational commitment, trust in leadership, organizational performance, organizational cohesion, leadership cohesion, job satisfaction, organizational processes, diversity management, help-seeking behaviors, and exhaustion. We were on the high end of near service average for sexist behaviors, sexual harassment, sex discrimination, racist behaviors, disability discrimination, racial discrimination, age discrimination, and religious discrimination. We were low, but within the average range, again for demeaning behaviors and hazing behaviors.

Nineteen Marines said they felt unmotivated to do their best; twenty-six said they didn't feel as if they belonged; eighteen said they did not feel proud to say they belonged to our unit. Again, those could have been the same people expressing all three statements. Forty-six respondents said members of the battalion did not support each other. Eighteen said they did. Twenty-nine said leaders did not work well together; thirty-five said they did. Eighteen said they did not like their jobs; forty-six said they did. Twenty-four said they were not enthusiastic about their work most days; forty said they were. Twenty-seven said people weren't accountable for their behavior; thirty-seven said they were.

Fifty-four respondents said they were mentally worn out; forty-five said they were physically worn out; forty-two said they were emotionally worn out.

Seventeen said they felt that newcomers were harassed and humiliated—hazed—before being accepted. Twenty-two said people were excluded from social activities. Thirty-four said some were reminded often of their mistakes.

As previously mentioned, I found out later from the investigation that Colonel Haas had tailored the essay questions for the survey to each battalion. So, while Kissoon's people would not have been asked if their leaders worked well together, Fourth Battalion Marines were.

The other battalions didn't get questions like the following: How many times have you seen your commander openly display her negative feelings toward others? Is there a fear of reprisal in the unit? What do you feel Germano's position on sexual assault is? Does she act differently to those she does not like? Is it visible?

Two points here: First, I don't think I was mean. Was I hard on them? Yes. It was a hard environment. Boot camp is tough. And we were working to increase the standards—that's hard work. I was especially hard on the Marines whom I felt weren't pulling their weight. And, second, this is the Marine Corps. I don't believe the environment should be tough-as-nails and miserable, but come on. I rolled my eyes? I wonder if, in the history of the Marine Corps, anyone has complained that a male battalion commander rolled his eyes or hurt their feelings.

My response was to chalk it up to the change-is-bad folks.

However, you can't make lasting change happen if the disgruntled people know your boss welcomes complaints. If he doesn't support what you're trying to do, and they know it, all they have to do is go over your head.

And that's exactly what happened.

In mid-May, soon after receiving the command-climate survey results, Colonel Haas instructed me to brief my action plan to correct the problems indicated by the survey. He didn't give me a lot of time—he shot me an email and said, "Come see me. Have your action plan ready." He didn't say what he wanted or how he wanted it presented. But I've done a brief or two before, and I had obviously been thinking nonstop about the survey results. So I put together the inevitable PowerPoint slide briefing.

I started by stating that I'm responsible for everything my Marines do, but that same level of responsibility needs to rest at every echelon of command.

In other words, just as my command philosophy laid out, my Marines also needed to understand that they were responsible for their actions and making positive changes in the battalion, and that they shouldn't be able to lob anonymous complaint grenades without taking every step to resolve problems themselves at the small-unit-leader level—exactly what we expect everywhere else in the Marine Corps.

After all, beginning at boot camp, we taught recruits to use informal resolution methods to solve problems at the lowest level. I fully expected my Marines to use the same methods to try to solve their problems at the unit level before they brought issues to me to address.

So, in the action plan, I reinforced much of what I had already said. I discussed how we would continue to focus on improving our conflict-resolution and mediation skills and the critical importance of my officers affecting change and achieving high standards. I talked about continuing to stress decision-making in the battalion on facts rather than emotions because, frankly, I was frustrated that so many of my Marines and officers interpreted my push for them to take responsibility as me just being mean.

For that to happen, we needed to communicate clearly with each other. Obviously, going to the XO's office to complain about the commanding officer or talking in front of recruits about how I was "making them" do something they considered unimportant wasn't going to get us there.

I told Colonel Haas I would ask my officers to present training to their Marines about small-unit conflict resolution.

I told him we should talk about the difference between perception and reality: Did my Marines feel they were being mistreated, rather than understand they were being held accountable?

Did that meet Colonel Haas's intent for creating a command-climate survey action plan to correct our deficiencies? You know, I don't think I was thinking that way. I felt as if I was constantly hard on myself and constantly trying to take responsibility. I felt as if I had worked hard for transparency and to make sure the Marines and officers knew what I expected of them.

But, most important to me, I knew the complaints in the survey came from my XO and the Marines who had fought hardest against change in the battalion, and I had tons of documentation showing that I was doing everything I could to address performance and behavior problems for these same individuals—things that would be expected of a leader anywhere else in the Marine Corps. I felt that, in directing me to come up with an action plan to correct my command-climate deficiencies, Colonel Haas was telling me I had to accept the results of the survey as factual, and my conscience would not allow me to do so.

Reading through the survey, I noted that the complaints were about the same incidents from the same company. Did the company commander I fired complain about me? It seems like it would have been a little strange for a woman I fired to say I was the perfect boss. Did my XO complain about me? After the counselings she had received for not doing her job and for fomenting dissent throughout the battalion, of course she did. The investigation that led to my relief laid out her complaints clearly. Did Papa Company's commanding officer and her drill instructors say bad things? The ones accused of hazing? Yeah. They did. These were the same Marines who made statements against me to the investigating officer a few weeks later.

I think Colonel Haas expected that I would come up with an action plan that included not rolling my eyes and being nicer to officers and Marines after they hazed recruits or fell behind on training. I'm sure I could come up with a PowerPoint presentation to that effect. But I don't feel like that would have addressed the real issues, and I think it would have reassured officers and DIs who performed badly that they could continue to do so.

I told Colonel Haas that if we continued to work on personal responsibility and transparency, everything would improve. When people are rewarded for success and held accountable for problems, everything else gets fixed. It makes things fair: Everyone knows what she's responsible for. So she will think to herself, "I know if I do this, I will be treated this way."

I did present my action plan in a PowerPoint, of course. But I also stated that I was aware that there was no requirement to fill out the survey—it was voluntary, and I said there were flaws in how it had been administered. I asked several times that we be allowed to do another survey in a controlled environment where every Marine received her own password and 100 percent of my Marines were required to take it. They could take the survey in an office where we saw them go in and out to ensure that the same people didn't fill out the survey several times.

I knew the results would be different.

"That's not what I wanted," he told me. "You're not taking responsibility. You're not being accountable. You're not listening."

In other words, it's nobody's fault but my own. I understood this to mean that he would never have my back. I could be nice or be mean, or lead or give up, and the results would all be the same: A couple of Marines would complain, and Colonel Haas would continue to try to fire me.

I went back to my battalion. I talked to my sergeant major.

"I'm at a loss here," I said. "I don't know what to do."

She tried to talk me down, to let me know I wasn't crazy or mean or a bad leader or any of the things I was being told. I depended on her to tell me if she disagreed with the way I handled things or if she thought there were a better way. She was as devastated about the chaos in the battalion as I was, because we knew that in presenting ourselves as a leadership team, it was a potential indictment of her leadership as well as mine if the assertions in the survey were true.

But I trusted my sergeant major with my life. There had been times when we didn't see things eye-to-eye, but we would sit in my office and talk through our different perspectives. Sometimes we compromised, and sometimes she changed my perspective. We always talked before I ever made a decision, and I considered her to be my trusted adviser who had never done me wrong. I knew that if she thought I was screwing up, she would tell me.

But she said that she didn't see it either.

My sergeant major said she thought I needed to ensure I had a mediator present whenever I had to meet with Colonel Haas.

Earlier, in March, we also concluded that I needed to reach out to the depot sergeant major, who happened to be a woman, for a sanity check. I started by apologizing for a long email, and then I spelled out everything.

"I really need some help and am not sure where I can turn," I wrote. "I am having significant issues with Colonel Haas that are affecting the welfare of my battalion, particularly pertaining to officer standing and his assessment of my leadership. . . . I am absolutely convinced that they are grounded in gender bias."

I explained that I had received no help in trying to address staffing issues, and that when I asked for backup on Marines behaving badly, I simply received an eye roll. I told her that I couldn't get maintenance problems addressed—that four of my Marines didn't have heat in their barracks rooms for three months—that we had no company-level executive officers, so my company commanders couldn't get a break, and that we had no replacement for my headquarters company commander.

These were things, I felt, that would help improve command climate. But I told her Colonel Haas had called me into his office to tell me he was worried about the command-climate survey and my approachability. He told me nothing more, so I could not defend myself.

"I feel like I am in a hopeless situation," I wrote. "We basically have no commander-commander relationship."

He had never attended a single training event with me to observe my interactions with my Marines. He knew only what was reported to him secondhand and through the command-climate survey.

Two days after my meeting with Colonel Haas, I told her, I received a phone call from a fellow battalion commander saying that a few of my Marines planned to make anonymous complaints to the inspector general about me, something that Colonel Haas had also warned me about. In my email, I told the depot sergeant major that was fine—that I felt the process is fair and that there would always be complaints. But I was angry that, while my battalion sergeant major and I talked every day about command climate, Colonel Haas heard a few complaints and took it as gospel. I believed that, in his mind, I was already guilty.

I told her about the work my sergeant major and I had done, and that our Marines often told us things were better than they had been in years. I told her of the problems Colonel Haas and I had had in not seeing things the same way.

"I knew coming to Fourth Battalion would be challenging," I wrote, "but I had no idea that the biggest struggle I would have would be in being considered credible and capable by my boss."

I hit "send," and I held my breath.

She got back to me within half an hour.

"Thank you for sharing this with me," she wrote. "I want to help."

"I'll find you today and share some interesting, but more importantly, helpful news for your end state."

"If you read just one thing from this message, please know that YOU are not alone in this fight. Hang in there."

Her response was very much the same as the commanding general: *We see it. We know what's happening. Keep doing what you're doing.*

Once again, I thought, "I'm not crazy. I just need to get through this."

She sent a second email asking about staffing and the response I had received when I asked for help, and asked me if I would consider men in my battalion, saying there had been men there when she was a recruit.

Yes! Of course! If they're the ones with experience, we want them. And if they're good and can fill my staffing slots, I don't care if they're purple, let alone if they're men. In fact, I felt that having men in the battalion would be good for diversity and would help reinforce the changes we were making to improve the performance of the female recruits.

She wrote back saying she planned to bring the commanding general to my area when their schedules permitted.

That night, I called Joe, as I had been doing every night. He and I have been

204   **FIGHT LIKE A GIRL**

together since we were kids, and he's never been afraid to tell me if I'm screwing something up—but usually in a way that makes me laugh. He's my best friend.

He had retired in March, but for several years, he had worked on the commandant's staff at the Pentagon, and he still had friends who fed him information about me, a battalion commander at Parris Island.

Why was that odd?

There was absolutely no reason for a battalion commander to be talked about at the Pentagon—unless I had been accused of some heinous crime. The decision whether to fire me should be a local decision, something handled by my immediate command.

Joe and I realized that Colonel Haas was probably looking for any excuse he could get to fire me. Colonel Haas acted as if the command-climate survey was a capital offense, despite all of the holes we had poked into the legitimacy of the results and the methodology used to administer it. It wasn't genuine.

"You need to request mast," Joe said. "Now."

"You've tried working through Colonel Haas. You tried writing an article to bring the issues to the attention of the Marine Corps. You heard from the commanding general that he was supporting you. Request mast."

In other words, Joe thought I should fill out a formal request to meet with Brigadier General Williams in person to discuss the problems I was having with Colonel Haas.

In my prior conversations with Brigadier General Williams, I had been very circumspect about my relationship with Colonel Haas. While he had tried to engage me in conversation about the problems I had experienced, I didn't want to be unprofessional and bad-mouth my boss with his boss, so I hadn't dimed out Colonel Haas to the commanding general. Without any invitation or information from me, he had approached me way back in January and said, "I hear things are going badly with your boss," and I gave him noncommittal answers, rather than specifics. His exact words to me had been, "It's my job to mentor colonels." And since he kept telling me I had his support, I figured he knew what was going on.

But Joe said, "You have to tell him everything that's happening, so he knows. Request mast now."

At about that time, I started having multiple sclerosis (MS) symptoms. I knew it was stress-related, and the symptoms scared me. I had had neurological symptoms before, but nothing I ever worried about after I received the initial diagnosis. The symptoms had never affected my work or my daily runs or any other aspect of my life, really, other than a vague wondering of what the future would look like. I was first diagnosed in 2001, and had experienced a few flare-ups but nothing significant.

According to the National Multiple Sclerosis Society, multiple sclerosis "is an unpredictable, often disabling disease of the central nervous system that disrupts the flow of information within the brain, and between the brain and body."[1]

Some people lose their vision; some people lose feeling in their limbs; some people lose their ability to reason; some people lose their ability to walk. But I was under a doctor's care, and none of these issues fit into my diagnosis.

My MS diagnosis and symptoms shouldn't have mattered at all, except that I'd never had to bring it up to my boss before. And I'd never had it used against me as a possible reason to fire me.

But heat and stress are well known to cause flare-ups, and I noticed in March that about ten minutes into a run, I would lose all feeling in the left side of my body. I couldn't control my trajectory, so I would find myself running from the sidewalk into the street, like I was losing my balance. It was terrifying.

Doctors determine whether you have MS by doing a brain scan and looking for lesions on the brain and spinal cord. The lesions are a sign of damage to the myelin shaft covering the synapsis, and they will show up as ghostly white spots on MRI brain scans. I knew what I was experiencing was a bad sign, so, in April, I went to the neurologist and said, "I can't run in a straight line."

After doing an MRI, the neurologist reported that I did indeed have some new active lesions on my brain.

I knew my symptoms were legitimate, and I was worried. As they age, most people with relapsing-remitting MS start developing symptoms or having exacerbations at more frequent rates, with shorter periods of recovery in between. Over time, the body loses its ability to recover, resulting in permanent damage, often resulting in an inability to walk. The neurologist put me back on medication and recommended that I be placed on limited duty for six months to see if I would recover from my symptoms. Being assigned to limited duty was a blow to my ego because it meant that I was officially nondeployable, and I worried my symptoms would prevent me from being able to continue to participate in all of the training at the battalion.

Guess who had to sign my limited-duty form?

Colonel Haas.

I took it to his office, but he wasn't there, so I emailed him. At that point, he didn't know I had MS. Nobody needed to know. I hiked every hike. I ran PT and had achieved perfect scores on the physical- and combat-fitness tests for years. I worked overtime and beyond. I didn't want there to be any question that I wasn't up for my job or any perception that I was using limited duty as an excuse for anything.

Within a few minutes of receiving that email, shockingly, Colonel Haas showed up at my battalion. When he pulled up, I was standing outside by the steps to the entrance of the battalion, getting ready to get into my golf cart to go observe training.

I may have mentioned before that Colonel Haas came to my battalion only exceedingly rarely. I think he was scared I was going to accuse him of causing stress that caused the symptoms to flare up.

We all have our own leadership styles, but I like to think that if I found out one of my Marines were sick, I would start with, "Oh my gosh. What can I do to help? Let's figure out a plan to make this easier for you."

As I stood by my golf cart, he started by demanding to know what my symptoms were, what was wrong with me, and what my doctor had said.

"Sir, I have MS," I told him. "I've had it since 2001. It comes and goes, and that's all there is to it."

He looked fully panicked and acted as if he didn't believe me—like I was making it up to get back at him. I definitely did not sense empathy, and he did not ask if I was okay or if there was anything he could do to help.

If he had known me at all, he would have known I would never have blamed him for something like that. Even if the stress contributed to my symptoms, it's not my style to place blame like that. And he should have known that I wouldn't want to make a big deal about it. I wanted to deal with it and move on, just as I had done for the previous fourteen years.

What I didn't fully understand at that point was that my MS symptoms were the least of my worries.

The bottom of my world was getting ready to fall out.

CHAPTER 25

THE RAPIST IS ALWAYS WRONG

I tried to teach our women not to be victims.

I was obviously all about girl power and equality and meeting and beating standards, but in the Marine Corps there are a lot of opportunities to get hurt, too.

Let me be explicit: The rapist is always wrong.

Rape and sexual harassment are not women's problems: They're men's problems. Men should know that there are consequences to abusive behavior, and they should know that we'll follow through after an accusation of sexual assault or harassment. Women do not invite rape by being flirtatious or drunk, or by wearing a short skirt or being cute, or for being known to have had sex with other men.

Most male Marines are pretty great—guys I trust with my life, literally. But in a unit made up of a majority of men, there is a strong likelihood that one or more of them has a history of violence toward women. That's all it takes. In that recent RAND report, 27 percent of female Marines reported sexual harassment at work.[1] Veterans Affairs reports that one out of five women who go to VA clinics for healthcare screen positive for military sexual trauma.[2] A 2015 American Psychological Association report found that as many as 33 percent of women in the military suffer through rape or attempted rape, but less than 15 percent of them report the assault.[3] We also know that rape victims tend to be victimized over and over again, and that's because creepy guys can spot them. In the military, if you've reported a sexual assault and no one helps you, you're unlikely to report it the next time it happens. The abusers know that— they know they can victimize you and that you won't report it, because you don't believe anyone will help you.

Purely because of the proportion of men to women, there are opportunities for men to assault women—which, again, is a men's issue and something that's been addressed in civilian business culture. But the ratio of men to women is not the only factor. We have a high number of young people living in close quarters. They often drink to excess to relieve stress or simply because they're twenty years old. There is, without a doubt, a machismo culture that contributes to the service's high rates of assault and harassment. The Marine Corps trains men and women about sexual harassment and sexual assault, but often that training is laughed off. Or it consists of PowerPoint slides that everybody sleeps through. And women don't always support each other. As I talked about before, most women Marines try to be "one of the guys." Often, women are the least supportive of other women when it comes to allegations of sexual assault, because they are afraid that their association with the alleged victim will impact their ability to fit in. Sometimes the accused is a well-liked team player, and we tend not to want to be seen as "men haters," so we support the accused man instead of the female who has been victimized.

This lack of support for each other is bullshit, but it exists.

I believe we could stop sexual assault and harassment with mentoring—even if that mentoring comes from veterans—and with officers, especially women, who model supportive behavior. If your culture is to lift each other up, and there's a trusted camaraderie, then women will feel more comfortable talking to each other and reporting harassment and assaults.

In my policy statement on sexual harassment and assault, I told my Marines exactly this: "The act of a sexual assault is equal to a violation of human rights. Every member of this battalion must do whatever we can to safeguard the human dignity of our recruits and our subordinates. As Marines, we deploy worldwide in order to protect men and women who are unable to protect themselves. Why would we tolerate an assault within our own ranks?"

And I talked to my recruits about risky behaviors. Here's why: I don't want them to become victims who then become re-victimized. I don't want them to be hurt and then find out that there's no one there to help them. I don't want them to go through the trauma of being assaulted in the first place.

Every high school, college, and military sexual-assault training course includes lessons about risky behavior—this is not to suggest, "It's your fault if you get drunk and are assaulted," but rather to advise caution: "The rapist is always in the wrong. And staying out of these situations can keep you safer."

I stand by what I told my Marines and my recruits.

Don't get so drunk that you can't make good decisions or weaken your response times should danger arise.

Choose your friends carefully, and be careful about spending time alone with someone you don't know.

Look out for your girls—if you arrive in a group, leave in a group.

"Look, don't make yourself a target," I told all of my recruits just before they graduated. "Toughen up. Don't compete at the bar; compete on the playing field."

In the investigation against me, three recruits complained about my comments related to sexual harassment and sexual assault.

All three were from November Company.

CHAPTER 26

WORST OF THE WORST

Those days—those months and months of days after the command-climate survey results came out—were like a bad dream. It was like I was swinging on a pendulum. I'd wake up in the morning and think, "Wait. Surely someone will see through what is happening here, and rational people will see that I am doing the right things for the right reasons and let this go." And then, as I pulled my car into the battalion parking lot, I would face the reality and be overcome by feelings of doubt and dread that it would be my last day in command. It was awful.

My sergeant major was great. She and Joe kept in close touch, with her reporting how I was doing each day. I couldn't fool him, because if I was having a miserable day, she'd text him to say, "Hey. You'll want to reach out to Kate today."

Most important, she helped me hold onto my sanity.

I was experiencing extreme cognitive dissonance. On one hand, I knew that all of the conversations I had with my Marines each day indicated that they believed in what we were doing and that things in the battalion were better than they had been when I arrived. And then seeds of self-doubt would sprout, and I would brood on Colonel Haas's comments about my leadership or the petty and cruel anonymous comments from the command-climate survey and think, "Man, maybe I really am a horrible person."

And she'd say, "Nope. That's nuts. Let's just get through today."

But every time sergeant major picked me back up and dusted me off, Colonel Haas cut me to the quick.

Just days before I submitted my request mast to Brigadier General Williams, Colonel Haas counseled me on my fitness report. Every officer gets an annual fitness report, which is basically like an annual evaluation in the business world: Your boss tells you what you do well, what you need to improve on, and how you failed (or, in business lingo, "your opportunities for improvement"). I've delivered average fitness reports to Marines who deserved averages, but I've never received an average, because I've always busted my ass. And I've always had tangible results to prove it—just as I had at Fourth Battalion.

You have to be pretty great to rate the highest, but you also have to be pretty damned mediocre to get an average ranking.

Haas ranked me last.

This was not only last out of all of the lieutenant colonels he wrote fitness reports for at Parris Island. He told me he had ranked me last of any lieutenant colonel he had ever written fitness reports for in his entire career.

Dead last.

Throughout my nearly twenty-year career, I've never had anything but great fitness reports.

Yet at Parris Island, I was ranked last.

Colonel Haas told me I was the very worst lieutenant colonel he had ever been in charge of.

And nothing in his evaluation was fact-based. Get this: For mission accomplishment—"results achieved"—he ranked me average. We had achieved significant success in improving the graduation scores for female recruits in a short period of time. But for proficiency—"combines training, education and experience"—average. Initiative—"action in the absence of specific direction"? Below average. Setting the example? Average. Intellect and wisdom? Below average.

And yet, this is what he wrote in the directed comments portion of the review:

> LtCol Germano has proven herself an operationally focused, organizationally capable officer. She displays a consistently high level of initiative, and relentlessly pursues achieving performance goals she sets for her Battalion despite any perceived obstacles. Decisive and self-assured; fully commits to her decisions once made. An energetic officer who drives her Marines to maximize unit output and personal performance. She is also a polished public speaker who regularly represents the Marine Corps to the public and distinguished visitors during ceremonies and official visits. Maintains a high level of fitness and an active professional reading program. Regularly volunteers at a local animal shelter. Fully qualified for promotion and resident PME.

But my review? Communication skills: average. Initiative: below average. Overall? Average.

Even worse, after giving me a copy of my review, Colonel Haas looked at me and said, "I've been giving you enough rope to hang yourself."

Wait. What?

While I had been working to mentor my Marines and improve my recruits, my boss had been giving me enough rope to hang myself.

Isn't that uplifting? I'd say downright inspiring, really.

He had never counseled me on what he expected and what I could do to improve in his eyes. He didn't offer suggestions. He didn't once come visit my battalion and sit in on a training session or observe my interactions and relationships with my Marines and recruits. Instead, when he realized I wasn't going to hang myself with his rope, he pulled the chair from beneath my feet.

He ranked me last.

None of our achievements at Fourth Battalion mattered, even though they were historic for the Marine Corps.

Nothing mattered.

When my Marines failed to correct mistakes, I had documented everything to show that I laid out my expectations to them, trained them, observed them, and attempted to improve their performance. He didn't have any documentation to support his review: No counseling statements. No memorandums for the record. No notes saying, "I spent time with her this day, this day, and this day to make sure she understood my guidance and my desires for her leadership."

Nothing.

He had no tangible evidence to base his perceptions on. It was all based on complaints from individuals who were seeking out something that they wanted for personal reasons—individuals whom I had counseled and issued counseling statements to. As revealed later in the investigation against me, it turned out that Marines who didn't like me (because I said they had to do their job the way I said they had to do it) would go to him and say I was being mean or unfair. That's all he had to back his decision to rank me last.

For Colonel Haas, there were no specifics on why I was considered substandard, even in the performance review.

There's more.

Despite being well aware of the unusual dynamic between Colonel Haas and me, Brigadier General Williams signed off on the report. He's the one who said he saw what was going on—the one who had asked me to wait it out.

He wrote:

An active commander who sought every opportunity to improve the operating results of her command. Fully engaged in the details of recruit training, she contributed to the improvement of initial marksmanship qualification rates by coordinating with WFTBn to ensure their efforts complemented each other. Maintained regular communication with recruiting stations to ensure they were aware of any challenges their recruits encountered. Focused on improving processes and outcomes, she developed a staffing structure to ensure the most capable leaders were in senior billets.

Average.

Not only that, he praised me for keeping in touch with the recruiting stations—something that came out in the investigation as a mark against me.

Two days later, after consulting with Joe and my sergeant major, I requested mast. I had asked Colonel Haas to have a mediator present in our meetings, which he had denied. I made the request again to Brigadier General Williams, but I also asked that a new command-climate survey be conducted, one that would require every Marine to participate using his or her own individual passwords. And I accused Colonel Haas of creating a hostile work environment by subverting my authority and allowing my subordinates to go directly to him to complain about me. I also laid out the case for gender bias at Parris Island due to segregated boot camp.

My request mast application had to be routed through Colonel Haas so he could ask if I was sure there was nothing he could do at his level to resolve my complaints. Of course I said no.

I handed the envelope to him, and then watched as his face turned bright red.

It was clear that he was pissed.

When a lieutenant colonel requests mast because of a bad relationship with her boss, including accusations of gender bias and a hostile work environment, that's a big deal.

As I mentioned earlier, my husband, Joe, had retired from the Marine Corps a few months before all of this, but he still had close friends and colleagues working in the commandant's office. As I was dealing with Colonel Haas at the regiment level, Joe was hearing about meetings and briefings happening all the way up to General Dunford's level. I wasn't being investigated for misconduct. There had been no official complaints about my behavior. But I was the subject of conversations by the most senior leaders in the Marine Corps at the

Pentagon. And the crazy thing is that these conversations were about how they could get me out of Parris Island.

That's bizarre—like *Alice in Wonderland* bizarre—for a couple of reasons:

1. No one at that level should have cared at all about what was going on with a lieutenant colonel in charge of a battalion. It would be like the president of the United States' cabinet worrying about a staff aide for a county official in, say, Nebraska. Battalion commanders are important to the people who serve under us, but our problems typically get handled at the local level—by the commanding general of the recruit depot, for instance—unless somebody dies or there's an abuse scandal.

2. No action should have been taken until an investigation into my request mast complaints had been opened, conducted, and completed. The point of an investigation is to have an objective report of a situation. In this case, it should have determined the actual facts in the situation, as well as who, if anyone, was at fault. In lieu of an investigation, all we had was a command-climate survey indicating that I rolled my eyes, and a company commander's fear that I was going to withhold her end-of-service award (which I had already signed off on); yet the Commandant of the Marine Corps—the highest-ranking officer in the Corps and a member of the Joint Chiefs of Staff—was already involved.

More than that, Joe heard rumors that the commandant and his senior Marine lawyer were trying to figure out how to get rid of me, no matter what.

We hoped that the request mast would somehow save me by allowing me to tell my side of the story.

The next day, I was at Page Field, where we conduct Crucible training. Despite being on pins and needles while waiting for a reaction by the depot leadership to my request mast, I was out observing my Marines and watching how the recruits were doing. My cell phone rang. It was General Williams.

"I've got your request for mast," he told me. "I want you to know I'm concerned. One of your Marines says she's afraid of reprisal." This was odd, because it had nothing to do with my request mast.

And then he said, "I had really hoped you could wait him out." Meaning the general had hoped I would simply stay quiet until Colonel Haas's change of command in a few weeks. I felt like the general was frustrated because he felt like I was putting him out by making him deal with an issue he had been hoping would just disappear after Colonel Haas left the depot.

Wow.

"I'm sorry, sir," I said. "There was nothing else I could do. He said I was the worst lieutenant colonel he had ever encountered—he wrote it down and put it in my record. He told me he was giving me enough rope to hang myself."

"I just think we could have worked this out," the general said.

"We'll do an investigation," he said.

I was relieved. I assumed that when Brigadier General Williams said he would do an investigation, he meant he would assign a senior officer to look into my complaints of a hostile work environment and gender bias. I naively assumed that once someone from outside of the regiment actually looked into the command-climate survey, he or she would see how flawed the execution had been, and sanity would prevail. I assumed that we would be able to finally get facts on paper about how I had tried to mentor, influence, and improve the performance of the Marines who made complaints against me. I thought that once a third-party officer reviewed the decades of graduation scores for male and female recruits, they would see firsthand how segregation limited the potential of the female recruits. I believed that there would be justice and that I would finally be able to refocus on continuing to improve the performance of my recruits.

I later found out that Brigadier General Williams had begun an investigation into my leadership on the same day that I requested mast, based on what he had seen in the command-climate survey. There would not be an investigation into the actions of Colonel Haas, nor would there be any effort to look into my complaint of a hostile work environment.

In the meantime, Joe's contacts were telling him about all of the meetings and briefings about my situation, which were taking place all the way up to the commandant level. He gathered that people were even asking about my medical status in these meetings, likely because they were looking for ways to get rid of me if they couldn't relieve me for misconduct. It seemed that they were playing out all of these options.

I thought, "What the hell? They're already talking about how they can get rid of me, and they haven't even investigated my request mast complaints?"

Here I was thinking that I was just a battalion commander fighting with her boss down in South Carolina.

A week and a half after I requested mast, I put in for my retirement. That had always been the plan—Joe and I figured we'd do our twenty years, and then we'd head off for a new adventure. It kept us honest, because we didn't have to keep our noses clean or play politics to move up in rank. It allowed us to be vocal about what we thought. I still planned to finish out my two-year tour at Parris Island, but I could buy a calendar and start counting down the days.

Short-timer.

Still, I had to submit my paperwork.

To whom? Colonel Haas.

I had just received the worst fitness report of my career—of anyone's career.

But I had already completed my forms and my letter resigning my commission, and I had already gotten the sign-off from Medical. I had it all lined up.

So I marched over to his office, just to get it over with.

As I walked up the stairs—his office was on the second deck of the regimental headquarters—I could hear him in the hallway, talking about me to his old sergeant major, who had just finished his tour.

All I wanted was for him to sign my paperwork. Instead, I heard, "Lieutenant Colonel Germano is mean to her Marines, and we've been getting a lot of complaints."

Yet another fabulous example of leadership: standing in a hallway at headquarters, gossiping about one of your subordinates.

I kept walking up the stairs. When I got to where he was standing, I stopped for a second, and then I handed him my retirement package.

"Sir, I need your signature on this," I said.

I'll never forget the look on his face. He knew I had heard everything.

CHAPTER 27

GENERAL RELATIVITY

**by Joe Plenzler, husband and
Marine Corps Lieutenant Colonel (ret.);
former press secretary and spokesman for the
34th, 35th, and 36th Commandants of the
Marine Corps, 2010–2015;
former battalion executive officer and director
of the Drill Instructor School, 2007–2009**

The person described in the command-climate report was 180 degrees out from the person I had known for more than two decades.

This is Joe, popping in for a second to give you a reality check because, by now, you've got to be wondering whom you should believe—Kate's chain of command or Kate. I'm going to provide you with some background on who Kate is, as well as some context to better help you understand the culture of the Corps and what she was dealing with—more of a tapestry than a chronology.

Not only is she my wife, but we've served together in the Marine Corps since the beginning of our careers, and I've watched, from the very beginning, how differently she was treated even when she led the pack in achievements.

Let's get started.

The accusation that Kate might be moody or that her instructions might not be clear, or that she'd mark someone out for retaliation, or that she was disrespectful or mean makes no sense to me at all. If anything, Kate is clear, focused, and always fighting for what's right—and encouraging me to do the same. She's fearless, one of the bravest and most principled people I've ever known.

When we were stationed in Okinawa from 2004 to 2007, we had this fifth-floor apartment that looked out over the seawall upon the East China Sea. One Sunday morning, we were lying in bed, and we could hear the surf and there was this cool, subtropical breeze floating through the curtains. It was one of those perfect mornings when you doze lazily—a moment of Zen. Then, in a flash, it was gone. I woke up to shouting down on the seawall, and it was clearly some domestic argument between westerners—people were screaming at each other in English. I figured it was some drunk Marine and his girlfriend, but the intensity of the argument was so hostile that it made the hairs on the back of my neck stand up. I could feel it, like static electricity in the air. I just knew something bad was happening.

Right about the same time, I heard the front door of our apartment clang shut—they used heavy aluminum doors on Okinawa because of the typhoons. I looked over to where Kate had been sleeping, and there was nothing more than an indentation in the mattress and our surly grey-and-black tabby cat, Baxter, curled up in a ball, nonplussed. I thought, "Oh man. Here we go." I realized immediately that Kate was heading down to help. She has a deep-rooted urge to take action.

I slid open the glass door to our balcony, and, looking down five stories to the seawall, I saw a fairly good-sized Marine holding his girlfriend by the hair, and Kate in her pajamas—all five-foot-four of her—walking up to him and demanding that he let the woman go.

I'm thinking the worst. It's a physics problem of force equaling mass times acceleration: a drunk, one-hundred-seventy-five-pound Marine versus Kate. I hurriedly grabbed a pair of shorts and ran down the stairs. I was like a cartoon character corkscrewing down the stairwell as fast as I could. The adrenaline flowed and I planned my next moves with this guy in my head.

By the time I hit the seawall, Kate already had the guy at parade rest—feet spread wide, elbows out, hands together at the base of his back. She had his ID card in her hand, and she had him giving her the "yes ma'am, no ma'am" routine.

She locked him up simply by force of will.

We called the Camp Foster emergency number to get a hold of the military police. When we gave them the name of the Marine, they started acting strangely.

It turned out that he was an MP (military police officer), so it took a while to get anyone to come to the scene, but we kept pressing the issue until the MPs sent someone to pick him up. Then we called the officer of the day at the general's command post to make sure he was aware and that the incident would be officially noted in the duty log for the command to follow up on Monday morning. Why? Because you don't allow Marines to act like that. And you don't ignore someone screaming outside your door who needs help. In Kate's world, it's not even something she has to think about twice. She just springs into action.

Kate is great in a crisis—quick and coolheaded. A few years back, we witnessed a car accident. While my brain was trying to make sense of what I was seeing, she was already out of the car and halfway to the accident site. There's something about her brain that allows her to think faster than most people in such situations—multiple times, I've seen her launch into action many seconds before everyone else can even comprehend what's going on.

Here's another example: We were at Officer Candidates School on staff in 2004, and an officer candidate, a young woman, fell off the monkey bars on an obstacle course. She snapped both of her forearms backward. That would have been enough to make me lose my lunch, but Kate took charge and acted like it was no big deal. She calmly and coolly reassured the young candidate that she was going to be fine, grabbed the nearest corpsman (medic), and supervised the medevac. The EMTs stabilized the candidate and took her to the hospital. Unfortunately for her, she'd have to re-apply to OCS after she recovered from her injuries.

And there's this: In 2010, we bought a historic home in Upper Marlboro, Maryland, and a year or so later our neighbor started subletting rooms to people. Two brothers from down South rented from him, and they liked to get drunk and fight in the backyard at 2:30 in the morning, which really sucked. We kept calling the landlord and trying to get him to do something about the problem, but nothing changed. So, one night, at about 2:30 a.m., they're yelling, and then I hear the front door slam shut. All of a sudden, there's an altercation between Kate and these two drunk Billy Bobs.

Having Okinawa flashbacks, I'm thinking, "Damn, here we go again." I grab the shorts, rush out of the house while figuring what to do next. . . . You already know the rest of this story.

I've been married to Kate since 1999, and I have known her since 1997. She's always been one to spring into action.

But she's also uber, Type-A organized. Each night, she lays out her clothes for work the next day. Her mind is very ordered—structured—and she's a clear communicator. Whether what's on her mind is good or bad, she'll let you know. She's got the moral courage to tell people the things that they don't want to hear, whether it's counseling an underperforming Marine or telling senior leadership she thinks they're wrong. That was her reputation in the Marine Corps: She's a straight shooter and a hard-charger. She was known as a "fixer," in that commanders would assign her their Gordian Knot issues to solve, and she always left the units she led better than how she found them. That had served her well for eighteen years of her career, and then she ran into some bad leadership at Parris Island that took umbrage at a strong woman speaking her mind and trying to make things better.

For me, her laser-like focus hasn't always been comfortable, but it's always been good—partly because I need that. I'm more of a right-brained, creative-type, free-spirit person, and she's more left-brained analytical, so we balance each other out like yin and yang. Left to my own devices, I'll ping from tangent to tangent. Kate helps ground me, and I help her not be as serious, and perhaps even be a bit more adventurous. She's a creature of habit and routine—I think most people are—but I think she finds a lot of comfort in order. Kate doesn't see the world in gray. If it's written in the book, and it's a Marine Corps rule, then that's the law. There's not a lot of debating about it, and she will enforce it without equivocation.

And she's not afraid to tell me when she thinks I'm off base. I've learned over the years that when someone offers you criticism, your first assumption should be that they're right, which is easy to say and tough to do.

She's damned difficult to argue with. She's always got her ducks in line—she's always a couple of steps ahead, with a well-thought-out, cogent argument. I find that if I pick an argument with her, I really need to have my homework done. She's thorough.

She's insistent.

And boy, is she good.

But I also know that many guys in the Marine Corps have a problem with direct women. At this point in the story, I've watched her deal with that for eighteen years.

Oh, and that women are "moody" or "emotional" crap? That's a gender stereotype. All human beings are prone to emotion. When men express emotions like anger or frustration, it's acceptable and perceived as "strong." It is more socially acceptable—especially in Marine Corps culture. If a woman expresses anger or is aggressive, she's seen as a bitch. Don't believe me? That's fine. There's thirty to forty years of research in the fields of human communication and behavior that supports this theory. It's called Language Expectancy Theory[1] and the main takeaway is that men are equally persuasive whether they use strong language or gentle language, but women are only persuasive when they use nurturing language; and women are typically penalized if they use strong language.[2]

But even with evidence right in front of me, it took some time for both of us to see what was happening all throughout her career, because sexism is so normalized in the Marine Corps. Just one example: One time, when Kate was a captain and she was talking about her marathon-training regimen, a colonel interrupted to tell the group his strategy was, "to find the woman with the nicest ass at the start and follow her for 26.2 miles." Everyone laughed—well, except two people. In any case, it's clear to me that, over two decades, she has had to navigate a very different Marine Corps, simply because she has two X chromosomes.

I regret not seeing it sooner or doing more sooner to address it with my peers.

Even when we were second lieutenants at Twentynine Palms in California, I was confused by my fellow lieutenants' attitudes toward women when, just two years earlier, they had been in a gender-split fifty-fifty environment in college. Here's the thing. If you had sexist beliefs prior to joining the Marine Corps, those views were reinforced during your acculturalization through thirteen weeks of boot camp or ten weeks of Officer Candidates School. Both are transformative experiences. Neither are about building warriors so much as they are about breaking you down, indoctrinating you with cultural norms and expectations and history, and challenging you to consistently perform better. All the real combat training comes after.

When I went to OCS in 1995, I hadn't yet realized that the sexism in the Corps was baked in. Hold that thought. I'll get to that in a minute.

By the time we left OCS and the Basic School at Quantico, we all embraced the thought that civilians were sloppy and slovenly and that we were better and more disciplined, and it was clear to me that women weren't welcome or part of the team.

I told you I met Kate in 1997; this was when I was assigned to Echo Company, Second Battalion, Seventh Marines out at the Corps' desert training center in Twentynine Palms—and, no, it wasn't as cool as the Led Zeppelin song.

We lovingly referred to that sunbaked, godforsaken base as "Twentynine Stumps." To make the desolation worse, some genius put the sewage-treatment facility in line with the prevailing westerlies, so a constant aroma of poop emanated from Lake Bandini and floated over the base.

Female officers were rare back then at Twentynine Palms. I joke that when Kate would come to my company area, it was like a prairie dog town with Marines popping their heads out of their little holes, peering around corners and over HMMWVs (Humvees)—like they had never seen a woman before. I think she was one of about four female officers on the base at the time, so it was an issue. The Stumps was essentially man-land filled with infantry, armor, and artillery units. As a rule, male lieutenants would typically write off any woman on base as someone's wife, someone's daughter, or an enlisted female Marine, so they didn't bother to romantically pursue them.

So how did we meet? Believe it or not, I first saw her at the officers' club pool on a Saturday in June 1997. I was there with my roommate, Lou Rhodes, and we saw two attractive women in bikinis there. They looked like they were our age. They were by themselves. I thought I was seeing a mirage. And then one of them appeared again, holding a baby. *Yep. They're each somebody's wife. Forget about it.*

The next Sunday I was bored, so I went to see Navy Chaplain Father Coyle's mass. He was a crusty, old combat-decorated Vietnam vet and former Marine. I'm a complete skeptic when it comes to religion—my parochial-school priest died in prison after being convicted of raping and murdering a nun in some crazy ritual—but Coyle was cool and made me think, so I went to mass.

I was looking around, and two pews behind me sat one of those attractive women from the pool. And she was alone. My mental gears began to turn. I looked back again, and some dude was next to her. *Damn. Foiled again.*

After mass, I went to the base department store and flipped through CDs, enjoying my day off. And there she was again. Alone. Quickly thinking of something funny to say, I turned around, and she was gone. *Damn.*

Then I was driving home in my blue BMW 328 lieutenant-mobile. A black Honda Del Sol pulled up, and it was being driven by that same woman. I looked at her. She looked at me. Our eyes locked. She scowled and sped off. *Damn.*

I was transfixed. Like the Hardy Boys, I was obsessed with solving the Mystery of Bigfoot Riding a Unicorn, in other words, the Mystery of a Rare, Beautiful, Single, Female Marine at Twentynine Palms.

I thought, *Okay, Plenzler, assuming she* is *an officer, there are only three or four places she could work on base.* So I got up a little earlier on Monday, cruised the base, and found it—that black Honda Del Sol.

Yeah, I'm not ashamed of it.

So I went to the company office and asked a fellow lieutenant in my company, this big galoot named Justin Anderson, if he knew of any single female second lieutenants with red hair and a black Honda Del Sol on base.

It went like this:

Justin (thick Long Island accent): Kate Germano?
Me: Dude, if I knew her name, would I be asking?
Justin: Yeah, we went to TBS together.
Me: And. You. Didn't. Let. Us. Know. That?!?!?
Justin: Want me to set something up?
Me: Does the Pope shit in the woods?
Justin: OK. Wednesday at the golf club.

The rest of the story is that Kate and I went to lunch on Wednesday; out for coffee in Joshua Tree, California, on Thursday evening; and to Palm Springs for a date on Saturday—and we have been together ever since.

You'd think my peers would be happy for me, right? Nope.

We'd be out in the field, training for a week or two weeks, and the lieutenants in my all-male battalion would say, "We're going to someone's house to drink beer Friday night. Are you coming with us? No chicks."

I'd respond with something like, "Man, the last thing I want to do after sweating my ass off in this godforsaken desert with you assholes all week is go to your dirty house and sit on your dilapidated couch and drink cheap beer. Nah, bro, I'll pass. I think I'm going to go to Palm Springs with my hot girlfriend."

I swear I wasn't rubbing it in.

Maybe a little.

But most of them were jerks about it: "Oh, you're pussy-whipped," they'd say. And they were clearly offended that I was choosing Kate over the tribe. Their jealous banter became boorish, so I just stopped going to unit social events.

I suppose they could have invited her. She was a Marine. She and they may have had Marine things to discuss, but the guys made it weird. Here's an example:

Every year on or about November 10, the Corps, every unit around the world, celebrates its birthday with huge, formal balls. They include full dress uniforms, formal gowns, a band, and all that pomp and circumstance.

Weirdly, the guys wanted to know what she was wearing to the ball.

I didn't know where this was going, so I said, "What in the hell do you care what Kate's wearing to the ball?"

"Well, she's not wearing her uniform, is she?"

"Yeah," I said. "She is."

"Well our dates are wearing dresses."

"Yeah, but they don't have a piece of paper hanging on the wall, signed by the president, saying they're a commissioned second lieutenant in the United States Marine Corps."

Like I said, they were weird about it. But this attitude about women ran deep.

I hadn't yet realized how systemic this attitude was. With the benefit of hindsight, I now realized that sexism and misogyny in the Marine Corps are baked in. I don't think it's by nefarious design, but it's being suffered, in the legal sense of the term, and they don't take the proper steps to correct it.

In fact, they encourage it.

For instance, when I was at the Infantry Officer Course (IOC) in 1996, our instructors told us that the INDOC, now called the combat endurance test, was specifically designed to keep women out. The INDOC, short for "indoctrination," is a day-long qualification course involving running, land navigation, military knowledge, martial-arts skills, swimming, and unknown events—all on unknown time limits designed to increase the stress.

Let me back up a second. The matriculation of a Marine Corps officer at Quantico involves about ten weeks at Officer Candidates School. If you pass that, you get commissioned as a second lieutenant and then spend six months at the Basic School (TBS), where you learn everything there is to know about being a provisional rifle platoon commander. In the Corps, every officer is expected to know basic infantry skills and tactics. Most lieutenants go on to other schools like flight school or intelligence school or, in Kate's case, administration school, but the grunts go to IOC.

At Quantico, IOC is shrouded in mystery. At TBS, we'd see those gaunt, sinewy, lieutenants in the shadows doing grunt officer training. They were the varsity and they never spoke to us. It was like Fight Club. Later, when I was attending IOC, we were ordered not to talk about IOC to anyone, ever.

Journalist Elliot Ackerman, who served as a Marine infantry officer from 2003 to 2011, recently was interviewed on a podcast talking about gender integration in ground-combat arms units, and listening to it brought back so many memories about IOC[3].

OK. I'm going to break the first rule of Fight Club: On the podcast, Elliot talked about low attrition at IOC, and I realized I can't remember anyone getting kicked out of my IOC class for performance, including some guys we thought had no business leading Marines. He also reminded me that the forced marches or hikes were all team events—we all passed or failed together as a group. During the hike briefs, the training staff would tell us that we had to go

X miles, but they wouldn't reveal the time limit, and they would say that if we didn't get there by the secret time, we'd have to redo the event the next day. The mental stress was designed to force us to go as fast as possible. The hikes were grueling and were usually held after a week or two of field training ops during which we'd get about two hours of sleep per night and one Meal-Ready-to-Eat per day. We were sleep- and food-deprived zombies frantically trying to put the pedal to what was left of the metal. IOC is a tough course.

It's hell.

When we would do these conditioning hikes during training there, I'd often end up carrying some other struggling lieutenant's M-16 (rifle) or someone else's pack across the finish line, because we were all committed to succeeding or failing together.

At IOC, everyone has good days, and everyone has bad days. You always help your buddy out. Some of the slower, weaker lieutenants were physically dragged along so that we all crossed the finish line on time and wouldn't have to do it again the next day.

Here's the thing the generals don't tell you: President Obama's policy of forcing the integration of women into all jobs—including the infantry—made IOC tougher. More on that in a second.

Elliot's podcast also reminded me that the brass moved the goalposts at IOC after women became part of the calculus.

The push to open all military jobs and units and stop discriminating solely based on sex forced the military—especially the Corps—to make their job-performance standards more rigorous and science-based, and even to establish new standards where none had existed before.

Now all training events at IOC are individual pass/fail, and attrition is upward of thirty percent.

But, still, there were the recalcitrant.

Elliot related a story: He was talking to a former infantry officer course director a few years ago when women first began attending as part of an experimental program.

Elliot asked, "So how's it going?"[4]

The course director said it was going fine.

Elliot asked, "So when do you think the first woman will pass?"

The course director said, "It's never going to happen."

Elliot asked, "What do you mean it's never going to happen?"

The director said the curriculum had completely changed when women started going through. Everything is now individual effort, and you're not going to see a woman pass the CET. Even if they pass the CET, they will never pass the heavy-weapons march. It's just never going to happen.

Elliot persisted in the questioning, "I'm sure, eventually, some woman who, you know, can pass the CrossFit challenge will come through and pass. What happens then?"

The director looked at him and said, "It's never going to happen."

During the podcast interview, Elliot said that he was unsettled by the idea that the standards had morphed to make it specifically more difficult for women.

Old prejudices die hard, and it's amazing what some men will do to keep their prerogative.

Well, as of this writing, it happened last week. Our first female Marine officer passed the course on September 25, 2017. I've talked to enough people to know it was absolutely legitimate. And before you get your boxers in a whirl about standards at IOC, the female officers are held to the *exact same standards* as the male officers—including how many pull-ups they have to do to max the physical-fitness test.

So now that a woman passed IOC, our work is done, right? Not by a long shot. The stories above, as well as Kate's story, represent just a few in a tapestry of what women face when navigating the Corps.

Here's another one.

In 2014, I was at an executive offsite meeting for the three- and four-star generals at the Navy Yard in Washington, DC, when the commandant, General James Amos, invited *Lean In* author and Facebook executive Sheryl Sandberg to speak. Kate touched on this earlier, but I'm going to give you my story firsthand here. There wasn't a single woman among the brass. The generals' body language in there—legs crossed, arms crossed, sitting back in their chairs—was awful. It was classic dominance posturing. As one of the commandant's personal staffers, I was one of the very few non-general officers in the room. My job was to be seen and not heard and to take copious notes. I remember making a comment to a colonel sitting next to me in the back of the room: "You'd think they'd rather jump physically into a chipper-shredder than let women into the infantry."

I took some twisted pleasure in seeing this super-successful woman tell these old codgers how they could improve outcomes for women in the Corps.

I think some of the resistance was them getting their minds around the thought that, while they were apex predators in the Corps, here was a woman who has kicked ass in the business world and probably pays more in taxes than all those generals' salaries combined.

When she finished her comments and asked if there were any questions, I shot out of my seat and said, "Commandant . . ." I felt the eyes in the room boring into my forehead. "I know I'm not supposed to speak at these things, but I just want to let everyone in this room know that everything she just said is real, and I've watched my wife navigate the same issues through our Corps over the past eighteen years." The commandant gave me a smile and a wink. Sandberg smiled. I sat down, breathed a sigh of relief, and shut up.

At first, it was hard to see how the institutional sexism impacted Kate, because she was so good at what she does. She was the exceptional female. She runs marathons, and now fifty-mile races. She climbs mountains like a beast. She's strong and fast. And she was a squared-away Marine.

The Marine Corps gives primacy to physical condition: If you can run fast, and you're strong, and you're fit, and you're not fat, then you're perceived as someone who is going to kick ass and get things done. Typically that's a good thing.

Kate has that covered.

But that's not what we heard at Officer Candidates School. Our instructors made a point of saying that women didn't carry as much weight, and that their obstacle course was shorter than ours. They pointed out that women had twenty-one minutes to max the three-mile run, whereas we had to do it in seventeen minutes. In short, our training staff was telling us that our female counterparts had it easier than we did. The message to us? The women don't have to do as much to earn their second-lieutenant bars. What impact do you think that had on the men of my platoon?

I remember Lieutenant General Carol Mutter, the Marine Corps' first female three-star general, was scheduled to preside over our commissioning ceremony to become second lieutenants in August 1995, immediately after we graduated OCS. I remember, especially with the prior-service guys, that this was a serious issue for discussion. They were pissed. Some candidates approached our staff and said they didn't want to be commissioned by "some fake-ass female general."

The father of one of the candidates was an admiral, and the platoon knew it. So the complainers asked our training staff if this admiral could commission them instead of General Mutter. Finally, the platoon sergeant said, "Everyone needs to shut the fuck up. She's the general in charge and everyone's going to get in line and get their bars and get commissioned by General Mutter."

Mutter had served in the Marine Corps longer than most of us had been alive.

By the time Kate hit recruiting duty in 2007 following our tour on Okinawa, she already worried about the lower expectations and standards for women. But I don't think either of us quite "got it" yet.

Over the following three years we spent in San Diego, Kate had several complaints filed against her. I remember asking her about one of them.

"What did you tell this Marine?" I asked.

"Well, I told him I was disappointed in him. He was completely happy to take his special-duty pay as a recruiter, but he wasn't writing any new-recruit contracts and hadn't in months," she said. "I told him, 'If you don't start doing your fucking job, I'm going to fire you.'"

"What would have happened if I had said that?" I asked her.

"Well, they would have said, 'Plenzler's a tough guy. Don't get on his bad side,'" she said. "But there wouldn't have been a complaint."

And that's a cold fact.

I think that's when I really started realizing how screwed up a lot of the guys were when it came to female leadership. Her results speak for themselves. The recruiting station had been failing before she got there. Her first year, they were most improved in the district. By the third year under her supervision, they were best in terms of quality west of Mississippi, and station of the year in the Twelfth Marine Corps District. The Corps began teaching things Kate innovated and implemented at the Recruiters' School in San Diego.

True to form, Kate was tough, and she was demanding. What was the difference between San Diego and Parris Island? In San Diego, her commanding officer on recruiting duty backed her up. That was the big difference, and it meant everything.

Oh, I didn't mention that I served with Kate's boss's boss, Brigadier General Terry Williams, at the Pentagon when I was on the commandant's staff and he was in charge of the Division of Public Affairs. Having been a career logistician, he was new to public relations, and I'd often find myself countering his advice to the commandant at staff meetings. He didn't like that, but we were on good terms when he left the Pentagon.

While at Parris Island, Kate told me that he was checking in on her periodically and was praising the work she was doing. I know command can be a lonely place, so I sent him emails thanking him for having Kate's back, and he'd say she was doing a great job. I think he knew Haas was weak. I still have those notes. Here's a few:

From me to him on April 17, 2015:

General,

Great to see you today.

Sorry we didn't have more time to chat, but I knew you were busy with the ceremony and guests.

Life is good on terminal leave. I landed a job as vice president of marketing for a local not-for-profit. I'm pretty excited about it and don't start till June.

If you ever need anything, my personal line is (xxx) xxx-xxxx.

Take good care, Sir.

Joe

And back from him the same day:

Great to see you as well!!! Your better half is doing great down here—I know, there's a little tension with the RTR CO—but in my book she is knocking it out of the ballpark. Best to you and if you need [something] that I can help you with, I'll try my best to get it done. My personal email is xx. My numbers change but for now: xxx-xxx-xxxx. You are a great American and Marine and it was an honor serving with you. Semper Fi!!!

V/R

Terry

I sent him another note to his personal email on May 1, as things started getting worse:

Sir, Kate has told me about the challenges she is facing and I just wanted to tell you that I appreciate you mentoring and supporting her as she works to improve the performance and culture of 4th Battalion. You and I both know that command can be a lonely place, and it means a lot to have the support of your senior leadership. Many thanks to you and Sergeant Major, all best, Joe

The same day, he wrote back with a quick note indicating that it was his pleasure to do so.

Later that same month, I was at Pimlico Race Course, betting on ponies in the Black-Eyed Susan races the day before Preakness, and I got a call from Kate.

"I just had this horribly hostile counseling session with Colonel Haas and

I think he was trying to bait me until he could fire me on the spot," she said. "I wasn't biting. What do I do?"

"Why don't you go to your reviewing officer," I said, meaning Williams. "He says you're doing good things—clearly, he has a sympathetic ear." The whole point of having a reviewing officer in the chain of command is to resolve differences between you and your reporting senior; in Kate's case, her reporting senior was Haas.

I didn't know it then, but this was the worst advice I could have given her.

As soon as she contacted Williams, he folded. He hit the panic button and asked higher headquarters to launch an equal-opportunity investigation into Kate's behavior and then set his dog, the Headquarters battalion commander, on an investigative trail to dig up dirt on her. From what I could tell, it wasn't much of an investigation—it was more of a kangaroo court. Essentially this guy set out a shingle that read: If you've got a gripe about Germano, come see me. The investigation wasn't thorough. It didn't include many of the statements of Marines who supported Kate. He never interviewed Kate. He never followed up with questions to her statement. It was a complete shit show, in my opinion. In grad school, we called this "purposive research"—studies done to find enough "evidence" to support a preconceived conclusion.

I think Williams didn't want to hold Haas accountable, because that's hard. But the hard things need to be done. If not, the next thing you know, you'll have a big abuse scandal with recruits jumping off balconies, and it will be no surprise to anyone who knew what was going on at the depot at that time.

Having spent two years at the Corps' boot camp in San Diego and served as the director of the Drill Instructor School there, I always saw the depot as this big machine made of muscle-bound DIs fueled by Red Bull, Copenhagen, and testosterone. The officers were supposed to serve as the governor on this powerful and wild-steam contraption spinning balls to the wall. When the officers failed to lead and supervise, bad things happened. Like Barnes said in the movie *Platoon*, "When the machine breaks down, we [all] break down."[5]

When you are working as a leader in what psychologist Phil Zimbardo calls a total environment—ala the Stanford Prison Experiment, like the depot at Parris Island—you need to have a strong spine.[6] You need to hold yourself and others accountable. You need to stand for something. When I worked at the depot, I read a lot about what Zimbardo and guys like Albert Bandura had to say about dehumanization and the potential for abuse, so I could identify symptoms. I also learned something important from Dr. John Steiner, whose ideas

Zimbardo discussed and expanded upon in a conference: "In any given situation, the roles individuals play have margins of discretion within which they can exercise freedom of choice in how they carry out the function of their roles. We call this the capacity for free will. Those margins are expanded when people have a high degree of moral and social intelligence, and trust, but I add that, those margins are compressed when situations become total and powerful."[7]

And that's the risk associated with putting young Marine leaders in positions of near total authority over recruits. Without firm, moral leadership like Kate's, bad things will happen and recruits will be abused, or worse.

Back to Williams and Haas and Kate. I had advised Kate to go to Williams for backing. I suppose her other option would have been to shut up and endure it, but that's not her style. She has never let anyone bully her, no matter the rank. She would always stand her ground and push back when it came to matters of principle.

Here's the other thing you need to know: By 2010, four years before Kate went to the depot, both of us had decided to get out of the Corps at the twenty-year mark. There was no question that we were going to retire by 2015 for me and 2016 for her. That decision had a single clarifying effect: When you don't care about making the next rank, the Corps has very little to hold over you when it comes to making hard decisions.

There's irony in that. The Marine Corps higher-ups put Kate at Parris Island because they were grooming her to become a colonel and a brigadier general. She had two successful tours on recruiting duty, had a solid tour in combat with the 31st Marine Expeditionary Unit, was selected for resident schools, and had been hand-picked to be an aide to the secretary of the Navy. The Corps was putting her in the right spots with the right visibility for advancement to top leadership. And, typically, you become a female general in the Marine Corps by doing a tour at Fourth Battalion. She went down to South Carolina with a clear conscious, a commitment to do the right thing, and the moral Kevlar armor that comes with not being beholden to any promotion board.

The Pentagon can be a morally nebulous place at times. When I started working there for the Commandant of the Marine Corps, Kate turned me on to this quote from Australian-born British intellectual Gilbert Murray, which I kept on the wall above my desk: "Be careful in dealing with a man who cares nothing for comfort or promotion, but is simply determined to do what he believes to be right. He is a dangerous uncomfortable enemy, because his body, which you can always conquer, gives you little purchase upon his soul."[8]

That describes my Kate.

But that doesn't describe everyone in the Marine Corps—especially generals. The way to top leadership in the Corps isn't by rocking the boat. The fastest track is to fall in line and go along to get along.

The entire time Kate was at Parris Island, we heard about investigations into complaints about leadership at Thumpin' Third Battalion, the male battalion associated with being harsh and abusive. The battalion commander there was the favored son of Colonel Dan Haas, the regimental commander. We thought something would come of those investigations, and that would help Kate because everyone could then see the turmoil in the regiment was due in large part to Haas's weak, laissez-faire leadership style.

But nothing happened. It didn't make sense.

We found out later that as Kate was strictly enforcing regulations, drill instructors in Third Battalion were putting recruits in industrial clothes dryers and hazing them in an old barracks called the Dungeon. Nobody in the depot's leadership took the situation at Thumpin' Third seriously until on March 18, 2016, Recruit Raheel Siddiqui allegedly shouted he would rather die than go on training and threw himself over a third-floor balcony rail to escape abusive drill instructors.[9]

I believe that the depot's leaders had to have known long before Siddiqui jumped off the balcony that there were problems with the regiment's leadership and the staff at Thumpin' Third. If they didn't, they should have been fired for negligence. It's not that hard to supervise DIs—it just takes a lot of time and personal engagement. You have to care.

On the heels of Kate's mistreatment and Siddiqui's death, my low opinion of Brigadier General Williams persists. I still have a fairly robust network in the Corps, and people regularly report back to me about what's going on in the commandant's staff and elsewhere. Even after Kate was fired, one of my associates at the Pentagon told me that General Williams told him that he was "voluntold" by his boss to fire Kate. If these allegations are true, this tells me that he didn't have the moral courage to stand up to his superiors about their decision to fire Kate. I heard from another contact that Williams's boss indicated that if the choice is between believing a colonel and a lieutenant colonel, he would pick the colonel every time. That's just the way the Marine Corps is. When a more junior officer is outspoken and calls the Corps out on its bullshit, the higher-ups circle the wagons and eat the young. Colonels will be sacrificed to protect generals; and lieutenant colonels, for colonels. That's the way it is. The fact that I had a

Pentagon source telling me that the commandant's staff was talking outcomes about Kate before any investigation was complete indicates to me that they wanted her out of the way at all costs. Despite her many successes in improving female performance, they saw her as the problem.

As I said, I had worked at the Pentagon for five years at the top of the Corps. I had five years to build relationships based on trust and mutual respect, a five-year record of superior performance, five years to develop my network. All to say I was wired-in, deep.

When the tide started turning against Kate, people who cared about me started tipping me off. In June 2015, I took my dad fishing in Michigan. One evening, about halfway through the month, I was standing on a dock when a Pentagon source called to tell me, "You need to get ready, because there's bad stuff coming your way."

At first I didn't want to believe it. My thought was, "As soon as this issue reaches the first level of adult supervision, it will go away. Maybe at a three- or four-star level, but preferably the two-star."

The two-star involved, General Williams's boss, and I had served together in Iraq in 2003 with First Marine Division. He failed to ensure Kate had a fair hearing and turned out to be a complete and utter disappointment. I was also hopeful that the commandant's lawyer, whom I personally medevacked in combat after he was wounded in action, would help, but he also turned out to be a complete and utter disappointment. That's the thing about the Corps: It's family business. When it goes south, it gets ugly quick.

I served with the Commandant, General Dunford, when he was the Regimental Combat Team Five commander back in 2003, then as his speechwriter in Afghanistan in 2013 for three months, and then again for the first five months of his commandancy. He too was no help.

It was pretty clear to me that General Dunford wanted to keep women out of the infantry at all costs. He was the only member of the joint chiefs (senior leaders of the Army, Navy, Marine Corps, Air Force, and National Guard) to ask the secretary of defense for an exception to policy in September 2015 to keep women out of ground-combat arms jobs and units.[10] That's one way of saying it. The other way is to say that he wanted to perpetuate the Marine Corps' policy of discriminating against women for some jobs based on their sex alone—regardless of whether or not they could meet the standards. His request made a lot of headlines because it placed him in direct opposition to his bosses, the Secretary of the Navy Ray Mabus and Secretary of Defense Ash Carter, who were pushing for all jobs to be open to any person, male or female, who could meet the standards. Even more disappointing, when Dunford didn't get his way, he skipped the secretary of defense's press conference on December 3, 2015, announcing the policy change.[11] It's practically a Pentagon tradition for both the secretary and his top general, the chairman of the joint chiefs, to attend together any press conferences announcing major policy changes.

In retrospect, it makes sense that the commandant would do nothing to ensure Kate's complaint about systemic gender bias was properly addressed. It's pretty evident that every advancement Kate made with her Marines at Fourth Battalion stripped away justifications for keeping women out of ground-combat arms jobs and eroded claims that women don't shoot as well, don't run as fast, and can't carry the same weight as their male counterparts. With every improvement to female performance, Kate was quashing critical elements of those arguments.

CHAPTER 28

KILL THE MESSENGER

On May 9, 2015, we planned to do an integrated Crucible hike with one of the battalions. The majority of the hikes had gone well, and it was still a point of pride for me that we had fought for integration and then proved ourselves successful.

I walked with my Marines—it was Papa Company and a company from Third Battalion that day—and almost as soon as the hike started, it became evident that the company commander and her first sergeant had not coordinated properly with their male counterparts. This was about two weeks before the change of command for the company commander, and I could tell she had completely mentally checked out by that point: She did not do anything beyond what she had to do. We ended up finishing about a mile and a half behind the male battalion.

Papa's CO let the guys get away with shuttling us to the back of the formation, but part of the delay was because the female DIs took too long on breaks and no leaders from the company or series staffs did anything to stay on schedule. I'm not just saying they needed to go faster; they actually were supposed to take a twenty-minute break at the halfway point so the recruits could eat some fruit and drink some Gatorade before getting on the road again. But that day, the company took much longer to start the second half of the hike, and then Third Battalion took off like lightning, seemingly to prevent the female formation from catching up. We walked with GPS, and it was clear that they hiked at a pace much faster than three miles per hour, which was the doctrinal hike pace.

Having them speed out ahead of us was the norm when we hiked with Thumpin' Third. We knew that before the hike, and we should have formed up our recruits and quickly gotten back on the road after the break so Third Battalion couldn't shoot out ahead of us.

Several times, I had talked to my Marines about stressing to their male counterparts during the planning for the Crucible that we expected them to follow the rules when it came to the conduct of the integrated hikes. I had also talked to the CO about this because she hadn't read the previous after-action review in which I had clearly stated that we need to make sure we don't let the guys undermine our integration efforts during the hikes. That we shouldn't undermine our own efforts seemed obvious.

A couple of days after that, on May 11, one of my drill instructors in Papa Company requested mast because she felt that she was being mistreated as a new drill instructor by her peers in her platoon. Like a lot of new drill instructors, she quickly became sick after her first few weeks, because of the strain of the duty and being exposed to recruit germs. (Sixty people in one room leads to a lot of germs.) The new DI's leadership had denied her request to go to Medical, and to her, that was the last straw after weeks of new-instructor hazing. She knew they were not acting in accordance with my command philosophy, so she brought her complaints to me.

By that time, I had already spoken to the hard-as-nails first sergeant and her disengaged CO several times about the command-climate issues in the company, but to no avail.

Because I had worked hard to eliminate any type of recruit and drill-instructor mistreatment and increase the transparency in the battalion, I thought it would be important to speak to the company about what had happened on the hike and about the request mast, so I had an all-hands meeting with Papa Company. We talked about the poor results of the hike and the request mast complaints, and I stressed the need for the drill instructors to treat each other with respect and common decency. At one point, the company commander tried to explain herself and why she didn't work harder to integrate the hike, and I cut her off. I didn't want to hear her excuses, and I needed her to set the standard for her Marines.

I talked to the company about holding each other accountable, and I related it back to the anonymous complaints in the command-climate survey about me. I told them I needed for them to understand the difference between feeling bad because you've been reprimanded and confusing that with the leadership being mean. I clarified that being reprimanded because you've done something incorrectly should be an expected outcome, no different from what we would expect anywhere else in the Marine Corps. This is a matter of feeling versus fact. And I'm much happier to talk with them about what a great job they've done. I wanted them to understand that we can't teach the recruits personal responsibility if we're not taking responsibility for our own actions.

But I was also angry about the request mast—not at the drill instructor, but that it had gotten to that point. The drill instructor's issues should have been handled immediately at the series- and company-commander level. That's what small-unit leadership and conflict resolution are for. I was irritated that the request mast was necessary because, in a properly functioning company, the problems would not have occurred in the first place.

The command-climate survey just added to the perception that there was "all that drama" in Fourth Battalion—women who couldn't sort out their issues because they're "too emotional," and yet, the company leadership was doing nothing to ensure their Marines were taken care of when they were sick, that they were being trained and mentored, and that we pushed back when Third Battalion tried to make us look like we couldn't keep up on hikes.

Then, Colonel Haas gave me my worst performance-evaluation ranking ever, and I requested mast, which is unheard-of for a lieutenant colonel to do.

I was mentally and physically exhausted from worrying about what Colonel Haas was cooking up. I knew from Joe's connections in the Pentagon that big trouble was brewing. I needed a break, and I needed to see Joe. I was supposed to meet him in Charleston, South Carolina, for Memorial Day weekend.

But before I could drive to see Joe, I was notified that General Williams had convened an investigation, and that the investigating officer wanted to meet with me. I was not provided any other information, so I assumed the investigation was about the complaints from my request mast. So I was thinking that this would be my chance to lay everything out with the investigating officer. Once again, the pendulum of hope versus fear had swung back to hope—surely, once I explained my side of the story and provided my documentation, the investigating officer would understand what was happening.

I walked in with all of my counseling statements, all of the documentation about people's performance, and the previous year's command-climate survey—which had similar results to mine but with comments that pointed to the main issues of discipline and accountability in the battalion. My paperwork rose five inches high. He said, "I need for you to write a statement about how you perceive your command climate to be. Make sure you explain the purpose behind your meeting with Papa Company Marines as well."

I must have stared at him for several seconds.

"Wait, wait, wait," I said. "I thought you here because of *my* request mast?"

"No," he said. "I don't know anything about that."

"Oh. Wow," I thought. "This is not going to be good."

He didn't ask me any questions or allow me the opportunity to defend myself. Instead, he told me to send him my statement via email. I had essentially no idea what the allegations were against me, other than that they were related to my meeting with Papa Company.

In other words, I had no idea what General Williams directed the investigating officer to look into for the scope of the investigation. As a legal officer and someone who had not only done command investigations but also had reviewed hundreds of them for accuracy and sufficiency, I thought it was extremely odd that the investigating officer didn't specifically lay out what I was being accused of. How could I defend myself without knowing what I had allegedly done?

I didn't know that the company commander had emailed Haas after our all-hands meeting and said she was afraid of reprisal. She had decided I wasn't going to give her an end-of-tour award, and so she claimed I was retaliating against her.

That wasn't even on my mind. I expected her to do better—I knew she was capable—so, throughout her tour, I had hoped I could influence her and that she would grow as a leader. Despite her lack of leadership, she had accomplished some good work, and I had already approved her end-of-tour award weeks before. Colonel Haas could have easily figured that out.

So, here I stood, being investigated for retaliation because one of my company commanders feared I wasn't going to approve an award I had already approved. (But I only learned that later.)

In any case, I left the stack of documentation for the investigating officer to review and consider, and I wrote a nine-page statement. I laid out what was going on at Fourth Battalion before I got there. I talked about the problems I was having with particular members of my staff. I wrote about the remedial actions I took to fix the problems. I wrote about the progress we had made.

I sent the investigating officer my statement by email, as he had asked; but he never called me in for an interview. I interpreted the silence as a good sign—clearly, he saw that my statement made sense. Now I know that I made a stupid assumption, thinking that my statement would be used to shed light on what I was trying to do to maintain good order and discipline in the battalion and how that had made some people who weren't performing up to standards unhappy.

The first week of June, when I was home for the weekend with Joe for the first time in two months, I got a call from Sergeant Major, telling me that the regimental XO was walking around the battalion with a female colonel. We had no idea what they were doing, but a day later I received a call from the female colonel, explaining that she had been appointed by General Lukeman, the two-star general in charge of Training and Education Command, and General Williams's boss, to conduct an equal-opportunity investigation into my request-mast complaint to Brigadier General Williams of gender bias and a hostile work environment. When I returned to Parris Island, we met, and I gave the female colonel an extensive statement, as well as a copy of the statement I gave to the other investigating officer who had been assigned by Brigadier General Williams to evaluate my leadership. She also talked to a few of my Marines, but that was all I knew.

As the investigation into my leadership was wrapping up, the female investigating officer completed her interviews and returned to Quantico during the third week of June, to brief General Lukeman on the results of the equal-opportunity investigation. I found out later that this represented the first of many mistakes by the Marine Corps to follow proper equal-opportunity investigation regulations. Not only did they fail to send out an official message to Headquarters Marine Corps, as required, when I made my complaints of gender bias, but they failed to ensure I was provided a copy of the investigation and given a chance to provide a rebuttal to it.

And then, out of the blue, the investigating officer for the inquiry into my leadership called and asked if I had any medical conditions.

This seemed to be a violation of my privacy, but I was honest with him: "Yes, I have MS, but it has never affected my performance. I can't even understand why you would ask."

By this point, I was a mess mentally and physically. I didn't know whom I could trust, and I swung from feelings of abject terror at the potential for being fired, to an unrealistic and naive belief that surely someone, somewhere would see the big picture and recognize that I wasn't the problem after all.

Sergeant Major tried to reassure Joe that I was going to be okay, but she also sent him pictures she had taken of me and my new executive officer, who was a breath of fresh air and had arrived at the battalion a few weeks prior, in which I look defeated. I had lost about ten pounds in about three weeks, due to stress, and my face looks gaunt and bony in those images. It's hard for me to look at them now, and I found out later that Sergeant Major and Joe were texting nearly daily to communicate about my well-being and the general state of affairs.

Joe knew, based on what he was hearing at the Pentagon, that things were going to get worse.

About the third week in June, Colonel Haas decided not even to pretend to play anymore: He was done with integrated hikes, probably because he knew the ax was getting ready to fall on me.

He didn't tell me about his decision.

November Company's commander had worked directly with her male counterpart on setting up for an integrated five-mile hike, which was great. Colonel Haas had only integrated the Crucible hikes, so we had to rely on cooperation with our male counterparts to do co-ed training events otherwise. She had reached out to Second Battalion for a final coordination call for the hike the next day, Saturday. Then her peer called her to say that he had just gotten a call from regiment, saying they were not allowed to do the hike together.

In a normal chain of command, a battalion commander would have received a call from his or her commander if the senior commander had made a decision to cancel a training event. But Colonel Haas apparently had talked to my peer, the commanding officer of Second Battalion. Obviously, this was not a normal chain of command.

To find out what had happened, I sent an email to the commanding officer of Second Battalion. He wrote back that he wanted me to know it wasn't his decision, and that Second Battalion had wanted to do the integrated hike. However, he said he had received a call from Colonel Haas the night before, saying the integrated hike was canceled.

Colonel Haas had simply excluded me from the notification chain. At that point, I knew I was doomed.

It was about then that I realized I needed to make sure my Marines were taken care of, and that they had what they needed to continue the work we had begun. After the final blow was struck, I wanted to hand facts to Congress and the Inspector General of the Marine Corps. Surely, someone would listen.

I still wanted women to win.

I copied all of the documents on my computer. I gathered all of my documentation. I wrote a letter to my Marines and sent it to Joe and Sergeant Major: "Do me a favor. Look at this, and tell me if there's anything you think I should change."

To the Marines of 4th Recruit Training Battalion,

I wanted to tell you it has been the greatest honor and privilege of my life to stand shoulder to shoulder with you over the past 12 months. I have always said that I am responsible for everything we do or fail to do, and my accountability begins and ends with my obligation to lead, mentor, and guide you. It is my responsibility, therefore, to inform you that I was relieved by BGen Williams as your commander due to his loss of trust and confidence in my ability to lead you effectively.

While this decision greatly saddens me, my sole concern at this point is for your health and welfare and that of the battalion. I have one final request for you, and that is that you pull together as a cohesive team and move forward as a battalion, for that is the true sign of resilience.

Despite considerable active and passive resistance throughout all echelons of the Recruit Depot and the Marine Corps, we each worked incredibly hard to improve the performance of our recruits to make them stronger, faster, smarter, and better shots—all to better the Institution. We achieved unprecedented and historic results in just a short period of time, and regardless of the controversy caused by our goal to improve the caliber of our graduates, I ask that you remain steadfast and committed to this objective.

Together, we redefined the perceived physical and mental limits of female recruits and Marines, which will have a lasting and positive impact on the Institution. Regardless of my departure, you must never, ever give up trying to change the status quo. You are so much better than the Marine Corps knows and it is the right thing to do for not only the Institution, but also our nation.

You deserve a seat at the table with your counterparts, but you must continue to earn it every day and never take it for granted.

Know that my year with you was precious to me, in spite of the personal and professional difficulties I encountered as your commander. I will forever value the funny and interesting conversations and laughs we shared, and I am immensely proud of each of you. I have full confidence that you and the recruits will continue to make history by improving the caliber of Marine we send to the operating forces, and I am extremely proud of all that we achieved.

You and the battalion will remain in my heart and thoughts. Thank you for giving me the best year any commander could ever have.

Sincerely,

LtCol Germano

I didn't want to come across as whining or pointing a finger. I wanted them to know how proud I was of them, and I wanted them to know how incredibly rewarding it had been to watch them achieve so much. But I also wanted them to know that they needed to keep demanding a seat at the table in order to level the playing field for women in the Marine Corps.

Because I knew I wouldn't be able to send it once I was relieved, I begged my sergeant major to make sure my Marines received the letter after I was relieved.

This was two weeks before Colonel Haas was supposed to have his change of command ceremony and leave Parris Island.

I packed up my belongings in my office, and then I waited.

It didn't take long.

Late that afternoon, Colonel Haas called me to say that I needed to be in the general's office the next morning. I told my sergeant major I thought I was going to be fired. At that point, she knew what side she needed to be on.

"Well, you know I've got two kids," she told me. "I gotta make it out of here."

In other words, she needed to make it until her retirement the next year and would do what she needed to do to survive. She was not going to fight for me or take my side publicly.

The next morning, I went into work, and she was nowhere to be found.

Later, I learned that she had been called into the depot sergeant major's office, where I suspect she was told something along the lines of, "You get in line, or you're not going to last either."

After I was fired, I returned to my office, and she met me at the door. She had clearly been crying and looked awful; she expressed to me how sorry she was about how things had turned out, as she helped me to carry out my stuff to the car. But, emotionally, she was already gone.

I got in my car, and I drove home.

CHAPTER 29

LEAKED LIKE A SIEVE

by Joe Plenzler, husband and Marine Corps lieutenant colonel (ret.)

As Kate made her way up the East Coast toward home, I was already making some phone calls.

So was the Marine Corps.

Kate and I both worried that the Marine Corps' leadership would try to come out ahead on this story. Typically, when an officer is relieved of command in the military under administrative reasons, the military releases a simple, generic statement with no details about its rationale for relieving an officer of his or her command.

It's only when an officer is found guilty at a court-martial—and these are typically for the most heinous things, like molesting children or accepting prostitutes as gifts in exchange for information—that the details are publicly released via the court proceedings.

But for political cases—when the military wants to make a point—the leadership will bend the rules, leak information, and use "cutouts" to pen op-eds in an attempt to control the message. In this case, we knew that the Marine Corps would not be thrilled about Kate having voiced concerns about systemic gender bias in the recruiting and training of women. It was pretty clear to me that she had been fired because (1) she was an outspoken, tough, aggressive woman; (2) Colonel Haas didn't like that; and (3) she was making too much progress in a direction that the senior leadership didn't want to go. She had shown that women can shoot well enough, run fast enough, and were tough enough to give the infantry a shot.

We were right.

Immediately after General Williams fired Kate, it's clear that the Marine

Corps started leaking information to the press—in a complete violation of their own release-of-information policies.

I was able to prove this.

I pulled up all of the cases of commanders who were relieved between 2012 and 2016 to see what information the Corps released and if the Headquarters staff gave a copy of the investigations to the press. When you look up all of the initial articles in the media about the administrative reliefs of commanders, the Corps followed policy and released only the information absolutely required by the Department of the Navy's instructions (SECNAVINST 5720.44c).[1] I am not surprised that policy was followed, because these were all male commanders. And because they were men, offenders were seen as damaged but still part of the tribe. In these cases, when the media asked about the reason for their reliefs, the Corps would respond, "Officer X was relieved of command of unit X due to a loss of confidence in his ability to lead." When the press would ask for details, the Corps would say, "Because this relief was administrative in nature and not punitive, we are unable to release any further information." Full stop.

Kate didn't receive the same professional courtesy. In fact, a reporter I knew from the Pentagon told me that a Marine Corps public affairs officer contacted her, emailed her a copy of the investigation, and made a comment that she understood to be an attack on Kate's character. It was pretty clear to me that the Marine Corps was taking active measures to damage Kate's reputation. That direction, I'm told, came from the Pentagon.

We had already seen from the command-climate survey that the basis for her relief was substantiated on individual uncorroborated testimonials: "Kate rolls her eyes at nonsense and yells when people don't do their jobs" had devolved into "Kate's mean and disrespectful to her Marines."

This is the Marine Corps, for crying out loud! I took an ass-chewing from a brigadier general in 2003 during the invasion of Iraq, and that guy now serves as the White House Chief of Staff.

Make no mistake, the cultural double-standard over what is acceptable from male and female leaders in the Marine Corps is strong.

Here's an example: just before Kate was relieved, she attended a retirement ceremony for a colonel, and during the ceremony, General Williams went on and on about what a tough guy the colonel was, even making jokes about how everyone called him the "Icepick" because he was so tough and demanding.

Obviously, I don't think Kate's a Lieutenant Colonel Icepick, but it does strike me that this trait was admired in a retiring male colonel—celebrated, even—but used as evidence to fire a female lieutenant colonel.

Heck, even General Mattis, whom I worked for twice, is celebrated for his no-nonsense, direct, tough, demanding leadership. Mattis used to say, "The only two qualities I look for in a Marine are initiative and aggressiveness." To this day, he's still celebrated among Marines for saying things like "It's fun to shoot some people."[2] Mattis was both tough and fair, and the Marines loved him for that. Well, except the non-performers. They hated him for that; and when it comes to initiative and aggressiveness, Kate has both in spades.

As I told you before, men, like Mattis, are praised for embodying the Corps' ideals of a tough leader, and women are generally penalized for the same. This is no different from what we see in the corporate world. There are decades of research out there on the subject of language expectancy in persuasion that support my contention. And some men wonder why women don't "smile" more? Ugh.

I've seen Kate deal with this double-standard before, but I had never seen her in a darker mood or more filled with doubt than during that month and a half following our phone call at Pimlico racetrack. She was suffering alone in South Carolina, in agony, awaiting her fate. There were multiple instances between the time when she made the complaint to Williams and when she was fired that I was truly concerned about her mental and emotional state.

I would call her and she'd be in such a dark place that I'd ask, "Are you going to hurt yourself? I need you to tell me you're not going to do something really rash, or else I will get in my car and be there in eight hours." There were times she was so low that I contemplated calling 911. I knew I couldn't count on Williams or Haas, or anyone else in leadership at Parris Island, to look after her, and I didn't know anyone else in Beaufort, other than her sergeant major, who was also very worried about her.

I felt helpless.

In any case, between the time when Williams fired her and the moment she pulled into our driveway in Maryland, the Marine Corps immediately started leaking out the details of her relief while refusing to provide her a copy of their investigations. Kate had requested copies of both the command investigation and the equal-opportunity investigation at the meeting when Williams relieved her.

It was clear to me that the Corps' leadership was playing political games.

What the Marine Corps leadership didn't know was that I was already a few steps ahead of them—both the media and my contacts in the Pentagon had been feeding me information for weeks.

Again, in the five years I spent in the Pentagon, I had seen some of the shady games that are played when senior leaders are scared and the wagons are circled.

As Kate drove home, I called our dear friends who lived nearby, Chris and Brian, to update them about the situation. Like us, these two dudes own a historic home. They are also the most caring and compassionate people on the planet, and I knew Kate needed the strength of people who love and respect her. Brian was out of town, but Chris came straight over and kept me company while I awaited Kate's return.

When she pulled into the driveway, she looked terrible, and I could tell her confidence was gone. Chris and I gave her big hugs, walked her inside, and told her we were proud of her for taking a brave stand. In a way, I think she was relieved for the drama to be over.

The next day, we hung out in Old Town, Alexandria—in Virginia—and I immediately started posting photos of her smiling on social media. I knew people from the Marine Corps were likely following my posts and reporting back to leadership, and I didn't want them to know they cracked her spirit. But, man, she was so skinny. She had lost about ten pounds and looked emaciated.

I needed them to understand that they hadn't destroyed her, and that she wasn't going to back down. For now, the best way I knew how to stick it to them was to not give them the satisfaction of knowing how deeply they wounded her.

That August, we went to Jackson, Wyoming, to climb the Grand Teton—a North American mountaineering classic—and I made sure they could see Kate on the summit, decked out in her climbing gear and grinning like she'd just won the lottery.

I wanted to project that she was both unbroken and indefatigable. In fact, she was just beginning to recover.

Shortly after Kate came home to Maryland and the news started to break, we got a flood of support from both left and right, and from people serving on active duty and veterans. Here's an interesting one.

About a month after she was fired, a male Marine Corps lieutenant colonel who was controversially relieved of his command in combat in Afghanistan in 2004 reached out to Kate.

In his case, the Marine Corps followed the policy concerning release of information, and there's not a lot out there in the open press on him. I knew this guy by reputation. He was a rising star within the Corps; he was very popular with his Marines; and it was clear that the brass were grooming him to be a general.

According to accounts, he was very intense, led his unit through a very tough combat deployment, and brought all but one of his Marines home.[3]

A major I served with and respect tremendously said he was the best officer he ever served with.

Some stated that this lieutenant colonel was hard on his officers.

Others stated he was relieved to protect the career-advancement potential of his boss, a colonel (who has since been promoted to lieutenant general), that the firing was due to personality conflicts between the lieutenant colonel and colonel, and that Marine Corps officials excluded the enlisted Marines of the command from taking the command-climate survey that fueled the investigation that led to his relief.[4]

The whole thing was murky, but when the lieutenant colonel was relieved, he followed the Marine Corps' script and went quietly, stating that his relief was his colonel's prerogative and that he was not embarrassed by it.

And this I immediately knew to be bullshit.

So much of a Marine officer's identity is wrapped up in being a commander, and it is a life-changing event when one is relieved. It impacts everything, including your sense of self and your reputation among the tribe.

I'm not trying to accuse or defend this officer, but I'll tell you that I wasn't surprised when he reached out to Kate after she had been fired.

"My biggest regret in life," he told her, "is not fighting back."

By that time, Kate and I were already well down the warpath. We were committed to fighting back.

OK, let me back up for a second.

Kate saw her relief coming about five weeks before I did. She's always had this prescient gift. On recruiting duty, they called her the "Great Carnac," after the old Johnny Carson skit, because of her incredible accuracy in predicting future events related to recruiting statistics. Kate always seems to be two steps ahead of everyone else and able to read people and react faster to events than most. As I mentioned earlier, when we were living in Southern California in the early 2000s, we saw an accident on the freeway ahead of us. It took me a few seconds to process all that just took place, and by the time I did, Kate had—once again—already shot out from behind the steering wheel and was going from car to car to check on people.

Let's just agree now that she has a gift for grasping the reality of situations before others do.

So, when I told her that all of the drama would go away when the issue reached the first level of adult supervision in the chain of command, she responded, "No, I'm fucked. They are going to screw me over."

At that time, I was still optimistic and clung to a few shreds of faith that the senior leaders, many of whom I worked with from 2010 to 2015, would be fair.

Kate, on the other hand, was being coldly realistic. She wasn't being dramatic.

I knew she was right. It took me a day or so to finally accept that. And once I did, I did what I do best: I went into crisis planning.

I had been doing public relations for the Corps for nearly two decades. I served in the Pentagon for five and knew where many of the skeletons were buried. I had a lot of solid contacts in the press, relationships built on years of trust. And I also had contacts on Capitol Hill.

In anticipation of what was coming, I started reaching out to people I trusted and giving them the details of what was happening.

You see, there is an old PR trope attributed to Mark Twain, "The only reason god is good and the devil is evil is because god got to the press first."

As a PR pro, I know this to be true. The race was on.

I suspected that the Corps' leadership would try to drag her name and reputation through the mud, and I knew that if she had any shot, we had to beat them and be first to speak. After the story broke, it would live on the internet forever.

The Corps is used to being the 400-pound gorilla in the room and getting its way. It also has a PR machine that, as President Truman once said, was "almost equal to Stalin's."[5]

Because of this, a commander's typical reaction to being relieved is to lie in the gutter and allow the institution to stomp on his head for a week and then slink off into oblivion, never to be seen again—just like the lieutenant colonel I described a few moments ago.

No. Fuck that.

It was pretty clear to me: Kate was right. Williams and Haas were wrong. And this wasn't about Kate. It was about the greater issue of gender equality and fairness.

It was about the fact that Kate was committed to doing the right thing and didn't give a whit about rank or promotion.

And it was absolutely about the fact that, for decades, the Corps had been recruiting women to lower standards, training them to lower expectations, and then sending them to combat—and everyone was cool with that.

Again, no. Fuck that.

Remember that Gilbert Murray quote I told you about? The one about being careful when dealing with a man who is committed only to doing what is right?

What I also forgot to tell you was that I was into punk rock in the '80s—well before I was a Marine officer. That anti-authoritarian streak runs deep. It's in my DNA.

We weren't going to lie down. We were going to fight. Not just because it was personal, but because it was the right thing to do.

We didn't just do it for Kate. We needed every other Marine to understand that it's okay—and necessary—to fight back when you have an ethical, just cause. Kate likes to say, "It's either a matter of principle or it's not. If it's a matter of principle, then you need to act."

But there's always a price to be paid. That's the thing nobody ever tells you as a young lieutenant at Quantico. It's easy for the instructors there to tell lieutenants to, "always do the right thing." What they don't tell you is that if that right thing bucks the system, you have to be willing to pay that freight all the way to the end of the line—and that end of the line is most likely the end of your career. They don't tell you that when you speak out, the institution you love will probably turn on you and attack you. People you think are your friends will slink off into the shadows and abandon you. It will come at the expense of your family, your future, your sanity, and your financial well-being. On the hard, controversial issues, most big institutions don't want you to do the right thing. They want you to shut up and row.

Well, we were going to row, hard, against the tide.

I started reaching out to a few very trusted friends and mentors for advice. When you are close to the flame on an issue as deep and emotional as this, you should always seek counsel.

I started calling this board of advisers the "Vikings" in my longboat, and started seeing the Corps as the monastery on the hill, stuffed with monks and gold.

For motivation and to build my resolve in launching an attack upon the very institution I had served for twenty years, I started watching Nicolas Winding Refn's *Valhalla Rising* as I was trying to go to sleep every night. I thought that maybe I was starting to lose it a bit.

I knew we had to be careful engaging with the press, because Kate was still on active duty. The Marine Corps likes to trick you into thinking your First

Amendment rights are completely gone when you join the military, but you're well within your rights to speak out to defend yourself.

The day Kate was fired, a Pentagon contact of mine called to tell me he heard that General Dunford, the Commandant of the Marine Corps, told his staff that he didn't care who they had to keep up for twenty-four hours, but that he wanted a copy of the investigation leading to Kate's relief in the hands of the press the following morning. The higher-ups wanted to get their side of the story out first.

My source said that a member of the staff questioned Dunford's decision, asking him if he knew to whom she was married and if he knew that I had deep contacts with the press. According to my source, Dunford doubted that I would get involved. While I was unable to confirm this with a second source, I believe it to be true. It sounds like the Dunford I know, so I'll let that thought float with you for a bit.

Still, I was astounded things got to this point.

Think about it. Let's do a mental experiment together based on game theory.

Any issue involving women in the military receives increased scrutiny from lawmakers on Capitol Hill and the press—especially since, for years, the military has been failing in its efforts to address the issue of sexual assault.

Now let's consider a situation in which a female commander in the last all-female unit in the entire Department of Defense is making historic and sudden gains in female performance after decades of poor performance. Additionally, she is tightening discipline and holding Marines accountable for their actions.

And let's also consider that this officer's boss, with whom she has clashed, is three weeks away from transferring to another job on another base. He is demanding her relief.

If you were the decision-maker, what would you do?

Let's draw the quad and examine the potential outcomes.

If you back the male commander and fire his subordinate, the female commander, you'll have a firestorm in the press.

If you back the female commander, and reprimand the male commander, you'll have a firestorm in the press.

If you fire both of them, you'll have a firestorm in the press.

The only clean way through this minefield is to have them both put their guns back in their holsters, have the male commander transfer as scheduled, have the female commander report to you for three weeks, and start again fresh with the next regimental commander.

It's the only win-win solution.

This is why I was hopeful that adult leadership would step in.

Game theory.

Boy, was I wrong.

Okay, back to reality.

Not only was this a viable solution, but also my wife isn't the awful person the Marine Corps said she is.

I had emails from Williams spanning a period of months, in which he praised Kate's performance and admitted Haas was an issue.

Does that sound like someone who wants to fire my wife?

Nevertheless, my contacts in the Pentagon started telling me that the Corps planned to kill the messenger who proved that women could succeed if trained to higher expectations.

Shortly after Kate's relief on June 30, a reporter from *Marine Corps Times* called me and said, "Hey. This is really weird. I think they're gaming this." She said that the Marine Corps is never forthcoming with information about someone who's been fired—they usually hide behind the Freedom of Information Act and administrative-relief rules. "But not only did they give me Kate's investigation," she told me, "they also made comments that I took as a swipe against your wife, which I thought was unprofessional."

This conversation corroborated my Pentagon source's account of the commandant telling his staff to release their investigation on Kate to the press.

Reporters are inquisitive by nature. That's cool. It's their job. But it is highly unusual to have a reporter call you to say that the Marine Corps was offering up *too much* information. That further confirmed my suspicion that the folks at Headquarters Marine Corps were mounting an information campaign against Kate.

I had to move fast and strike from an unexpected direction.

The brass would be watching for the story to first break in *Marine Corps Times*.

That's the way things usually go.

So I reached out to Gretel Kovach, a war correspondent I knew at the *San Diego Union-Tribune*. Gretel had spent a lot of time covering Marines in combat, and she was also reporting on the Marine Corps' gender-integration efforts. I gave her a call and caught her as she was driving from Twentynine Palms back to her office in San Diego. She was willing to hear me out. During the conversation, she told me that she had been getting jerked around on the gender-integration story, as far as getting correct information, so she was already cautious about what the Marine Corps was putting out about Kate.

From what I gathered, her impression was that the Marine Corps wanted the narrative to be that Kate was a toxic commander and they did something about it, but Gretel wasn't buying that.

On July 2, 2015, Gretel published a story titled "Marines Sack Commander of Female Boot Camp Training" and described Kate's repeated clashes with her leadership over the issue of gender bias and its negative impacts on female performance. Here's a snippet.

Kovach wrote: "Germano . . . has been outspoken about what she sees as lower expectations for female recruits and a lack of male-female competition at boot camp, which she feels hurts performance."

And an officer who served with Kate said she "lost her job because of a difference in philosophy about the future of women in the Marine Corps."

The officer said: "She is the kind of strong-caliber leader the Marine Corps needs. Firm, with high expectations, fair and compassionate. . . ."

In the PR industry, we call this the moment a story starts "going sideways" on you. Clearly there was more to the story than the Corps' "toxic commander" narrative. I wanted the public to know that.

Gretel also told me that while she was researching my claim, a Marine Corps general called her to tell her that he had served with Colonel Haas, that he thought Haas was a weak leader, and that his one regret was not being in a position to do more to protect Kate. Unsolicited from me, she was getting information from her contacts in the Marine Corps.

In the meantime, the Marine Corps seemed to be doing its best to disparage Kate and was handing out copies of the investigation into Kate's command, which we had not yet seen, to reporters.[6] I have no doubt that the Corps expected its negative version to come out in *Marine Corps Times* and set the tone for the story going forward.

Gretel's story came out first.

My contacts in the Pentagon told me that this had an "unbalancing" effect on the leadership. They started to realize we weren't following the lay-in-the-gutter-and-take-it pattern of behavior for relieved commanders.

I asked several people to speak up for Kate to help us tell her story. They did, unanimously.

I also asked Kate if we should contact her sergeant major.

"She and I have talked about this," Kate said. "I'm sure she will."

But when Kate called, nobody answered the phone.

So she tried emailing her as she was heading home to Maryland from South Carolina: "Would you be willing to speak, without attribution, to the media?"

Sergeant Major responded by saying that she'd really like to put this behind her, that she was sorry, and that she wished she could help.

I texted the sergeant major and she responded that she wasn't turning her back on Kate but that she needed to get into recovery mode after everything that went down.

It was pretty clear to me that Judith Iscariot was taking her thirty pieces of silver and going home.

I suspect that the sergeant major had received the loyalty speech from the depot sergeant major, which probably went something like: "This is going South. Germano's a sinking ship. You're either going to stay afloat and be strong for the battalion and the Marines, or it's curtains for you. It's your choice."

So she did what most people would do and went with the flow.

Marines always want to thump their chests and talk about what's important and matters of principle. But when it comes to standing up to the institution, most Marines will flinch most of the time. It's the rare few who take action and speak out against the tribe.

It was supremely disappointing, but mobbing theory explains why she gave up on Kate.

Loyalty to the institution is important in the Corps, and it carries a tremendous amount of pressure.

Recently, a friend of ours broke the story on the Marines United scandal—in which nearly 30,000 Marines and Marine Corps veterans were cyber-stalking active-duty women and posting nude photos of women they didn't like online—a classic case of revenge porn.

Our reporter friend had served in the Marine Corps but had been out for a few years. He told me that he went to the Corps in good faith with the evidence he collected, but the Marine Corps' leadership and public affairs officials didn't like where he was going. During a meeting, he said these officials questioned his loyalty to the Corps and asked whether he was a Marine first or a reporter first.

Loyalty.

So much for the Corps' stated organizational values of honor, courage, and commitment.

Don't get me wrong. I love the Marines, but I want to see the Corps live up to its ideals.

Here's the thing: the Marines and the Marine Corps are two entirely different entities. It took me a while to understand that.

Navigating the media onslaught was tough. It's not easy when your house becomes a glass box, but, in a crisis, you just have to embrace it and use it to your advantage. You have to fight on the ground you are on—not on the ground you wished to be upon.

The media's coverage helped Kate see that she had it right and she wasn't alone. Crucibles like this inevitably make you start to question your own sanity. At one point, she said, "Isn't it sad that the American public gets it, and the military doesn't? The public expects female Marines to be able to run and shoot. I'm not losing my mind."

For us, this never was about Kate. It was about the greater, higher purpose: creating a better training environment for women so that they could perform better. By increasing female performance, Kate and her team were helping build a more operationally capable Marine Corps. This is obvious. It's common sense. But the Corps leadership wasn't getting it. I don't think they wanted to get it, because it eroded their arguments against integrating ground-combat units.

As we engaged the media, we carefully reinforced that point. Kate didn't wallow in self-pity. She didn't complain about the command. She unrelentingly pressed her point that the Corps was failing women, that decades of data proved this, that the leadership didn't care or were oblivious to the fact that they were sending women to combat with inferior training compared to men, and that this was wrong. If the Corps is going to send Marines into harm's way, the women need to be trained as well as the men.

A few days later, Dave Philipps at the *New York Times* released a story titled, "Marine Commander's Firing Stirs Debate on Women in the Corps."[7]

Presto! Now we were firing on all cylinders.

Philipps wrote: "To many advocates of full gender integration, Colonel Germano's dismissal has raised questions about the willingness of the Marine Corps, the most male-dominated of the services, to open the door to women in leadership roles. Why, those advocates ask, should a service that reveres its tradition of tough and demanding male commanders have problems with one who is a woman?"

When I read his article, I had a mental image—that moment in the movies when a lit match floats through the air and touches a puddle of gasoline. Contact.

A few days later, Kate heard from Colonel Keenan at the *Marine Corps Gazette*, who told her he was tabling the piece she submitted in April criticizing the Corps' recruiting and training practices and offering recommendations for improvement. It would not be published. Like many retired colonels, Keenan was stepping to the commandant's tune. Kate was dejected.

I reached out to my friend Chris Chivers, who ran the *New York Times* blog *At War*, and let him know what was going on.

Chivers, a former Marine Corps infantry officer and Pulitzer Prize winner, has, shall we say, a very robust understanding of the politics of the Corps.

On July 28, he published a piece in which he asked Keenan to explain his decision to suppress Kate's article, and then Chivers published the paper Kate wrote in full. Chivers is a fair man and a solid reporter, and he always calls it like he sees it. I'm eternally grateful he published Kate's piece and allowed her ideas to come to the light of day.

As he summarized it: "Colonel Germano was relieved of command at Parris Island in June under circumstances that remain contentious, setting off a controversy about whether she was being punished for what the Corps calls an abusive leadership style, or for forcefully expressing her views about the how the Corps trains and integrates women into its male-dominated ranks."[8]

A funny thing started to happen.

Kate's willingness to speak up forced the Corps into having a national discussion about gender integration about six months before they wanted to, and people on both the right and the left started rallying behind her.

We had people on the left contacting us to say, "Proud of you and all that you are doing to advance rights and fair treatment for women!"

At the same time, we had the Fox News crowd contacting her to say, "Go Germano! She's calling for higher standards for women! (And she's saying all the non-PC stuff I didn't have the balls to say while I was on active duty.)"

It was bizarre. It was amazing. It was beautiful.

As I see it, in trying to deliberately torch Kate's reputation, the commandant and his generals had unintentionally set their own house on fire.

My Pentagon contacts started reporting back that leadership was confused by and fixated with her. They told me that every new media report about Kate was briefed at the next commandant's staff meeting.

Eventually, we started to see some humor in the situation. The next time a story posted that included her position, I told her that I could hear the Headquarters Marine Corps brass in the Pentagon standing up with the article clenched in a shaking fist, veins bulging, eyes popping, and screaming, "Germaaaaaaaaaaannnnnnnnooooooooooo!" It was the first time I saw her laugh in months. To this day, every time one of our op-eds gets published, we look at each other, shake our fists, and scream, "Germaaaaaaaaaaannnnnnoooooooooo!" and laugh and laugh. If you don't laugh, you'll go insane. Trust me.

I'd like to think that, in some small way, we contributed to the gender-integration policy change of December 2015 when we saw Secretary of Defense Ash Carter rescind the policy excluding women from ground-combat jobs and reaffirming that women could join the infantry, armor, artillery, and other ground-combat arms units if they could meet the standards.

Shortly after Kate was fired, General Bob Neller was selected to replace Dunford as the Marine commandant. Dunford had been selected to serve as the chairman of the Joint Chiefs of Staff. During Neller's confirmation hearing on July 23 before the Senate Armed Services Committee, something special happened. Senator Kirsten Gillibrand, when it was her turn to question Neller, asked about where he stood on gender integration. She also mentioned Kate by name after discussing the issue of chain-of-command retaliation in the Corps:

> I know in the case of Colonel Kate Germano, she was trying to create even tougher requirements for them so they can meet standards. As you look at your standard review and as you look as to whether you are going to ask for waivers for any positions today, I would urge you not to seek waivers, because all you are saying is that there is no one who can meet the standards today. If we begin to create tougher standards to come into the Marines and begin to make them gender neutral, you will begin to have women who can meet those standards. They just might not be able to meet those standards today. So asking for a waiver says under no circumstances can any woman ever meet the standard. I would caution you not to take that action.[9]

It's rare for a Senator to name a field-grade officer by name. The implied message: I'm watching, so stop messing with Germano.

We kept a steady drum beat in the press during the summer and fall of 2015. It had to start dawning on the brass that this story wasn't going away.

I was in New York City on December 3, 2015, when my phone rang. A Pentagon contact called to say Secretary of Defense Ash Carter was going to announce the repeal of the Combat Exclusion Policy for women and open all military jobs and units to women who can meet the standards.[10] I rushed back to my hotel room to watch the press conference on my laptop. It felt really good to know that Kate contributed in some way to that decision.

On March 23, 2017, I learned that Private First Class Maria Daume graduated from the School of Infantry and would be the first woman to be awarded the 0311 military occupational specialty. She headed out to the fleet and was assigned to our friend Lieutenant Colonel Warren Cook's 2nd Battalion, 4th Marine Corps Regiment.[11] She was in good hands. A few Marines in the unit made some sexist remarks about her. Warren stomped that out quickly.[12] We hear she's hard as a coffin nail and doing great. She was born in a Siberian prison camp.[13] No joke.

"I like to prove people wrong," Daume told Voice of America in her first interview since completing her training at the Marine Corps School of Infantry at Camp Lejeune, North Carolina. "No matter what your belief is, you can't argue that I didn't do it, because I did."[14]

On September 28, 2017, we learned that a female second lieutenant graduated from the Corps' Infantry Officer School.[15] As of today, the senior leadership seems to be playing games by not releasing her name. We don't know her identity, but we do know she is remarkable and we celebrate her success.

I like to think that Kate had a little something to do with helping create these conditions. She certainly forced the conversation.

It's gratifying to see these women smashing through walls of low expectations—proving the naysayers wrong. These are clear wins.

But we can talk about mobbing theory and we can talk about the future of gender integration, and we can talk about wins, and none of it will change how it felt for Kate to have the senior leadership of the Corps attack her reputation. She's a Marine. She's a good Marine. She's kind and strong and stable, and they attacked every piece of her, bit by bit, until she questioned everything she had known about herself.

Two weeks after she was relieved, we went back down to South Carolina to retrieve her belongings from her apartment. We still hadn't received an official copy of the investigation, despite Kate having requested it during the meeting in which Williams relieved her, and despite the Marine Corps leadership releasing it to the press.

With her in the passenger seat of a big U-Haul truck, I pulled into the parking lot next to the depot headquarters—Williams's headquarters.

On a quiet Saturday morning, I met with Williams's executive officer to pick up her official orders assigning her to a dusty closet at the Navy Yard—heading the Department of the Navy's parole board.

It was awkward as hell, and I was still pissed.

The XO met me at the door and offered a cheery, "Good morning!"

I just bored into him with my eyes.

The look on my face cut him short.

He turned away and unlocked the door.

I followed him in and picked up her orders, and I saw that the heavily redacted investigation was included.

I was still pissed that the press had it immediately after her relief; but it took us two weeks to get a copy.

Let's just say I was devoid of warmth in my interaction with the XO.

He couldn't get me out of there fast enough.

As I pulled away behind the wheel of that U-Haul, all I could think of was Kate and how glad I was that she was still next to me in one piece.

I told her that she'd be okay.

And that we'd figure out the next steps together.

She did the right thing.

She stood up for what she believed in.

I was so goddamn proud of her that it took all of my strength not to break down on the spot.

CHAPTER 30

COMMAND PERFORMANCE

That drive from South Carolina to just outside of Washington, DC, where Joe and I lived was always a long one. After you get to North Carolina, it's essentially nothing but flat farm fields occasionally interrupted by scraggly pine trees and signs for barbecue joints and strip clubs. But that day, that awful day, it felt like the longest ride of my life. Luckily, I had Mr. Fitzwizzle to keep me company.

I think I might have mentioned that there were days leading up to my relief of command where the pendulum would swing, leaving me feeling despondent and confused. Late in the evening on those days, I would pull up to the crazy pink Victorian house where I rented a small ground-floor apartment, and I would think about quitting.

Worse, I questioned my own sanity. I simply could not understand what was happening.

When I began my tour at Parris Island, I thought it would be my redemption tour as a CO. Unlike when I was a CO on recruiting duty, I was not going to handle every problem as if it were a nail and I was the hammer. I would not use profanity or raise my voice with my Marines, because I didn't need to prove how tough I was. I was going to be authentic. Me.

And I had done just that.

Yet, there I was, pulling up to that apartment, with complaints against me piling up. Although I knew that I had done the right things for the right reasons, the investigation caused me to question myself. Did they see something I didn't? Were they right and I wrong? I felt like I couldn't quite grasp reality, even with the facts so glaringly obvious in front of me. By the time mid-June rolled around, I was a wreck. I had lost a ton of weight, and I cried every day. I felt terrible for Joe and my dad, because all I could talk about was the investigation and the complaints about my leadership. They dominated every second of every waking hour.

In May, as things started deteriorating with Colonel Haas, I remember texting my dad and telling him that no matter what, I knew I was doing the right things, but that I never wanted to cause him any embarrassment. He always responded that I could never embarrass him and that he was proud of me for taking a stand. He and his girlfriend, Kathy, whom Joe and I love, were well aware of the struggles I had with Colonel Haas and my executive officer. My dad especially understood because he had experienced similar situations in the Army. But for as much comfort as he, Kathy, and Joe provided, I was putting a lot of pressure on myself to not let people down, and that pressure made things even worse.

When I got home from work at night, the darkest thoughts would swirl around in my brain.

Maybe it would be better for everyone if I just killed myself.

But then, as I sat in my car, thinking these awful things, Mr. Fitz would appear at the window by the front door, meet my gaze, and meow.

He may have been just asking for his dinner, but I swear he is the most empathetic animal on the planet, and he provided me with so much comfort during those dark days. That long drive home to Maryland was no different. For eight hours, that cat sat curled up on my lap, while I alternated between crying and being angry. I kept thinking about the meeting with Brigadier General Williams that morning, and how he had started off by saying how much it hurt him "to do this because I am a big fan," and then had proceeded to say that the equal-opportunity investigator had not substantiated my complaints regarding gender bias and a hostile work environment, and that the investigation into my leadership had revealed that I had been abusive to my Marines.

As I drove, I thought about the note I had sent to my company commanders:

> Ladies,
>
> I am so very sorry to have to burden you with this, but I wanted you to hear it from me first. The commanding general just relieved me for loss of trust and confidence in my ability to command. The results of my EO investigation did not substantiate gender bias on the depot or a toxic environment with the Recruit Training Regiment, but [the investigating officer's] investigation did substantiate that I had established a hostile work environment in my own battalion.
>
> They have already identified a replacement for me, and the XO and Sergeant Major will ensure a sound transition. Please go to them for support until

the new CO is on board. I would also ask that you treat her with the same professional courtesy and warmth you have shown me.

Many battalion members past and present will celebrate my departure. I ask, for the sake of the Marines, that you do your best to control the message. The last thing the battalion needs is more conflict, gossip, and rumors.

I so have appreciated the opportunity to work with you and see you grow, and wish you the very best of luck.

Please let me know if I can be of assistance to you in the future.

V/R,

LtCol Germano

And I thought about the response I received on my Blackberry about ten minutes later, from the new Papa Company commander:

Ma'am,

I am so very sorry to hear this news.

I want you to know that I truly appreciate everything that you have done for us, and for me personally. You are an amazing example of what strong leadership is supposed to be like, and I have learned more lessons from you than I probably realize now.

I hope that you are proud of what you have done for this battalion, even if some people don't understand. My brother-in-law once told me to never forget that I don't work for my superior officers, I work for my Marines.

You have done that for us, ma'am, and there are many of us in this battalion who see that.

You should leave here with your head held high, ma'am.

I will do my best to do as you have asked ma'am, but I will also continue to hold Marines accountable.

Thank you for your support and advice.

For eight hours, I distilled my thoughts into two problem areas: first, that Colonel Haas had succeeded in firing me because I hadn't fully appreciated his guidance from our initial meeting that he "prized harmony above all else." I was foolish to have thought that he wasn't keeping a secret list of my transgressions.

Second, something didn't smell right about the equal-opportunity investigation results. After all, the legal definition of *gender bias* is the "unequal treatment in employment opportunity (such as promotion, pay, benefits and privileges), and expectations due to attitudes based on the sex of an employee or group of employees."[1] Decades of substandard performance results by the female recruits at Parris Island substantiated that there were clearly lowered expectations for their performance because they were women.

Worse, I didn't know exactly what was in the investigation into my leadership, and had no idea what the specific allegations had been about my leadership. I was sick about it, and by the time I got home to Joe, I was frazzled.

I would find out what was in the investigation in an unexpected and public way.

Normally, when a CO is relieved of command due to reasons not involving legal misconduct, the Marine Corps public affairs department sends out a generic statement to the press stating that the officer was relieved for "lack of trust and confidence" in their ability to lead.

In my case, the Marine Corps took an unprecedented approach. I learned from a reporter that she had a copy of the investigation within twenty-four hours, which corroborates what Joe had heard.

Continuing to deviate from normal public-affairs protocol, when asked why I had been relieved, depot representatives said that I had disobeyed orders, I had abused my Marines, and that the depot had investigated because my Marines had told the leadership they were being mistreated.[2]

Twelve days later, the *New York Times* posted a detailed article about my relief, as well as links to both the damning command investigation into my leadership and the equal-opportunity investigation based on my complaints.[3] They were posted online for all the world to see.

The investigations consisted of pages and pages of redacted, or blacked-out names—horrible statements about someone named Kate Germano, a female Marine who was mean and abusive to her subordinates.

I didn't recognize this person.

As I laid out in my command philosophy, I was accountable for everything my Marines did or didn't do. I get that 100 percent. For any of my Marines to say that I never admit when I'm wrong is simply unfair, because I'm the first one to say I make mistakes every day. I'm not the smartest person on the planet, and making mistakes is part of learning. I admit that there were times when I did things wrongly and my frustration got the best of me.

Were there times I rolled my eyes during meetings? Most likely.

Were there times I got irritated with my executive officer in front of others? I think that is true.

Did I take issue with DIs who were cruel to each other and their recruits? Yes.

Did I express dissatisfaction with company commanders who did not take ownership of their companies by leading, mentoring, and holding their Marines accountable? Absolutely.

But here's the thing: I was not wrong for having high standards for my Marines and recruits.

I was right about the rifle range.

I was right that the recruiters weren't holding female recruits accountable for preparing mentally and physically to succeed in training.

I was right to try to bring order to the chaos of Fourth Battalion by eliminating DI and recruit abuse, and by leading with facts and not feelings.

And after trying to get the regiment and depot leadership to see how segregation perpetuated negative expectations for women in training, I was absolutely right to pen my article.

I knew some of my Marines didn't like me. But had I ever been mean, used abusive language, or blamed victims for being sexually assaulted? Absolutely not. Never. Ever.

I knew that I had held those same Marines accountable for abusing recruits or for not doing their jobs, and that there were malcontents in the battalion. But when I read the investigation into my leadership, I was struck by the lack of evidence to support the findings. As I read page after page, the legal officer in me kept expecting to find some damning statement: Germano slapped a recruit. Germano gave an unlawful order. Germano mouthed off to her commander. Instead, the investigation is filled with unsubstantiated complaints related to whether or not my Marines thought I was nice or I was mean.

The first part of a command investigation is the "findings of fact." Each finding of fact is not just a statement, it's a statement that should be corroborated by multiple witness statements. After all, as in the American justice system, under the military justice system, the rights of the accused are just as important as the rights of the accuser.

But instead of ensuring each finding of fact was corroborated by multiple witnesses or sources, the investigating officer had turned unsubstantiated claims made by some of my Marines into incontrovertible truths. It was also striking that in the statements included as enclosures to the investigation, several Marines said good things about my leadership and the command climate. Yet out of more than one hundred findings of fact, only a handful of positive observations were included.

And the most damning thing of all for the Marine Corps? I was never interviewed by the investigating officer. As a legal officer having completed and reviewed countless investigations, I knew that I should have been interviewed and asked specific questions about the accusations, but, shockingly, that never happened. And I was dumbstruck when I realized that the five-inch stack of counseling documents I had provided to the investigating officer was not included in the investigation as an enclosure. The papers had simply disappeared.

The investigating officer had only asked me to write a statement about how I perceived my command climate. I provided him a detailed nine-page statement describing the environment of the battalion when I took command, all of the changes we had made, and friction points due to some of the personnel and Marines who were averse to change. But my statement was only referenced in the finding of facts four times.

It is clear to me that the investigation was heavily biased to come to a particular conclusion: that I was the problem and the culture of the Marine Corps was not.

If you look at only the investigative report, you'll see that the Marines who had received bad counseling statements from me came off looking like they were performing flawlessly, and I came off looking like a ranting lunatic whose high standards were somehow impossible for my Marines and recruits to achieve. The investigating officer made it sound like it was irrational of me to want my female recruits to be able to shoot as well as their male counterparts. He implied that somehow, by requiring my Marines to ensure our female recruits were able to run faster and shoot more accurately, I was making impossible demands of them, despite the fact that these same high expectations were levied in each of the male training battalions daily.

He stated that I was "obsessed with equality" and that, in seeking to make my female recruits competitive with their male counterparts, my standards for performance were unattainable.

The equal-opportunity investigation into my complaints of gender bias and a hostile work environment with Colonel Haas wasn't much better in terms of legal sufficiency. Oddly enough, the investigator interviewed all of my peers to figure out if they thought there was gender bias on the recruit depot. But the investigating officer never defined what gender bias actually is, and, instead, she asked them about whether they knew of any instances related to gender "discrimination."

But discrimination and bias are not the same thing. In fact, the legal definition of *gender discrimination* is "any action that specifically denies opportunities, privileges, or rewards to a person (or a group) because of gender."[4] If gender bias is having different expectations for a group of people based on gender, it seemed to me that the decades of substandard performance by female recruits clearly indicated gender bias existed at Parris Island. Despite being provided the same slide deck laying out the differences between the male and female recruit graduation scores that I had provided to the battalion, the equal-opportunity investigator did not refer to the data in her findings.

And while she did note that there was evidence that the relationship between me and Colonel Haas was a bad one, she did not find that it met the definition of a hostile work environment.

In reading the equal-opportunity investigation on the *New York Times* website, I found that the investigating officer did make several recommendations based on my complaint. But the really odd thing is that the commanding general of Training and Education Command, Major General Lukeman, didn't concur with any of her recommendations. In his endorsement to the investigation, he basically said that there was no gender bias and that Colonel Haas was not the problem, I was, and that I wouldn't admit it. Because he overturned the investigating officer's findings, which, legally, he was permitted to do, he was able to say in his endorsement that the investigators found nothing to substantiate my claims.

In other words, the Marine Corps was an equal-opportunity employer.

Until I saw the statement Haas gave to the investigating officer, I never knew how many things I had done wrong, in his eyes, as a commander. I never knew that he was angry with me for the recruiting emails. I knew that we had disagreed, but by the end of the conversation, all he said, was, "Okay, I got it, just make sure you cc me on the emails."

Going off of that, I was thinking, "Okay. Minor victory," and then I was moving forward (copying him on those emails, as he requested).

In his statement, he said that that was when our relationship started to go downhill. He also claimed that I fired the November Company CO in December expressly against his guidance. That's not true.

The complaints made me sound like a horrible officer, but not one worthy of being fired. And I could easily connect most of the complaints to the person whose name had been blacked out based on what he or she said. Digging in, the people who had gotten in trouble had the most to say.

Papa Company's commander alleged that she was losing weight because of the stress of dealing with me and that I blamed her when her recruits fell behind on an integrated hike with the male recruits. Guilty. She said I lectured her and her Marines for not taking responsibility, for being afraid of adversity, and for blaming me for being mean when I held them accountable for poor performance. Guilty, guilty, guilty.

One Marine said in her statement that I yelled at my XO when she was "openly defiant" with me.

Yup.

The company commander I fired after a month's worth of morning mentoring sessions? She said in her statement that she didn't enjoy that. I imagine anyone required to meet with her boss every morning because her performance had been so poor would feel the same way.

Another company commander said that, even though she was proud of the progress her recruits had made, I was upset because they had performed below average on the rifle range and in physical fitness.

Seriously?

In statements, several Marines wrote that I had said that sexual assault is "100 percent preventable" and that "by drinking, you are putting yourself in a position to be sexually assaulted." I did not. I told them not to put themselves in a position where they could be hurt, and that although the rapist is always wrong, you never want to have to deal with that after the fact.

My XO complained that I isolated her from the other officers after she decided to survey them about whether I was a good commander.

I stand by that decision.

It gets "worse": The XO said that I said only "congratulations" to one drill instructor after good results at the rifle range, while going out of my way to say nice things about everyone else. Sometimes, she said, I hugged one person but not another. And she said in her statement that I used extreme language with her, such as saying she was "allowing [the staff] to run amok!"

Clearly some of these "offenses" seem silly now, but if I can see that, why didn't anyone else question it?

The operations officer who gave me the hand and walked out on me to do pull-ups after I admonished her for not setting up an all-hands meeting when I requested it? She talks about it in her statement, but no one questioned that this lower-ranking officer walked out of my office while I was talking to her. Anywhere else in the Marine Corps, that kind of disrespect would be considered unbecoming of any Marine, much less an officer.

In their statements, the Marines said I was moody; that, in front of recruits,

I corrected drill instructors who had behaved badly; and that I treated Marines who performed their jobs well in a more friendly manner than I treated Marines who were not performing well.

In the investigation, the whole problem was me. Full stop. Kate is the only problem.

I'm sure I was bawling by the time I got to Sergeant Major's statement from the investigation into my leadership. While she didn't say anything bad, she didn't say anything amazing, either—nothing that speaks to the fact that we spent all of our time together and that she was texting my husband to say that she wished she could do more to support me.

After the command-climate results came out, about three weeks before I was relieved, she had told me the Sergeant Major of the Marine Corps called her and asked what the heck was going on at Fourth Battalion. She said that her response to him was that the command-climate results were not accurate. But, after reviewing her statement from the investigation, I think he was already talking to her about what she needed to do to continue her career in the Marine Corps. And, clearly, that meant distancing herself from me, or she might not make it through her tour successfully.

One of her comments hurt me deeply. In her statement about my leadership, she claimed that because I was out with the Marines three quarters of every day, they couldn't trust me. In other words, I micromanaged them by spending so much time with them, thereby creating a sense of distrust. In her statement, Sergeant Major said that our relationship was "not personal," even though she acknowledged that she was the person I was closest to at Parris Island. She said we didn't go to many events together, because she felt like "our Marines won't trust us if we are always around." Sergeant major said I "was always 'so there' that even the good ones feel they are not trusted."

This contrasts sharply with our shared experiences. My sergeant major and I went everywhere together, both to set the example of what a command relationship should look like and to ensure that the Marines knew there was no daylight between us. We were a united front. I cared about her deeply as a human being, and she and I had the deepest conversations about everything from family and kids to slavery and racism. She would send me thank-you notes, thanking me for everything I was doing for the Marines, for the battalion, and even got a container of Goldfish crackers personalized with our photo because she knew I was crazy about snacking on them. When she worried about not being able to participate in morning physical-fitness events with the recruits and Marines because she had morning "kid duty" or was injured, I allayed her concerns. After she had surgery, I visited her and her kids at home and brought her all kinds of "get well" goodies. I even went to her daughter's birthday party.

Reading her statements and then reflecting back on the relationship I thought I had with her was like having an out-of-body experience. The weirdest part? It was as if her statement to the equal-opportunity investigating officer had been written by someone else. It was much more upbeat about my leadership, and it laid out the challenges I had experienced with the regiment.

In the equal-opportunity investigation, the tone of her statement is akin to, "Hey, we're trying to make all this progress here. We've had some problems, but we've made progress. Yeah, she's out there a lot. She sees what's going on. She's had run-ins with her boss. It's bad for the battalion because it creates a tension that doesn't need to be there." But that was the worst thing that was in her statement.

Her statement in the investigation about my leadership, on the other hand, was completely damning. It seems as if you have one person giving two different statements to different people who have two different agendas, and they're both writing their statements to reflect their specific agenda. Yet no one looked at that and said, "Hey, wait a minute. Why is the sergeant major saying in one report that there were problems, but progress was being made, but in another report that everything is terrible"?

Ironically, after reading the two investigations online, it became more clear to me than ever before that the Marine Corps has serious cultural problems related to gender. Segregated boot camp for men and women and decades of substandard performance by female recruits? They were just the tip of the iceberg.

And while the Marine Corps might have thought that by trying to humiliate me in the media, I would crawl away from Parris Island with my tail between my legs and my mouth shut, they were sorely mistaken.

To me, gender equality in the military is a matter of principle, and I had just found my voice.

I was not going to go away quietly.

CHAPTER 31

EQUAL OPPORTUNIST

Kate-

You don't know me, but we met a couple of times in the Pentagon- I saw you in the gym here almost every day.

I think what has happened to you is a miscarriage of the Marine Corps system, and that you are being held to a ridiculous double standard. You are precisely the kind of officer and leader we need over the next ten years, and the Marine Corps has made a big mistake in how they handled your situation.

Hang in there. A similar thing happened to me, and I have recovered. You will, too. Keep your chin up- a lot of people are behind you.

Semper Fidelis-

Stan Coerr

GS-15

Marine Aviation

When I got home, I was so depressed that there were days when I didn't want to get out of bed. I was exhausted mentally and physically. I didn't want to eat and was so skinny that Joe later said I looked like a scarecrow. But he forced me to focus on our action plan. Joe would not let me quit, and every day before he would head to work, he would brief me on my "to do" list.

We knew I had to have a clear plan for engaging with the media. But I insisted that I didn't want the stories to focus on me. Even in my haze of depression and utter humiliation, I knew that my firing was never about how I had treated my Marines. It was bigger than that: The Marine Corps simply did not want to change the status quo for women, no matter the negative impact on our ability to fight and win battles.

I focused on telling the media the story of how the Marine Corps had systematically held women back from greatness through poor recruiting practices, and then by segregating them in training and holding them to lowered expectations for performance. And the funny thing? I didn't tell the story to give the Marine Corps a black eye. As anyone who is committed to an institution, faith, or belief will tell you, those who care most for the success of organizations are often the change agents who create the most friction by rocking the boat. The institution was not the problem—the senior leaders were.

The Marine Corps talks a big game about how it is the service with the highest standards and most stringent qualification requirements for enlistment. Yet, for decades, this has not been true for women. With less than 9 percent of the total force made up of women, historically there has been no real focus to ensure that recruiters work to enlist the highest-caliber women. I knew this from two tours on recruiting duty and my year-long stint at Parris Island. Instead of focusing on recruiting top female high school athletes the way we do for men, we have allowed less-qualified women, with little screening or scrutiny, to join.

While data shows that the most successful recruits in boot camp are those who go to training fresh out of high school, the women who typically join the Marine Corps walk into the recruiting office a few years after high school, when they have failed at college, employment, and relationships. In essence, these women join the Marine Corps as a last resort. That, though not optimal, might be okay. But Marine Corps recruiters further their female recruits' odds of failure by not properly preparing them mentally for what to expect in recruit training, as indicated by the high rate of mental-health discharges for female recruits. Historically, recruiters have not done a good job of holding their female applicants to improving their physical-fitness ability before going to boot camp, which explains the high rates of failure on the initial strength test and lower-extremity injury rates for women at Parris Island. Female applicants are nothing more to their recruiters than a check in the block—they are quota satisfiers as opposed to people the recruiters actually invest in to the same degree that they do with their male applicants.

There is also a high discomfort factor for many recruiters in working with female applicants. Sadly, this is a reflection of the poor state of gender affairs in the Marine Corps. Because so many recruiters get into trouble for having inappropriate relationships with their female applicants, the perception by many is that they should avoid female applicants for fear that the recruits will raise allegations of impropriety. Just as we are seeing with the backlash against the #MeToo movement today, there are a whole lot of male Marines who think that the only way to protect themselves is to avoid one-on-one interaction with female applicants and Marines at any cost.

I can't tell you the number of times I have heard a male Marine say that he would never have a closed-door counseling session with a female Marine in his charge, because he didn't want to risk his career. We hear men in the corporate sector saying the same thing following the #MeToo movement. To me, this is a cop-out. If male Marines treated women as valued members of the team, just as they do with their male counterparts, there would never be a need to fear allegations of wrongdoing. Here's my proof: As a woman Marine, I was still expected to lead male and female Marines throughout my career. When I was in command on recruiting, I was expected to lead my male and female recruiters and applicants—including one-on-one. Leadership and performance expectations should be no different for women, and I wanted to stress this point with the media.

I also wanted to educate the public about the limitations presented by the very construction of Fourth Battalion itself. Want to know why there aren't more women in the Marine Corps? Look no further than the squad bays on the female recruit compound. I don't think there was some nefarious thinking that went into the design of the battalion to keep the percentage of women at 10 percent or less. It isn't a conspiracy issue—it is reality. If you were to compare a male training-battalion squad bay with a squad bay from Fourth Battalion, you would see right off the bat how much smaller the female squad bays are. There's simply not enough room for more female recruits at Fourth Battalion.

It doesn't take a genius to add up the potential bed spaces at Fourth Battalion and see that the maximum throughput per year is capped at approximately 3,200 female recruits, compared to male recruit throughput of 5,300 per male training battalion each year. When you add that women are trained at only one of two recruit depots in the Marine Corps, you see that there is an enormous difference in the throughput of male and female recruits. By my calculation, a total of approximately 32,000 male recruits are trained at Parris Island and San Diego each year, compared to just 3,200 women.[1] Since women make up 51 percent of the US population, it is staggering to consider how much talent the Marine Corps misses out on each year, all because of space limitations and a reluctance by male senior leaders to increase the number of women in the force. And, in my view, for the Marine Corps to solve its sexual assault and harassment issues, increasing the number of women in the service would help change and improve the culture.

Finally, I wanted to ensure that the public was made aware of the major disparities in performance and expectations for male and female recruits. The

Marine Corps has long justified segregated boot camp by saying that separation is the only way to instill confidence in women. I believe that confidence can only come by helping a person achieve higher results than she ever thought she could—just as we expect from our male recruits. It might be different if the Marine Corps had never held women to lower standards in training because of assumptions about gender. If, for example, they had maintained segregated training and produced results on par with those of the male recruits, it would be harder to argue that segregation was bad. But forty years of recruit graduation scores don't lie. This data is collected and maintained by the regimental operations section, so it isn't as though the scores are not readily available for comparison and analysis by the regimental CO. I wanted people—the media and members of Congress—to start asking the Marine Corps hard questions about its recruiting and training methods for women.

During my year at Parris Island, my Marines had shown the Marine Corps that women were capable of achieving better results than anyone had ever thought possible. I wanted the public to know that women could keep up with men, both on the rifle range and on the PT field, as long as we expect them to do so. In other words, all of the Marine leaders who espoused the idea that the female form is inherently limiting were wrong.

And it was a critical time to get the message out to the public about why the Marine Corps couldn't afford to maintain the status quo for how it recruited and trained women. Just a few months after I was relieved, the secretary of defense announced his intention to open up all jobs and units to women, including the infantry. Truth be told, I was originally not a fan of women in the infantry. When I first got to Parris Island, I harbored doubts that we would ever be able to find women who were capable of doing the job, because I knew the Marine Corps had historically not focused on recruiting physically fit women and then training them to high standards.

But after we implemented our action plan to improve the performance of our female recruits, I quickly realized that when women were held to higher expectations, they could keep up with their male counterparts. My thinking on women in the infantry changed when I realized that we would arbitrarily limit the talent pool if, simply because of their gender, we denied the opportunity to women who were capable of doing the job. The more I thought about it, the more I realized that allowing women to serve in the infantry—the most exclusively male club in the Marine Corps—would help eliminate negative stereotypes about women and reshape the culture. Joe and I knew that the media could help us shape public opinion on the issue, and so we constantly stressed the need to change the status quo for female recruits and Marines.

In the beginning, I was anxious about engaging with the media, particularly because I still had a year to go on active duty. But it didn't take long for me to realize that the worst had already happened. The Marine Corps had fully expected me to leave Parris Island cowering and ashamed, and I think I shocked the leadership when I began to fight back. My own confidence grew as the summer days turned into fall, and I began to receive more and more emails from men and women—both military and civilian—expressing their support for what I was trying to do. I was finding my voice.

After I returned home, I also continued to use all possible avenues to draw attention to the unjust manner in which I believed I had been relieved of command. But although I still believed that justice was possible, as September turned into October and then fall turned into winter, I recognized that if I was going to see my reputation restored, it was not going to come through official Department of Defense channels.

I tried submitting a request for an investigation into my relief as reprisal through the Department of Defense inspector general, or IG. By the IG's own definition, "Reprisal happens when a management official takes (or, under certain statutes, threatens to take) an unfavorable personnel action against an individual, or withholds (or, under certain statutes, threatens to withhold) a favorable personnel action, because that individual made or was thought to have made a protected communication or disclosure."[2] In my request to the IG, I explained that I had been fired as a form of retaliation for making allegations of a hostile work environment and gender bias.

I knew that the criteria for substantiating reprisal through the IG is extremely narrow, and it can be difficult to prove, even with extensive documentation, which I had. In fact, I learned that IG investigators substantiate less than 11 percent of all reprisal cases each year. Although these are fairly overwhelming odds, I was hopeful that an impartial investigator would see the injustice in the way I had been fired.

I carefully and thoroughly laid out my case, explaining that the Marine Corps had failed to conduct the equal-opportunity and command investigations by the book. I also explained that, because General Williams and his officers knew I had requested mast before the investigations were conducted, my relief represented reprisal.

When I finally received a final copy of the IG investigation, I found out a little more about what Colonel Haas had been thinking.

Those emails I sent to recruiting-station commanders? The ones on which I had copied Colonel Haas? He told investigators that he had counseled me that they were "counter-productive to the relationship he worked to build with the recruiting force."[3] He said he told me my emails were critical and not helpful, and that he told me to stop sending them. As I've already made clear, he did not say this to me or convey any of this to me. Later, he said he learned I was still sending them and asked me to send him a courtesy copy of each email.[4] This is not true.

Brigadier General Williams, who at that point been stopping by to tell me I was doing good work, told investigators that he recalled me "really laying into them about the types of recruits they might be sending to the depot and to Fourth Battalion in particular."[5] He said he had asked me to "tone it down."[6] Again, completely not true.

Colonel Haas told the IG investigator that when I told him I wanted to relieve November Company's commander of duty in December, he responded to me with, "Do nothing while I look for another solution," but that within ten minutes, I had fired her and violated his explicit directions.[7] I imagine if that had been what he had actually told me, I could be accused of violating explicit directions. But it's not what he said. Haas's comments in the report are simply not true.

In the IG investigation, General Williams claimed that he didn't believe I intentionally disobeyed orders, but that I had misinterpreted what Colonel Haas had told me. "Brigadier Williams believed the frustration between [Colonel Haas] and [me] had reached a point where they were not communicating clearly and that led to [me] disobeying [Colonel Haas's] order," the investigator wrote.[8] Yet if this was truly what Williams believed, why did he then do nothing, as a senior leader, to solve the problem? If he believed Colonel Haas and I were not communicating clearly, he should have, as a leader, helped us overcome that problem. He did not; and, I suspect—based on the feedback I received from him at the time—that he didn't see me as the problem.

Colonel Haas also told the IG investigator that he didn't learn that I had requested mast against him until long after I did it, which is of course untrue, because I had to deliver the signed envelope to him in person for him to then hand-deliver to General Williams. He said he became aware that "there was some sort of allegation against me" in mid-May, but that he didn't know what my request mast entailed until he was told by the investigating officer on June 12, 2015.[9]

When I spoke to him on the phone after I requested mast, General Williams had told me he was going to look into my complaints and get back to me. He didn't. But Williams told the investigator that he informed me he was already conducting an investigation, and that he would include my request mast as part of the investigation.[10] Except this part of our phone conversation never happened. In fact, I was unaware that he had convened an investigation into my leadership until I was contacted the week of Memorial Day by the investigating officer. Brigadier General Williams also told the IG investigator that he later talked with his lawyer, who determined it might be better to keep the request mast separate from the command investigation.[11] Williams stated to the IG investigator that within ten days of receiving the opinion of his counsel, he talked with General Lukeman and that they decided to have a female colonel look into my complaints of gender bias and a hostile work environment.[12]

As I've already mentioned, the female colonel assigned to look into my request mast found no gender bias or hostile work environment. She recommended that Fourth Battalion's staffing levels be reviewed, that they do a fitness report by the book for the commander I had fired, and that a new command-climate survey be conducted. In other words, she knew that the one that was being used by Williams and Haas was full of holes. Unfortunately, General Lukeman did not concur with her recommendation, seemingly because he had already made the decision to fire me.

And Brigadier Williams said he did say he was a big fan of me just before he fired me.

"Brigadier Williams explained that his decision to relieve [Germano] was not an easy decision and that, 'I'm a fan of [Germano], but I think at the end of the day, as I'm seeing these things unfold, this is what I think I need to do,'" the investigator wrote.[13] Brigadier Williams explained in his statement to the IG that no one told him to relieve me, and they all told him, "It's your call."[14] Ultimately, the inspector general determined that Brigadier General Williams and Colonel Haas had not been responsible for retaliating against me.

However, the investigator did substantiate that Williams had failed to adhere to military regulations by failing to investigate my request-mast complaints and providing a response to me within seventy-two hours—or at all—as is required. The investigator also found that Training and Education Command had failed to follow the equal-opportunity investigation regulations by ensuring I was out-briefed about the results of my gender-bias complaint and given the opportunity to provide a rebuttal statement regarding the outcome of the investigation. Finally, the investigator substantiated my allegations that Colonel Haas had failed to follow the regulation on Marine Corps fitness reports.

But that was it.

I was supremely disappointed and continued to wrestle with bouts of depression and anger about the injustice of the situation. It was exhausting to feel like every day I had my shoulder against a huge boulder, pushing uphill, only to gain an inch and then slide backward. I continued to wrestle with angst about whether I had really done the right things. After a while, when you read over and over that you are abusive and mean, it's hard not to start doubting that you are not that person.

But every time I stepped to the edge of the abyss of self-doubt and self-flagellation, Joe would coax me back to reality. He would point out that I was a good, kind person, one who cared about animals and little kids, and that I was right in pushing for greater equality and better treatment for women in the military. If it weren't for Joe, Lord knows I wouldn't still be here.

It was, of course, Joe who convinced me to pick up my pen and start writing again. After the *Marine Corps Gazette* scuttled my article on training women at boot camp, the *New York Times* picked it up as part of a piece Chris Chivers wrote about my firing.[15] I was relieved that the facts about how women are recruited and trained by the Marine Corps would see the light of day, but knew that I couldn't just let it go at that. So I started writing about the issues affecting women in the military, like gender bias, sexual harassment and assault, and how benevolent sexist tendencies by senior male leaders hold women Marines back from achieving equality. The more I wrote, the more feedback I received from women—and men—who felt the same way. I also received a lot of negative comments from readers, many of whom were current or former Marines, but their remarks only reinforced the points I made about the need to reform the culture of the Marine Corps to level the playing field for women.

To me, equal opportunity for women in the military was a moral imperative, and I was determined to fight like a girl to achieve it.

CHAPTER 32

FIFTH DIMENSION: A LIFETIME OF DEVOTION

For my birthday in March 2015, Joe got me a bottle of champagne from Pol Roger. Winston Churchill used to drink it every day. Have you read *The Last Lion: Winston Spencer Churchill, Defender of the Realm, 1940–1965*, by historian William Manchester? Churchill fascinates me because every time he'd fall down politically, he'd fight his way back to the top.

When I was on recruiting duty, Joe got me a framed black-and-white picture of Winston Churchill making the victory sign. Joe has been there for me—every step of the way, that guy. When my mom died, to save me and my dad the agony of having to identify her at the funeral home, he went in our place. He's a good man. When he gave me the bottle of Pol Roger champagne, I just cried and cried and cried. It was so thoughtful of him. We have fights, just like any couple, but he's my best friend.

He's there for me through everything. When he invited me to climb the Grand Teton with him in August 2015, that was the first time in four months that I hadn't thought about being relieved. My thought process was *hand, foot, hand, foot* placement. On the mountain, you can't focus on anything else. It was cathartic, and he knew it was exactly what I needed.

Since 2015, I have continued to work on my mental health. As I've mentioned, my time at Parris Island, dealing with mobbing, gender bias, and everything else, took a toll on me, physically and mentally. Faced with all of that stress and paranoia about whom I could trust, I started to question both who I was and what was happening to me. There were many days when I was so overcome by the humiliation of it all that I didn't want to be here anymore. It has taken time to believe in myself again, and I have learned that when things seem unbearable, as the memories of those events often do, I need to focus on the things that make me feel happy—like my dad and Kathy; Joe; and, of course, our furry and feathered friends.

I have two cats besides Mr. Fitzwizzle, and they're a pain in the butt. I left them at home with Joe, along with our chickens, when I went to Parris Island.

Poor Joe.

They lay eggs. The chickens, not the cats. And, yes, we keep the chickens and cats separate. Our hens, Sylvia, Maude, and Big Bertha (and now the recent addition of a baby rooster for which Big Bertha was a surrogate layer) are so nice, and they lay the most beautiful blue-green eggs. They also eat all of the bugs in our garden. It's therapeutic to come home and watch them strut around the garden, looking for things to nibble. Because their brains are only the size of a pea, you wouldn't think this were possible—but they each have such a distinct personality that they're hilarious, and they bring my blood pressure down.

We spoil them. For instance, Joe built them a penthouse coop with one-and-a-half times the space they need. This is a mistake, because then there's no incentive for them to go outside. They won't lay eggs without getting vitamin D from the sun. As soon as the temperature hits fifty degrees, they decide it's time to camp out in their condominium. This means we don't get eggs after September.

Like I said: they're spoiled.

We make fun of their "fowl" language.

But even with the animals to take my mind off things, I find myself thinking about Parris Island. I poured my heart into that place, and I worry that things will go back to the status quo. Of course, I'm curious about what has happened at Fourth Battalion since I left, but I haven't checked in. I do stay in touch with many of the Marines—I don't contact them, but if they reach out to me because they need help or advice, or simply want to talk, I am always here for them. I try to avoid talking about Fourth Battalion, because things needed to settle after my relief. But I'd love to know what has changed, if anything.

I continue to receive emails from people saying they believe that what I did at Parris Island was right. Those messages—from men and women—have helped me rebuild my self-confidence. I know that many of these people read the two investigations online, which are still available today, and they understand that what I said about why I was relieved is true.

I keep all of the messages I receive—whether it's from my Marines, people I worked with then and before, or people with whom I never worked but who just send kind thoughts. While my outlook on life has improved with time, there are still days that are so bad that I need to go back to those messages for a mental pick-me-up. The day recruit Siddiqui died? That was a bad day.

I've gotten other bad news, too.

Remember the fitness report I wrote for the CO I fired? After sitting on that report for seven months, Colonel Haas finally completed it, but only after he had gotten rid of me for good. Even though Marine Corps regulation states that he was required to contact me for my input if I did not agree with his remarks, Colonel Haas non-concurred with my evaluation without talking to me, and then he wrote her up like she was the best thing since Tabasco sauce in a Meal-Ready-to-Eat. I know this because every Marine has a file of fitness reports he or she either received or wrote. When I reviewed those files to prepare for my IG complaint submission, I saw Colonel Haas's remarks.

Not surprisingly, Brigadier General Williams agreed with Haas's remarks, despite the stack of documentation that showed how poorly she had performed as a company commander. Williams's remarks were also in my file. So even though Colonel Haas gave me permission to fire her based on her performance, there will be no adverse remarks in her file to indicate that she was relieved for cause. Instead, her file will show that she was removed erroneously, because I was a bad commanding officer.

And what about that XO? The one who did not do her job and who caused incredible turbulence in my command by inviting my company commanders and subordinates into her office to gossip about me? I read in my fitness-report files that Colonel Haas and General Williams recommended her for command and promotion, as well as school. They non-concurred with my report for her, too, despite the reams of documentation I had provided them regarding her substandard performance. Get this: in his report comments in the file, Colonel Haas said that she was the glue that held the battalion together in an extremely stressful environment with bad leadership.

Lieutenant Colonel Kissoon, the CO of Third Battalion who protested against our integrated training hikes, was relieved after Recruit Siddiqui died and investigations uncovered a longstanding pattern of recruit abuse in his command.[1] So was Colonel Paul Cucinotta, who replaced Colonel Haas.[2] I had worked with Colonel Cucinotta briefly at the Pentagon before I went to Parris Island, and I respected him as a leader. I know what he inherited when he took over from Colonel Haas. He was the right leader in the wrong time.

There's been some nonsense among the positive messages, though. Occasionally I receive ridiculous emails, like this one from some old Vietnam-era dude (I'm quoting it exactly, including the misspelled words):

Ms. Germano,

    After having the misfortune of reading your article I am unable to address you in any military terms. The assertions you make that gender bias and sexism is the reason why female Marines underperform, I find to be troublesome, especially coming from a person who has spent their last twenty years occuying a Marine Corps uniform. Your assertations and arguments are based on a logic that escapes reality and is a pretext to expouse your liberal femenist beliefs.

    During my three years as a Marine, one of the years being 1968 was spend in Vietnam. I am not going to go into a disertation describing my combat experience, except for the fact I damn well experienced the taste of battle on numerous occasions. You know that no matter how hard you try to decieve or decept those who don't understand what you are trying to do or who have not tasted the battle, it does not work on me or my fellow Marines that have endured. You have betrayed the honor of Marine Corps and for what it stands for. The only difference between you and a Jane Fonda is the uniform you wear. God forbit if you are successful in what you are trying to do to the Marine Corps, because the blood on your hands will be the blood of Marines and not the blood of the enemy.

    [Name Redacted], Sgt.

    USMC 1967-70

While I respect his service, apparently this vet missed out on the intervening years between his service and today, when thousands of women have "tasted battle."

And there have been some surprises. After I was relieved, I had champions both on the far left and on the far right. The response I received from the far left was as expected: *If women can meet the standards, then—hell, yeah—they should be allowed in the infantry.*

As it turns out, that's been a big argument from some of the more-conservative infantry guys, too: *Don't let them in if they can't carry my ass out of the zone after I've been hit.*

WeaponsMan is a blog about guns, and it's written by a former special forces soldier who doesn't exactly cater to the "*Kum ba yah*" crowd. While Joe and I were packing up my apartment in South Carolina, we saw that he had written a blog post about what had happened at Parris Island, and I cringed automatically, preparing for the worst.

But when the author saw how we had bumped the rifle-qualification scores, he said, "You can't argue with facts."[3]

He quoted an officer who said I was hard-charging but fair, and that I expected people to do the right thing, and he acknowledged why some party-line followers would have a problem with that.

Further, he wrote that commanders should have known the limitations of the online command-climate survey that allowed the same people to take it multiple times or to "spread the word among critics" to take it.[4]

The author noted that I was working for true equality for women, and that, now that I had been relieved of command and would be retiring, the Marine Corps had just given me carte blanche to be loud about it.

So I will.

In some ways, I can't help it. My relief, and the injustice of it, follow me everywhere I go. My experience dealing with gender bias and sexism on Parris Island pushed me to be more interested in women's issues. I read and do research constantly, send emails to people who can help me better understand what happened and how we can fix it, and write editorials for newspapers when I see issues that should be addressed—or women to be proud of. For example, Joe and I just co-wrote a column—See? Gender-integration!—about the first female Marine Corps officer to graduate from infantry school.[5] The Marines have decided not to name her or track her progress. But we are trying to put her in the spotlight.

Why? Two reasons:

(1) We want other female Marines to watch and learn and cheer.
(2) We want the public to know about it, to make sure the Marines treat her fairly.

There's also some irony: For a year after I retired, I worked as chief operating officer for the Service Women's Action Network (SWAN), the only nonprofit in the United States entirely focused on supporting the needs of and advocating for the rights of service women and women veterans. Sexual harassment and assault were big issues for us, but everything else I learned at Parris Island also came into play on a daily basis with my work at SWAN.

I've talked about gender integration on Capitol Hill, and I've talked about the hyper-masculine culture of the Marine Corps and how we lay the foundation for sexism and gender bias at Parris Island in segregated boot camp. Representatives and senators are finally asking when the Marine Corps intends to integrate boot camp and change the culture of the service to level the playing field for women.

For instance, when General Neller appeared before the Senate Armed Services Committee about the Marines United scandal, he tried to tell Senator

Elizabeth Warren that boot camp was integrated because men and women are within five hundred yards of each other, training at the same time.[6]

She and several other senators on the committee fought back and grilled the crap out of him. He then sidestepped the question by repeating himself: He said that male and female recruits perform the same activities while in the same area of the base, and, therefore, they were integrated.

Although the hearing ended and boot camp still isn't integrated, it feels good to know that folks on the Hill and people in the non-military world (and actually quite a few in the military world) get it. They know separate is not equal. After all, the benevolent sexism and gender bias women experience every day in the Marine Corps is exactly the same as what women face in the corporate sector.

I have come into contact with two networks of women, mostly from the Army and Air Force, and I've learned that, to a certain degree, gender bias exists in all of the services. But it is incredibly pervasive in the Marine Corps, in great part because we pride ourselves on being tough as nails so we can serve as the first responder for the nation when the stuff hits the fan. By maintaining segregated boot camp, because it is allegedly the only way to create confidence in female recruits, from the start, we create a negative perception about women not being as strong or tough as their male counterparts. And by separating the women in training, the men don't see the female recruits pushing themselves past their perceived limits. All that the male Marines and recruits know is that the women have to train separately because they can't mentally handle training with their male counterparts. We teach the men from the second they arrive at Parris Island that the women are inherently frail. Imagine the impact this has on the culture. The Marine Corps culture shapes who we are and what we do. But if all of our heroes are men, most of them white, and most of them from the conservative Bible belt, there isn't a place for women. The myth that only men can be warriors on the battlefield exists partly because we don't celebrate the victories and contributions of female Marines in combat situations.

That comes, in part, because there aren't enough women in the Marines to begin with. Many male Marines go their whole careers never having worked with women, because, let's face it, with a population of just 9 percent for the entire force, the women are spread thin throughout the entire organization.

Of all the services, I think the Marine Corps has the hardest time overcoming institutionalized bias, in large part because we are so tied to our history that we end up confusing "the way we have always done it" with tradition. And for a Marine, it is tantamount to sacrilege to buck tradition. The Marine Corps has always been the service most resistant to change, as evidenced by the service's reluctance to integrate African Americans into regular units or when it fought against lifting the "Don't Ask, Don't Tell" ban on gay men and women in the military.

You want to talk about resistance? It was especially evident in the lead-up to integrating ground-combat jobs and units.

Despite the existence of studies from academic organizations like RAND indicating that the integration of women into ground combat would not cause cohesion problems, the Marine Corps insisted that allowing women into these new fields would pose a risk to the service's ability to win battles.[7] It was interesting to see how Marine spokespeople cherry-picked items from their Integrated Ground Task Force experiment to support the idea that women physically are not capable of ground-combat jobs, while glossing over other portions of the study that supported how integration would actually improve the force.

Having seen the lowered expectations for female recruits firsthand at Parris Island, I was also struck by the fact that the women who participated in the Marine Corps study were recent graduates of Fourth Battalion. I knew that even though many of the female participants performed at the highest levels on the female physical-fitness test, this would automatically set them up for failure, as they would not be as fit as their male counterparts. As I had witnessed firsthand, this was less due to physiology than it was to lower standards for performance.

In the end, the Corps had to be dragged across the line, kicking and screaming, with the commandant (General Dunford) being the only service chief to request a waiver to deny women the opportunity to pursue infantry jobs.[8]

In other words, the Navy, Air Force, Coast Guard, and Army had no issues with opening the doors to women in these new roles. The Army is way bigger than the Marine Corps and has a lot more ground-combat jobs at stake. You would have assumed, if anything, they would have joined forces with the Marine Corps in asking for a waiver if indeed there were viable reasons to believe that women would pose a risk to the lethality of the force.

And how embarrassing is it that, after he was promoted from Commandant of the Marine Corps to the chairman of the Joint Chiefs, General Dunford didn't show up to the press conference given by his boss, the secretary of defense, to announce that all of the services would be required to integrate women into ground-combat jobs and units?[9] It seemed petty to me. Imagine this for a second: How might the outcome of the Marine Corps combat-integration task force study have turned out had the female Marine participants been held to higher standards in boot camp? It probably would have made it more difficult for General Dunford to say that women were slower, more injury-prone, and worse shots than the male participants.

The Marine Corps has struggled with gender issues like the Marines United scandal on a regular basis since I was fired, and I am pretty torn up about that, and I'm torn up by that, because I'm still a Marine in my heart, even if I was kicked out of the gun club. Marines United, which involved the illegal sharing of explicit photos of female Marines by up to 30,000 male active-duty and veteran Marines, was a clear indication of how screwed up the culture of the force is.[10] Think about it—out of a service with a total population of around 172,000, up to 30,000 men shared and commented on naked photos of female Marines on social media.

And although many women have completed the Army's enlisted and officer infantry courses, the Marine Corps only recently had the first female infantry officer complete its course, and the enlisted female Marines graduating from schools for ground-combat jobs has remained a trickle. Why the difference? I believe it's because the Marine Corps doesn't want women in these fields. Unlike the Army, which has taken a much more aggressive stance on welcoming women into the jobs, starting with how they recruit women, the Marine Corps has been slow on the draw. As a result of the Army's recruiting campaign, the service has consistently exceeded its goals for women in the newly opened jobs, and they see that as a success story.[11] I'd like to see the Marine Corps do the same.

It hurts me to see the differences between the Army and the Marine Corps, because I know it doesn't have to be that way. With the lessons learned about foot-dragging during the integration of African Americans into the Marines or the lifting of the ban on gays in the military, what would you think if the Marine Corps were on the vanguard, leading the Department of Defense in cultural change? Then each Marine could feel like he or she is part of an organization that both believes in equality and high standards and really does lead from the front.

And I know what is possible when it comes to women in the Marine Corps. I went to Parris Island and said, "Let's make sure they're living up to their potential." They lived up to their end of the bargain and were amazing. It makes me sad, now, thinking about it. They had to work so much harder to make change happen. But after they did, the credibility and the changed relationships they had with their peers was tangible, palpable. That's amazing. The Marine Corps as a whole could experience that change.

Joe and I don't believe in fate, but there has been a weird convergence of events in our lives. Joe always says that things happen for a reason, and it is interesting that in being relieved of command, I was able to be an even louder squeaky wheel. But if nothing good were to come from my constructive dissent, I would be truly devastated.

I know that women join the service to be Marines—not to be held to lower standards because of opinions about the female form that are based on feelings and not facts. The more we subcategorize ourselves, the less whole we are as an institution. The more distinctions there are between men and women, the more we're set apart. We become the "other." It makes it harder to just be Marines. In other words, segregating women from men is undermining the unity and functioning not only of the women themselves but of the entire Marine Corps.

In the general public, the biggest fitness trends right now are CrossFit and high-intensity interval training. The focus for women is no longer on doing aerobics and being skinny. It's about being strong, mentally and physically.

CrossFit is about creating a different standard of beauty, and if we Marines are smart, we will recruit these women. That is because they will, without a doubt, be able to handle carrying two-hundred-pound men. It doesn't mean all women will want to go into the infantry, but let's be fair here. Not all men want to, either.

It's becoming a self-leveling playing field. In the civilian world, the women who compete in CrossFit competitions get paid the exact same money that their male counterparts do, and there is a culture of mutual respect between men and women. We're seeing women winning in endurance events, like running and biking, and participating in obstacle courses. They upload videos of themselves in weight-lifting competitions. Talk about pride. Right now in this country we are seeing a self-leveling athletic adventure going on with women and men, but the Marine Corps isn't harnessing the power of it. What a wasted opportunity.

I am still baffled by the fact that the Marine Corps has never been required to provide any data to prove that segregated boot camp is an effective practice.

The gender bias that women in the Marine Corps face every day is not only sad but also dangerous. The leadership's lack of focus on how to make the Marine Corps better means zero positive growth for the service that I love and that keeps our nation safe.

It's exasperating and nonsensical. Despite the support of key members of Congress, no one on the Hill or in the Department of Defense is saying, "If you're doing this right, why do we have women failing at boot camp at such an exponentially higher rate than men at boot camp? Why are they getting broken when science says . . ."

The American public is not holding the Marine Corps accountable for showing data that backs up the claim that segregation is necessary to make better female Marines.

I think I'm always going to feel a little angry about my relief of command. It was the worst thing I have ever experienced, personally and professionally, and it almost cost me my life. If Joe had not been my Kate whisperer, telling me every day that it would be okay and that everything would work out, I know I would have taken my life after I was fired. I battle with feeling shame every day because of what the Marine Corps said about me and what many people persist in believing, even when confronted with the facts. But Joe is patient and kind and never lets me stay down long. And even on my darkest day, I know in my heart I am not the evil person they painted me to be.

Joe said recently, "We've already done what we need to do to make this a win. It's already a win," meaning not only that we were able to get my side of the story out in the media, but also that I was able to take on a bigger advocacy role for women in the military as a result.

But I said, "No. It's not a win." As somebody who is a rule follower (I am an I/ESTJ for those who have taken the Briggs-Myers personality inventory), it is practically in my DNA to make sure that people are taken care of and that those who screw up are held accountable. It's disturbing for me to know that no one has been held to task for how resistant the Marine Corps is to cultural change. Sixty years ago, Marine leaders said African American Marines shouldn't be integrated into the rest of the service, because they were not as capable as whites. How much talent did the Marine Corps miss out on then, due to misconceptions about the abilities of African American men? And how much longer is it going to take to ensure there is a level playing field for women in the Marine Corps, by ending segregated boot camp and ensuring high performance standards and expectations for men *and* women?

If I have learned one thing over the past few years, it is that timing is everything. I know I will never get my job or reputation back, and that is not the purpose of this book.

I want this to be a wake-up call that the Marine Corps can't deny and must answer to, even if it means I get slammed in the press again—because I know the Marine Corps isn't done with me yet. When this book comes out, I have no doubt they will, once again, attack my reputation.

The leadership needs to understand this isn't about me: it's about ensuring that women who join the service ten years from now do not have to deal with the same sexist attitudes and treatment that female Marines have had to deal with for decades. By shedding light on the longstanding training deficiencies for women at Parris Island and how they negatively influence the culture of the Marine Corps, my hope is that people will ask serious questions. I want to have better treatment for female Marines, to improve the quality of Marines who come out of boot camp to keep the nation safe, and to eliminate any perceptions that women can't achieve high standards and compete.

My hope is that my story, and the story of the struggle against gender bias in the Marine Corps, will create a bridge between civilian and military women to demonstrate that the issues we face are the same. When women threaten the established male hierarchy, we face backlash. Women everywhere, whether they are first responders, professors, or executives, all face the same challenges.

The fact is, we can't change the culture of the Marine Corps without the public being in the fight. Countless studies have demonstrated how diversity in thought makes organizations more powerful, and the military is no different.

When I started on this journey, it was important for me to tell my story, but I wanted to do it in a way that would help provide context to nonmilitary people about the gender-related challenges women in the Marine Corps face. I wanted to show the public that the root cause of sexual misconduct in the military—namely, the lopsided power dynamic between men and women—is the same as it is in regular society.

As we began work on this book, I had no way of knowing that the Harvey Weinstein Hollywood sex scandal would explode into the mainstream media in 2017, leading to the resurgence of Tarana Burke's 2006 #MeToo movement, and the birth of the Time's Up Legal Defense Fund for the victims of sexual misconduct in the workplace.

And at the 2017 Golden Globes Awards ceremony, in a rousing speech as the first African American woman to receive the Cecil B. DeMille Award for lifetime achievement, Oprah Winfrey laid it out. She said that the issues of sexual discrimination and misconduct impact every aspect of society and the workforce—including the military.

Wow.

For the first time, military women are being included in the movement to change the way we view gender in America. As the Time's Up initiative grows, I want to ensure military women have a seat at the table for discussions about gender and the workforce. I want to ensure that we are able to show that we aren't that different, even if our jobs involve weapons and camouflage, rather than golden statues and formal gowns.

We know that without public scrutiny and left to its own devices, military leaders will likely continue to fumble the sexual misconduct football. I want Sen. Kirsten Gillibrand's Military Justice Improvement Act (MJIA, or Senate Bill 1752), which aims to reform the military justice system to ensure justice for sexual misconduct victims, to pass—and that won't happen without the strength of a movement to drive the momentum. The act takes the decision about whether a sexual assault case should be moved to trial out of a military commander's hands and into those of trained, independent military prosecutors. This would help victims feel safer about reporting crimes without facing repercussions within their units, as well as taking away the conflicts of interest that come when a commander bases his or her decisions on keeping a unit ready to deploy, rather than what's best for an individual.

I want military women to be responsible for developing strategies to combat gender bias and sexual misconduct in the military. And there should be a consistent approach, adopted by all of the services, to eliminate foot-dragging and resistance (ahem—Marine Corps) to those proposals. Such strategies should be based on successful interventions from other industries.

I want military leaders to be held accountable for the sexual harassment and assault rates in their units. If commanders are responsible for maintaining good order and discipline, they should be evaluated, on their performance evaluations, about how they prevent and deal with sexual misconduct.

Of course, I want Marine Corps boot camp to be integrated.

But, most importantly, I want for young women to know that if we do these things, there will be a place in the military for them, where they can thrive and succeed. I want parents to be confident that if their daughters choose to join the military, that they will be taken care of by their brothers- and sisters-in-arms.

Military leaders do not own the military establishment—the American people do, and it is time for them to start asking questions about why, for so long, women have been held to lower expectations in the Marine Corps. Without the public and members of Congress acting as checks and balances for the military, most senior leaders in the Marine Corps will continue to resist leveling the playing field for women, by maintaining segregated boot camp and having lowered expectations for female performance.

So listen up, Marines.

I am here to stay, and this time, I've surrounded myself with women and men who have my back.

I will never again allow anyone to make me feel like my life isn't worth living.

And I still have plenty of time to push to the fire the boots of those who have tried to hold women back, as well as to cheer for the accomplishments of women who will continue to serve as the tip of the spear.

After all, I'm a Marine.

MARINE-SPEAK 101: GLOSSARY AND RANK STRUCTURE

Note: Marines think of everything as boats. You aren't "at" a base; you're "on" it. Building floors are "decks." Bathrooms are "heads." And so on . . .

after-action review (AAR): after completing an exercise, such as a hike, a review of what went well and what went poorly

attrition rate: number of recruits who don't complete a training program

battalion: A military unit, typically commanded by a lieutenant colonel (such as Germano), made up of about one thousand people. Within the battalion, there are typically about four companies, usually commanded by a captain and made up of between 80 and 150 people.

BOLO: fail

Bradley Fighting Vehicle (BFV): thirty-ton armored fighting vehicle

Chesty Puller: Lewis Burwell "Chesty" Puller, aka the most decorated Marine in US history. He lived from 1898 to 1971, and served in World War II and the Korean War.

CO: Commanding officer. This can apply to any level of command, so the officer in charge of a company is the CO, as is the officer in charge of a battalion.

commissary: military grocery store

commission: military appointment as an officer

company: A military unit, typically commanded by a captain and made up of about 250 people. Within the company, there are typically about four platoons, each of which is usually commanded by a lieutenant and made up of about 60 people.

court-martial: when a military court is called upon to enforce military law

cover: hat

Crucible, the: A 72-hour training exercise that is the final step before recruits become Marines. The final event is a nine-mile road march, and it ends with the emblem ceremony.

cyber-bullying: harassing someone online

deadly explosively formed penetrators: self-forging rounds that penetrate armor

deck: floor. (Remember, buildings are like boats.)

delayed entry program: the time between when a person signs up as a Marine and ships to boot camp

depot: the military installation at Parris Island

DI: drill instructor

early/late check officer (ELCO): the person assigned to make sure the recruits are safe late at night and early in the morning

emblem: the Eagle, Globe, and Anchor (EGA) symbol seen on Marine Corps uniform brass

EWS facad: faculty advisor

expert: highest level one can attain on the rifle range

fitness report: annual job review

Golem effect: the idea that if you have low expectations for a group of people because of their race, gender, or ethnicity, they will underperform

head: bathroom

hooch: a small building or trailer where service members live, typically in a war zone

IEDs: improvised explosive devices, or roadside bombs

Infantry Officer's Course: rather than boot camp, officers go to Infantry Officer's Course

IST: initial strength test

liberty: off duty and away from the base

"making" a Marine: the process a person goes through to transform from a civilian to a recruit to a fully trained, physically fit, confident Marine

Marine Combat Training (MCT): The training all Marines attend after boot camp (if they aren't in ground-combat fields), to learn more combat skills before going to their job-training schools. Other services don't have this training.

marksman: lowest passing level one can attain on the rifle range

Mean Girl/Queen Bee syndrome: Mean Girl or Queen Bee syndrome is when a woman in charge treats women who work for her worse than she treats men

military occupational specialties: jobs

Mr. Fitzwizzle: the best cat ever

Navy corpsman: medic

Navy Cross: second-highest decoration granted in the United States for valor

NCO: Non-commissioned officer, an enlisted leader

nonjudicial punishment: a process that allows commanders to punish offenders by lowering their paychecks, giving them extra duty, or reducing their rank without going through an actual court-martial

officer: commissioned officer

Officer Candidates School: an officer's training to become an officer

"on": What Marines say when they're *at* a base: "I worked on Parris Island." Recall, they think of everything in terms of ships on water.

Parris Island: base in South Carolina where Fourth Battalion is located

platoon: a military unit, typically commanded by a lieutenant, made up of about sixty people

pogue: anyone who's not infantry

poolee: what recruiters call people who have been recruited but have not yet shipped to boot camp

post exchange: military store

PT: physical training

Queen Bee syndrome: *see* Mean Girls/Queen Bee syndrome

R & R: rest and relaxation, or time off

recruit: someone who has joined the Marine Corps but hasn't yet completed boot camp

Recruit Training Order: written guidance laying out how recruits should be trained and treated

regiment: A military unit, typically commanded by a colonel and made up of about four thousand people. Within the regiment, there are typically about four battalions, each of which is typically commanded by a lieutenant colonel and made up of about one thousand people.

relational aggression: when you try to negatively affect how other people see someone

request mast: the process by which Marines ask for help from someone above their commanding officers because they believe they are being treated unfairly

series: two platoons of recruits that train together

Service Alphas: dress uniforms

sharpshooter: the middle badge one can obtain on a rifle range

surge, the: General David Petraeus's move to flood Iraq with American troops as a show of force, but also to enact his counterinsurgency measures to build trust and hope among the local people

The Basic School (TBS): six-month-long course of instruction all commissioned officers in the Marine Corps must successfully complete before being assigned their military occupational specialties

Uniform Code of Military Justice: the legal code for the military

Structure of Parris Island

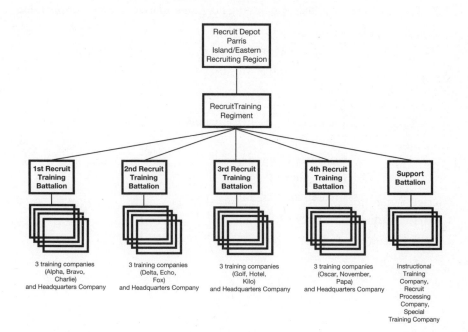

```
                    ┌─────────────────┐
                    │  Recruit Depot  │
                    │     Parris      │
                    │ Island/Eastern  │
                    │Recruiting Region│
                    └─────────────────┘
                             │
                    ┌─────────────────┐
                    │ RecruitTraining │
                    │    Regiment     │
                    └─────────────────┘
```

| 1st Recruit Training Battalion | 2nd Recruit Training Battalion | 3rd Recruit Training Battalion | 4th Recruit Training Battalion | Support Battalion |

3 training companies (Alpha, Bravo, Charlie) and Headquarters Company

3 training companies (Delta, Echo, Fox) and Headquarters Company

3 training companies (Golf, Hotel, Kilo) and Headquarters Company

3 training companies (Oscar, November, Papa) and Headquarters Company

Instructional Training Company, Recruit Processing Company, Special Training Company

Rank Structure

Enlisted:

      E-1 Private

      E-2 Private First Class

      E-3 Lance Corporal

      E-4 Corporal

Non-Commissioned Officers (including the higher-ranking enlisted—drill instructors are NCOs):

      E-5 Sergeant

      E-6 Staff Sergeant

      E-7 Gunnery Sergeant

E-8 Master Sergeant (First Sergeant)

E-9 Master Gunnery Sergeant (Sergeant Major)

Commissioned Officers (including platoon leaders, company commanders, me, my boss):

O-1 Second Lieutenant

O-2 First Lieutenant

O-3 Captain

O-4 Major

O-5 Lieutenant Colonel (my rank)

O-6 Colonel

O-7 Brigadier General

O-8 Major General

O-9 Lieutenant General

O-10 General

NOTES

Note: Except when quoted from a document or email, all references to conversations are based upon my recollection and to the best of my knowledge are accurate and complete.

Chapter 2: The Firing Squad

1. Eyder Peralta, "Marine Corps Study: All-Male Combat Units Performed Better Than Mixed Units," NPR, September 10, 2015, https://www.npr.org/sections/thetwo-way/2015/09/10/43919 0586/marine-corps-study-finds-all-male-combat-units-faster-than-mixed-units (accessed January 8, 2018); 1992 Presidential Commission on the Assignment of Women in the Armed Forces, quoted in "Marine Corps Force Integration Plan—Summary," p. 1, https://www.documentcloud.org/documents/2394531-marine-corps-force-integration-plan-summary.html (accessed January 8, 2018).

2. Morris J. MacGregor, *Integration of the Armed Forces, 1940–1965* (Washington, DC: Center of Military History, United States Army, 2001), p. 336. Originally published 1981.

3. Ray Mabus, *Morning Edition*, NPR, November 4, 2015.

Chapter 4: Data Geek

1. "We Hear You, Ladies," *Outside*, April 11, 2017, https://www.outsideonline.com/2169326/we-hear-you-ladies (accessed January 8, 2018).

2. Karen Rubin, "Research: Investing in Women-led Fortune 1000 Companies," Quantopian, edited February 11, 2015, https://www.quantopian.com/posts/research-investing-in-women-led-fortune-1000-companies (accessed January 8, 2018).

Chapter 5: The Rest of the Story

1. Ann Dunwoody, *A Higher Standard: Leadership Strategies from America's First Female Four-Star General* (Boston: Da Capo, 2015), p. 86.

2. Ibid., p. 131.

3. Ibid., p. 132.

4. Carl Prine, "Most Veterans Groups Remain Silent on Marine Nude Pix Scandal," *San Diego Union-Tribune*, March 10, 2017, http://www.sandiegouniontribune.com/military/veterans/sd-me-marines-united-20170310-story.html (accessed January 8, 2018).

Chapter 8: Iron Ladies

1. Quoted in Steven Carlton-Ford and Morten G. Ender, eds., *The Routledge Handbook of War and Society: Iraq and Afghanistan* (London: Routledge, 2010).
2. Richard Cohen, "Victimizer and Victim," op-ed, *Washington Post*, May 6, 2005, http://www.washingtonpost.com/wp-dyn/content/article/2005/05/05/AR2005050501682.html (accessed January 8, 2018).

Chapter 14: Preaching Integration

1. For example: Agnes Gereben Schaefer, Jennie W. Wenger, Jennifer Kavanagh, Jonathan P. Wong, Gillian S. Oak, Thomas E. Trail, and Todd Nichols, "Implications of Integrating Women into the Marine Corps Infantry," RAND Corporation, 2015, https://www.rand.org/pubs/research_reports/RR1103.html (accessed January 9, 2018); Margaret C. Harrell and Laura L. Miller, "New Opportunities for Military Women Effects upon Readiness, Cohesion, and Morale," RAND Corporation, 1997, http://www.dtic.mil/docs/citations/ADA332893 (accessed January 9, 2018); Margaret C. Harrell, Megan K. Beckett, and Chiaying S. Chen, "The Status of Gender Integration in the Military: Analysis of Selected Occupations," RAND Corporation, 2002, http://www.dtic.mil/docs/citations/ADA407514 (accessed January 9, 2018).
2. "The Risk Rule," *New York Times*, August 15, 2009, http://www.nytimes.com/2009/08/16/us/16womenbox.html (accessed January 9, 2018).
3. For example: Lynette Arnhart, Blair Crosswhite, Jennifer Jebo, Michael Jessee, Dominic Johnson, Sara Lechtenberg-Kasten, Peter Kerekanich, Amy McGrath, and Blair Williams, "Gender Integration Study," US Army TRADOC Analysis Center, April 21, 2015, https://www.defense.gov/Portals/1/Documents/wisr-studies/Army%20-%20Gender%20Integration%20Study3.pdf (accessed January 9, 2018); "Fact Sheet: Women in Service Review (WISR) Implementation," https://www.defense.gov/Portals/1/Documents/pubs/Fact_Sheet_WISR_FINAL.pdf (accessed January 9, 2018); Anne W. Chapman, *Mixed-Gender Basic Training: The US Army Experience, 1973–2004* (Fort Monroe, VA: Government Printing Office, US Army Training and Doctrine Command, 2008).
4. For reference of studies at the time: Mickey R. Dansby, James B. Stewart, and Schuyler C. Webb, eds., *Managing Diversity in the Military: Research Perspectives from the Defense Equal Opportunity Management Institute* (New York: Routledge, 2017), first published 2001 by Transaction Publishers; Mark E. Gebicke, "Gender Integration in Basic Training: The Services Are Using a Variety of Approaches," testimony before the Subcommittee on Personnel, Committee on Armed Services, US Senate, June 5, 1997, https://www.gao.gov/archive/1997/ns97174t.pdf (accessed January 9, 2018).
5. Schaefer et al., "Implications of Integrating Women into the Marine Corps Infantry," p. 14.
6. Ibid., p. 51.
7. Ibid.

Chapter 20: While the Cat Is Away

1.   United States Marine Corps, "Command Investigation into the Circumstances Surrounding Alleged Abuse of Authority by the [Redacted], 4th Recruit Training Battalion, Marine Corps Recruit Depot, Parris Island, South Carolina," June 18, 2015, p. 253, and enclosure 35, p. 4.
2.   Ibid., p. 164, and enclosure 35, p. 4.
3.   Ibid., pp. 159 and 161, and enclosure 35, p. 5.
4.   Ibid.
5.   Ibid., enclosure 35, p. 8.

Chapter 21: Thumpin' Third

1.   Alex French, "The Mysterious Death of a Muslim Marine Recruit," January 11, 2017, http://www.esquire.com/news-politics/a52195/raheel-siddiqui-marine-corps-death/ (accessed January 9, 2018).
2.   Rory Laverty, "Marine Drill Instructor Sentenced to 10 Years in Prison for Targeting Muslim Recruits," *Washington Post*, November 10, 2017, https://www.washingtonpost.com/news/checkpoint/wp/2017/11/09/military-jury-convicts-marine-drill-instructor-who-targeted-muslims/?utm_term=.d483ba4d2a1f (accessed January 9, 2018).
3.   Todd South, "Heads Roll at Parris Island," *Marine Corps Times*, https://www.marinecorpstimes.com/news/your-marine-corps/2017/06/11/heads-roll-at-parris-island/ (accessed January 9, 2018).
4.   Wade Livingston, "He Wrote This Letter to Parris Island When His Marine Son Bragged a DI Choked Him," *Beaufort Gazette*, October 29, 2017, http://www.islandpacket.com/news/local/community/beaufort-news/bg-military/article181357386.html (accessed January 9, 2018); Wade Livingston, "Former Parris Island Drill Instructor Found Guilty of Abusing Muslim Recruits," *Beaufort Gazette*, November 9, 2017, http://www.islandpacket.com/news/local/community/beaufort-news/bg-military/article183811511.html (accessed January 9, 2018).
5.   South, "Heads Roll at Parris Island."
6.   Ibid.
7.   Ibid.
8.   Dan Lamothe, "Marine Recruit Needed Skin Grafts to Treat Chemical Burns Suffered at Boot Camp, Documents Reveal," *Washington Post*, May 3, 2017, https://www.washingtonpost.com/news/checkpoint/wp/2017/05/03/marine-recruit-needed-skin-grafts-to-treat-chemical-burns-suffered-at-boot-camp-documents-show/?utm_term=.e11d6ad7ed30 (accessed January 9, 2018).
9.   Ibid.

Chapter 22: Good News Travels Fast

1.   Lolita C. Baldor, the Associated Press, "Officials: Marine Commandant Recommends Women Be Banned from Some Combat Jobs," *Marine Corps Times*, September 18, 2015, https://www.marinecorpstimes.com/news/your-marine-corps/2015/09/18/officials-marine

-commandant-recommends-women-be-banned-from-some-combat-jobs/ (accessed January 9, 2018).

2. United States Marine Corps, "Command Investigation into the Circumstances Surrounding Alleged Abuse of Authority by the [Redacted], 4th Recruit Training Battalion, Marine Corps Recruit Depot, Parris Island, South Carolina," June 18, 2015, enclosure 5, p. 5.

Chapter 24: Climate Change

1. National Multiple Sclerosis Society, "What Is MS?" https://www.nationalmssociety .org/What-is-MS (accessed January 10, 2018).

Chapter 25: The Rapist Is Always Wrong

1. Andrew R. Morral, Kristie Gore, and Terry Schell, eds., *Sexual Assault and Sexual Harassment in the US Military*, vol. 2, *Estimates for Department of Defense Service Members from the 2014 RAND Military Workplace Study* (Santa Monica, CA: RAND Corporation, 2015), https://www.rand.org/pubs/research_reports/RR870z2-1.html (accessed January 10, 2018).

2. Sara Kintzle, Ashley C. Schuyler, Diana Ray-Letourneau, Sara M. Ozuna, Christopher Munch, Elizabeth Xintarianos, Anthony M. Hasson, and Carl A. Castro, "Sexual Trauma in the Military: Exploring PTSD and Mental Health Care Utilization in Female Veterans," *Psychological Services* 12, no. 4 (2015): 394–401, https://www.apa.org/pubs/journals/releases/ ser-ser0000054.pdf (accessed January 10, 2018).

3. Ibid.

Chapter 27: General Relativity

1. Michael Burgoon, Vickie Pauls Denning, and Laura Roberts, "Language Expectancy Theory," chap. 7 in *The Persuasion Handbook: Developments and Theory and Practice*, edited by James Price Dillard and Michael Pfau (Thousand Oaks, CA: Sage Publications, 2002), pp. 117–36.

2. Chi Luu, "Bad Language for Nasty Women (and Other Gendered Insults)," *JSTOR Daily*, November 9, 2016, https://daily.jstor.org/the-language-of-nasty-women-and-other -gendered-insults/ (accessed January 10, 2018).

3. Elliot Ackerman, interview with James W. Weirick, "More Marines United," July 25, 2017, in *Military Justice*, podcast, ep. 23, 58:50, available via Stitcher at https://www.stitcher .com/podcast/audioboom/military-justice/e/50911522 (accessed January 10, 2018).

4. Ibid.

5. *Platoon*, directed and written by Oliver Stone (Los Angeles, CA: Hemdale, 1986), 120 min.

6. Philip G. Zimbardo, http://www.zimbardo.com/zimbardo.html (accessed January 10, 2018).

7. Philip G. Zimbardo, "Transforming People into Perpetrators of Evil: Why Does Genocide Continue to Exist?," Robert L. Harris Memorial Lecture, Holocaust Studies Center, Sonoma State University, March 9, 1999, http://web.sonoma.edu/users/g/goodman/zimbardo .htm (accessed January 10, 2018).

8. Quoted in Deepak Chopra, *How to Know God: The Soul's Journey into the Mystery of Mysteries*, 1st ed. (New York: Three Rivers, 2000), p. 99.

9. Janet Reitman, "How the Death of a Muslim Recruit Revealed a Culture of Brutality in the Marines," *New York Times Magazine*, July 6, 2017, https://www.nytimes.com/2017/07/06/magazine/how-the-death-of-a-muslim-recruit-revealed-a-culture-of-brutality-in-the-marines.html (accessed January 10, 2018).

10. Lolita C. Baldor, the Associated Press, "Officials: Marine Commandant Recommends Women Be Banned from Some Combat Jobs," *Marine Corps Times*, September 18, 2015, https://www.marinecorpstimes.com/news/your-marine-corps/2015/09/18/officials-marine-commandant-recommends-women-be-banned-from-some-combat-jobs/ (accessed January 10, 2018).

11. Tom Bowman, "Pentagon Opens All Combat Positions to Women," December 3, 2015, in *All Things Considered*, podcast, 3:52, available via NPR at https://www.npr.org/2015/12/03/458361180/pentagon-opens-all-combat-positions-to-women (accessed January 10, 2018).

Chapter 29: Leaked Like a Sieve

1. Department of the Navy, *Department of the Navy Public Affairs Policy and Regulations*, SECNAVINST 5720.44c, February 21, 2012, http://www.jag.navy.mil/distrib/instructions/SECNAVINST5720.44CPublicAffairsPolicyRegulations.pdf (accessed January 10, 2018).

2. Quoted in "General: It's 'Fun to Shoot Some People,'" CNN, February 4, 2005, http://www.cnn.com/2005/US/02/03/general.shoot/ (accessed January 10, 2018).

3. C. Mark Brinkley, "Sacked," Leatherneck.com, October 11, 2004, http://www.leatherneck.com/forums/showthread.php?16947-Sacked (accessed January 11, 2018).

4. Ibid.

5. Harry S. Truman, letter to Gordon L. McDonough, August 29, 1950, available at "Public Papers: Harry S. Truman, 1945–1953," Harry S. Truman Presidential Library & Museum, https://www.trumanlibrary.org/publicpapers/index.php?pid=864 (accessed January 11, 2018).

6. For example, the investigation was made public through *Marine Corps Times* on July 7 and the *New York Times* on July 12; Kate was not provided with a copy, despite her requests, until after these articles and the report were released to the public. We picked up a copy of the report in person, on June 12, but she was not sent a copy of the investigation until several weeks afterward. See Hope Hodge Seck, "Controversy Surrounds Firing of Marines' Female Recruit Battalion CO," *Marine Corps Times*, July 7, 2015, https://www.marinecorpstimes.com/news/your-marine-corps/2015/07/07/controversy-surrounds-firing-of-marines-female-recruit-battalion-co/ (accessed January 11, 2018); Dave Philipps, "Marine Commander's Firing Stirs Debate on Integration of Women in Corps," *New York Times*, July 12, 2015, https://www.nytimes.com/2015/07/13/us/marine-commanders-firing-stirs-debate-on-integration-of-women-in-corps.html (accessed January 11, 2018); "The Marine Corps' Command Investigation into Alleged Abuse of Authority by Lt. Col. Kate Germano," *New York Times*, published July 12, 2015, corrected July 16, 2015, https://www.nytimes.com/interactive/2015/07/16/us/13marine-document-one-286-pages.html (accessed January 11, 2018).

7. Philipps, "Marine Commander's Firing Stirs Debate on Integration of Women in Corps."

8. C. J. Chivers, "Lt. Col. Kate Germano on the Marines and Women," *At War* (blog), *New York Times*, July 28, 2015, https://atwar.blogs.nytimes.com/author/c-j-chivers/ (accessed January 11, 2018).

9. "Marine Corps Commandant Confirmation Hearing," C-SPAN, July 23, 2015, https://www.c-span.org/video/?327285-1/marine-corps-commandant-confirmation-hearing (accessed January 11, 2018); "Stenographic Transcript before the Committee on Armed Services, United States Senate Hearing to Consider the Nomination of Lieutenant General Robert B. Neller, USMC, to Be General and Commandant of the Marine Corps," July 23, 2015, https://www.armed-services.senate.gov/imo/media/doc/15-65%20-%207-23-15.pdf (accessed January 11, 2018).

10. Matthew Rosenberg and Dave Philipps, "All Combat Roles Now Open to Women, Defense Secretary Says," *New York Times*, December 3, 2015, https://www.nytimes.com/2015/12/04/us/politics/combat-military-women-ash-carter.html?_r=0 (accessed January 11, 2018).

11. James Clark, "Born in a Russian Prison, She's Now a Trailblazing infantry Marine," *Task & Purpose*, March 28, 2017, http://taskandpurpose.com/born-russian-prison-shes-now-trailblazing-infantry-marine/ (accessed January 11, 2018).

12. Carl Prine, "Two Camp Pendleton Marines Disciplined for Online Misconduct in Wake of Sex-Shaming, Cyberbullying Scandal," *Los Angeles Times*, April 7, 2017, http://www.latimes.com/local/lanow/la-me-ln-marine-sex-scandal-20170407-story.html (accessed January 11, 2018).

13. Clark, "Born in a Russian Prison."

14. Carla Babb, "Female Marine Trailblazer Graduates From Infantry School," VOA, https://www.voanews.com/a/female-marine-trailblazer-graduates-from-infantry-school/3779372.html (accessed January 11, 2018).

15. Jeff Schogol, "First Female Marine to Graduate from Infantry Officer Course," *Marine Corps Times*, September 21, 2017, https://www.marinecorpstimes.com/news/your-marine-corps/2017/09/21/first-female-marine-to-graduate-from-infantry-officer-course/ (accessed January 11, 2018).

Chapter 30: Command Performance

1. *USLegal Dictionary*, s.v. "Gender Bias Law and Legal Definition," https://definitions.uslegal.com/g/gender-bias/ (accessed January 11, 2018).

2. Dave Philipps, "Marine Commander's Firing Stirs Debate on Integration of Women in the Corps," *New York Times*, July 12, 2015, https://www.nytimes.com/2015/07/13/us/marine-commanders-firing-stirs-debate-on-integration-of-women-in-corps.html (accessed January 11, 2018).

3. Ibid.

4. *USLegal Dictionary*, s.v. "Gender Discriminations Law and Legal Definition," https://definitions.uslegal.com/g/gender-discriminations/ (accessed January 11, 2018).

Chapter 31: Equal Opportunist

1. US Marine Corps, "Marine Corps Recruit Depot: Eastern Recruiting Region; Parris Island, South Carolina," http://www.mcrdpi.marines.mil (accessed January 11, 2018).

2. Department of Defense, "The DoD Hotline—Whistleblower Reprisal Complaints," http://www.dodhotline.dodig.mil/hotline/reprisalcomplaint.html (accessed January 11, 2018).

3. Inspector General, US Department of Defense, "Lieutenant Colonel Kate Germano 4th Recruit Training Battalion, Marine Corps Recruit Depot, Parris Island, SC, Whistleblower Reprisal Investigation," November 28, 2016, p. 5.

4. Ibid., p. 4.

5. Ibid., p. 5.

6. Ibid.

7. Ibid., p. 6

8. Ibid., p. 7.

9. Ibid., p. 13.

10. Ibid.

11. Ibid.

12. Ibid.

13. Ibid., p. 19.

14. Ibid., p. 14.

15. C. J. Chivers, "Lt. Col. Kate Germano on the Marines and Women," *At War* (blog), *New York Times*, July 28, 2015, https://atwar.blogs.nytimes.com/author/c-j-chivers/ (accessed January 11, 2018).

Chapter 32: Fifth Dimension

1. Wade Livingston, "Update: Recruit Commander, Sgt. Maj. Dismissed at Parris Island," *Beaufort Gazette*, June 7, 2016, updated June 8, 2016, http://www.islandpacket.com/news/local/community/beaufort-news/bg-military/article82227107.html (accessed January 12, 2018).

2. Ibid.

3. "Keelhauling Kate Germano, Part II," *WeaponsMan*, July 14, 2015, http://weaponsman.com/?p=23915 (accessed January 12, 2018).

4. Ibid.

5. Kate Germano and Joe Plenzler, "Female Marine Officer Smashes Glass Ceiling of Infantry—Let's Learn from It," *San Diego Union-Tribune*, September 25, 2017, http://www.sandiegouniontribune.com/military/guest-voices/sd-me-germano-plenzler-infantry-officer-graduation-20170925-story.html (accessed January 12, 2018).

6. "Marine Corps Social Media Nude Photos Investigation," testimony of Marine Corps Commandant Gen. Robert Neller and Acting Navy Secretary Sean Stackley, C-SPAN, March 14, 2017, https://www.c-span.org/video/?425339-1/senators-press-marine-corps-commander-accountability-nude-photo-controversy (accessed January 12, 2018).

7. Joanna Walters, "'Flawed' Study Casts Doubts on Mixed-Gender Units in US Marine Corps," *Guardian*, October 17, 2015, https://www.theguardian.com/us-news/2015/oct/17/marines-study-casts-doubts-mixed-gender-units (accessed January 12, 2018).

8. Lolita C. Baldor, the Associated Press, "Officials: Marine Commandant Recommends Women Be Banned from Some Combat Jobs," *Marine Corps Times*, September 18, 2015, https://www.marinecorpstimes.com/news/your-marine-corps/2015/09/18/officials-marine-commandant-recommends-women-be-banned-from-some-combat-jobs/ (accessed January 9, 2018).

9. Tom Bowman, "Pentagon Opens All Combat Positions to Women," December 3, 2015, in *All Things Considered*, podcast, 3:52, available via NPR at https://www.npr.org/2015/12/03/458361180/pentagon-opens-all-combat-positions-to-women (accessed January 10, 2018).

10. Daniel Brown, "A Marine Was Just Sentenced for the First Time in Connection with 'Marines United' Nude-Photo Scandal," *Business Insider*, July 11, 2017, http://www.businessinsider.com/marine-sentenced-in-connection-with-marines-united-photo-scandal-2017-7 (accessed January 12, 2018).

11. Sean Kimmons, "More Women Than Expected Pursuing Combat Arms Positions," US Army, December 16, 2016, https://www.army.mil/article/179741/more_women_than_expected_pursuing_combat_arms_positions (accessed January 12, 2018).